TOM HENRY

Confession of a Killer

BY HIS FORMER PRISON CELLMATE
David Hendricks

// CRIME SCENE DO NOT CROSS //

ISBN: 0988495112

ISBN-13: 9780988495111

Printed in US by Hendricks Publishing

TOM HENRY
Confession of a Killer

By David Hendricks

Table of Contents

Foreword

Soon after I arrived as chaplain at Menard Correctional Center I started a Bible study that included both David Hendricks and Henry Hillenbrand. Henry impressed me as a street-wise inmate while David appeared out of place in a foreign environment. Henry understood criminal thinking and behavior. David was quickly learning to live in a culture where criminal thinking was the norm. If an inmate exhibited the trust and openness we expect in the civilized world, he soon found himself in trouble. Both Henry and David had a great sense of humor, a key to keeping your sanity where the behavior around you often lacks it.

Henry's own criminal behavior had led him to jail, then to life as a fugitive, and finally a prison sentence. David also went to prison because of criminal behavior, but not his own. David suffered both in losing his family and then his freedom, as well as his business and, in the end, life in his community. So David first became the victim of a terrible crime and then of a judicial system that seeks to solve crime but often fails to achieve justice.

During his seven years in prison, David came to see a different world. He came to see sin and brokenness in its depths on all levels of society in a way few people ever experience it. He'd been a loyal member of society, helping people with physical disabilities, and a faithful church member who zealously proclaimed the truth of the gospel. Suddenly everything had been taken from him, and he now was an innocent yet convicted "murderer" fighting for justice. He saw that prisoners were not all demons, though some came close, nor were all those in the judicial system saints. There is a strange mix of saints and sinners in every area of society, even among prisoners.

During my many private and group meetings with David I was struck by several things. First, I don't think I ever met a person in the prison system with such impeccable integrity. Whether it is staff or prisoner, you're never certain a person is telling the truth. With David it was different. He clearly lived by a standard of integrity rarely seen in our society today and non-existent in the prison system. He was even honest with himself, which seems to be too painful for many inmates and, frankly, a rare trait in most outside of prison.

Second, David has an exceptionally keen mind. His clear thinking was a sharp contrast to that of the inmates as well as their keepers. His boss, a Ph.D.

and the director of the University Studies program at the prison, was clearly the intellectual inferior of his prisoner subordinate. Intellectually David had no peers in the institution.

These qualities gave him insight and discernment. In that strange environment—a brilliant, honest, innocent man living among convicts and their keepers—David observed things most inmates never saw. This experience gifted him to write a story like *Tom Henry* and in the process give us a unique perspective on the prison system, which is failing so miserably in doing what society expects of it.

For this reason alone, *Tom Henry* is an important book.

Henry Bouma
Grand Rapids, Michigan

Preface

This is a true story.

Not an account suggested by a true story, not a novel based on a true story—all of this really happened. I, David Hendricks, really was sent unjustly to a prison where I met Tom Henry, a man who really told me how he murdered two people, escaped from jail, and lived for thirteen years as a fugitive under an assumed identity. He really attempted to commit suicide, an act which resulted in his rebirth as a committed Christian, and three years later he really was recaptured and re-incarcerated.

So this is a true story, with three caveats: First, the chronology of events has been altered to allow me to condense six years of prison into the two years Tom Henry and I lived together in prison cell West 3-49. Second, I've occasionally combined multiple conversations and events into a single scene or conversation. And third, some names have been changed to respect the privacy of this book's real characters.

In prison I kept a daily journal and captured most of Tom Henry's story on tape, but human errors tend to creep in unnoticed. Should you discover any, please let me know. There's a feedback area on my author website, www. authorhendricks.com, for just that purpose.

We don't read books from people like Tom Henry because people like Tom Henry don't write books. Which is too bad in this case, because Tom Henry is a born raconteur and his stories follow Hitchcock's axiom: "Drama is life with the dull parts left out."

I've tried to let Tom Henry speak for himself. This book contains the story just as he would tell it if he could write, organize, and edit himself. The most difficult thing to get out of Tom Henry was his account of the murders. He appears to have blocked much of it from his mind, perhaps to retain his sanity. Reconstituted from the bits and pieces he told me and from what others have told me, I've presented it as if he dictated it complete and uninterrupted, which was not at all the case. If you want to know how Tom Henry sounds, think of a midwestern-southern accent. When you see "creek" read crick, when you see "ride," read rod.

Although this is a book set in prison, I've limited obscenities, both of action and of language. A few violent scenes and some vulgar language remain, but neither the f-word nor the n-word will be found here, though both are as common in prison as "move" or "cut that out." Prison slang I've also minimized, though I couldn't avoid it entirely. At the first appearance of an expression most readers are unlikely to know, I define it in a footnote.

At Tom Henry's request I've omitted two events I would have otherwise included. In each, he's protecting someone in his life. "I've hurt them too much already," he says. I should add that Tom Henry never asked me to squelch any fact or event on the grounds that it might hurt *him*.

In the sentence-hearing chapters I compressed 2,000 pages of transcript into 20 pages of manuscript. I did this by condensing the direct examinations of witnesses and omitting the cross examinations in order to present the facts without the bickering.

Finally, since many of these events may be difficult to believe, I confirmed as many of them as possible in interviews with the people involved. Some events weren't confirmable—no available witnesses—but for those I could confirm I footnote witnesses' comments so as to share the information without impeding the flow of Tom Henry's story.

Like all of us, I have many people to thank for bringing me to where I am today. Let me mention a few who gently prodded me toward the completion of this book: Tom Henry for his advice, friendship, and incredible patience, waiting some twenty years after my release from prison for this book to be finished; Winkie, his daughter, for resetting my perspective about the tragedy Tom Henry left in his wake in Streator; Aron Aji (currently Dean of the College of Arts and Sciences at Ambrose University in Iowa), who as a young graduate student taught primary composition classes at Menard Prison, for devoting the time he could spare to teach me elements of story structure; Reverend Bouma, the prison chaplain, who never lost faith in me even as I lost faith in the God he knew and loved; the many people from this story for allowing me to interview them; my brother, Jim, and friend, Donavan, for reading the manuscript; Sherry Mascal and Thomas Elliott for locating people; and last but never least my wife, Gazel, for her support—and for keeping me humble. Just when I begin to consider myself something of a wordsmith, she brings me back to earth by thrashing me in on-line Scrabble, using a language which is my first but her third.

When I went fishing for an editor, so good was my luck that I landed none other than Renni Browne (in tandem with Shannon Roberts) of The Editorial Department. Renni, for those few writers who don't know about her, co-authored the "bible" of editing (*Self Editing for Fiction Writers*). A month after receiving my manuscript she told me, "This is a terrific first draft for a true crime story, one of the best I've seen in my fifty years as an editor." She followed that with forty pages telling me what was wrong and how to fix it. But she and Shannon were right about what was wrong, and I'm grateful.

Prologue

When I tell people about Tom Henry, almost everybody asks me the same question: "Why would you write this story?"

In 1983 I was twenty-nine years old with a wife and three children, a successful businessman fulfilling my dream to design orthopedic braces, and a Christian—I'd done missionary work in Bolivia and was a Bible-reading believer down to my toes.

That life ended when I returned from a business trip to discover my wife and children viciously murdered in our home.

From the moment I showed up I was the first and only suspect. One year in hell later I found myself convicted of a quadruple murder and given a never-get-out prison sentence.

I suffered through more than seven years of incarceration before the legal system found me not guilty. During those years, a best-selling book was published about my case: *Reasonable Doubt*, by Steve Vogel.

Tom Henry was one of the first inmates I met in prison. In a place populated by violent inmates and ignorant guards, he stuck out as a guy you could count on for sound advice, a helping hand, or a light-hearted witticism just when you needed it.

At a time when I struggled not to lose my faith, Tom Henry was a testimony to God's love in a sea of moral darkness—not the kind of "witness" who drums his religion into you but one who lives his faith even in the depressing conditions of prison life.

A good man.

I found it difficult to reconcile this goodness with the fact that this particular good Christian man had murdered two people. And not just murdered—he'd struck the head of the woman he loved, the mother of his child, with his rifle, over and over again, so severely that parts of the stock broke off.

It's easy to label someone like Tom Henry a monster, suggesting that he doesn't share our humanity. This is a comfortable but dangerous fiction—comfortable because it allows us to feel superior, dangerous because it enables us to ignore the truth that within each of us lies the capacity for evil. The truth is there's a man inside the "monster."

I wrote this book because I discovered in Tom Henry a man whose life demonstrates violence and gentleness, cruelty and compassion, selfishness and benevolence. The only way to reveal the complexity of the man was to tell the whole story of the man.

And I wrote this book because Tom Henry's story is hands down the best story I've ever heard.

One

"You guys mind if I join you?" I said.

Three inmates were waiting their turn to play handball in Menard prison's south yard. One of them broke off from a cockamamie story he was telling about shooting seven deer with six bullets.

"It's a free country." He glanced up at one of the yard's gun towers. "Although this ain't exactly the free part of it."

"So I'm free to stand here but not to climb the fence?" I said.

"Naw, you're free to climb the fence." He was a wiry guy with dark hair, friendly eyes, a jaunty walk, and an air of mischief about him. I liked him immediately. "But let me place a couple bets first."

I paused a second. "Well, I do need the exercise, but I was thinking more of handball. How's it work here? Do you sign up, or …"

"Winner stays," he said. "I'm third, you're after me. Games are to seven." He looked me over. "I'm Henry Hillenbrand," he said. "You new here?"

"I'm David Hendricks and you're right, I just got here a couple of days ago."

"Mind if I give you some advice?"

"Happy to have it. This is my first time to yard."

Henry grinned.

"I saw you carrying a color TV in from commissary yesterday. Hauling one into your cell your first week here, you're asking for trouble."

In Menard, you could have a TV, but only if you bought it at commissary. Most TVs were tiny, black and white, and cheap, but lately they'd started offering color TVs. They were a little bigger and a lot more expensive.

"Thanks—I'll keep that in mind for the future." My turn to grin. "But don't let me interfere with your story. Seven deer with six bullets? This I've got to hear."

So Henry started over for my sake.

"I was headed for old Cheese Eye's store that day," he said. "It was just down one hill and up another from Mac's Salvage. So I left Mac's and right after I walk out of the garage, Lester opens the back door and sees seven deer in the field. Buck and Lester didn't have a gun there but they knew I'd just left, so they jump into the pickup and race up to get me.

"Now, both of them liked to joke around with me, especially about deer. They'd put signs up around my place, 'Deer beware, Tom lives here!'—I was Tom to them—so I wasn't about to believe them telling me they saw seven deer in their back yard!

"They pull up to the store in an all-fired hurry, slide to a stop in the loose gravel, and lean on the horn. I didn't know what they were about, so I come on out the store.

"'Tom!' they said, 'Let us use your gun! There's seven deer in the field back of Mac's!'

"Now, heck, if they'd of said one or even two, I'd of dashed down lickety-split. But seven?

"'Come on, guys. How gullible you think I am?'

"'No, really! *Seven* deer! Hurry up—give us your gun!'

"'Be right there.'

"I go back in the store and tell Frankie and we're still laughing about it when they call on the phone. 'Tom! Come on, Tom—they're *still here*!'

"Now, I know seven deer aren't about to hang around like that but I decide to play along, and they come running up the minute I pull in at the garage. 'Where's your gun! Get the gun, goddammit!' Well, heck, they're serious. Look like they're about to pee their pants. I grab my gun and ease around back. When I seen all them deer I was like a dog with lighter fluid up his butt.

"So I holler, 'Run out there, you two, and watch the road!' So here I am, sneaking between these junk cars behind Mac's garage. Now, I don't have an extra clip, and EF Hutton's only got six shells in it—one of my friends nicknamed my rifle EF Hutton, said when it spoke, the animals listened. Anyhow, there are still seven deer in the field. No way I'm getting more than two of those buggers, even with a semi-automatic, 'cause with the first shot they'll bolt. And they're right next to the woods.

"I'm close as I can get and still stay hidden in the junk cars. This one taillight had the red lens missing. Whoever took it just bent the chrome on either side of the screw, making a vee for me to rest EF Hutton in. I steadied it there, took aim, and BAM! I shot this one deer, and my bullet goes right through his neck and hits the one behind him in the side. So I got two deer with my first shot, but the second one didn't drop. Ran into the woods with the other five.

"So now I got five shots and six fleeing deer, far as I knew. I go running into the woods after them, see one in a patch of trees and shoot him, which leaves me four shots. I saw one ahead of me, laying low behind brush in a ravine. I was ready to plug him but I'd have to shoot him in the back so I try to sneak up to him for a cleaner shot, but he never moved. I got right up to him and found out why. He was the deer I killed with the first bullet.

"I was coming out of the woods, and the four deer left was jumping over a fence down by the road going up to this other patch of woods. So here I went—see, you don't ever go behind deer, 'cause wherever they come from, they stand and look behind them to see if they're being chased. I circled around the side of them, way around so I was ahead of them, so they'd come to me. Now, this works perfect if you got two guys. One goes up ahead, the other waits till the first one's in position then feeds him the deer just by moving. The deer will see the guy behind them and go forward.

"Took me about two hours to track all four deer down. I got every one of them and I was on my way back to Mac's with an empty gun when Buck and Lester spotted me walking along the road and picked me up—they'd been riding around looking for me, of course.

"'Got all seven of them buggers,' I said when I climbed in.

"Now it was their turn not to believe. 'With six bullets? Uh-huh! Tell us another one, Tom!'

"'Nope, I got something better to do. I'll make believers of you, 'cause you'll be picking up seven dead deer. Here, I'll draw you a map.'

"So I did and they did. Picked up all seven."

ᐧᗒᗕ

In May of 1997, I traveled to Missouri seeking confirmation of this outlandish story from the owner of Mac's Salvage, Raymond "Tudie" McAnally.

"Yeah, it happened just the way he told you," Tudie said. "I'll tell you, Tom was the most amazing shot you ever saw."

Ricky Cleaver, another Missouri friend of Tom's, said, "I'd rather have the law shooting at me than Tom."

To this day, some thirty years later, they still tell stories about the legendary hunter Tom Elliott. They're the same stories but now they come with a twist, for the last sentence always starts something like this: "But I never knew …"

What they never knew was that Tom Elliott had a past he was keeping to himself, a secret that, were it to leak, would cut short his career in woodsmanship. For Tom Elliott's name wasn't Tom Elliott. His real name was Henry Hillenbrand, and he was wanted by the law for the double murder of the woman he loved and the man he found her in bed with, and like the deer he hunted, he was constantly looking backwards over his shoulder.

Two

In jail, while awaiting transfer to the maximum security prison that was to be my home for the rest of my life, a counselor had given me some advice.

"David, I like you. You've been a model inmate here and for all I know you may be innocent. You're intelligent, you've got social skills, and you're a big guy, but none of that's going to mean a damn thing when you get to prison. I've seen the guys there, and let me tell you, they're all big, they all lift weights, and they're all mean.

"And in their hierarchy someone who killed his children is way low. Maybe above child molester, but not much. And you—you've got another problem. Money. You've got it, they want it. So you want my advice? The second you come off that bus, get yourself to PC[1] and stay there! You've got appeals, you've got a chance, but only if you're still alive."

That was probably good advice, but it wasn't for me. I'd lost my family, my reputation, my dignity, most of my money, and now my freedom. But there's prison and there's prison. General Population is still incarceration, but at least you get to go to work, play sports in the yard, visit in the chow hall. In Protective Custody you're locked down. Period. The idea was to guard your life. But what kind of a life? Didn't sound like one worth guarding to me.

I'd never shied away from risk. I flew airplanes, rode motorcycles, ran my own business, and gave up the profitable prosthetic and orthotic practice I'd developed to pursue my dream of designing orthopedic braces.

And while the Bible had taught me the meek shall inherit the earth, I now had serious doubts about that. To be fair, I had doubts about everything when it came to my once unshakable faith.

And so when I stepped off the bus with chains on my ankles and manacles on my wrists, I didn't even *think* of nodding when they asked if any of us wanted protection. And when the gangs came around to hook up the new fish, I told them I respected them but I didn't want to ride with an organization. "I'm too old for that shit," I said. And they said okay and marked me down: Hendricks – independent.

---

1 Protective Custody, a relatively safe part of the prison where a threatened inmate is kept separate from the general population, locked in his cell except for meals and limited activities.

I tried to fit in. When I went to chow hall I sat on the white side. Half the chow hall was populated by blacks; the other half by whites, Latinos, and the overflow of blacks. Blacks and whites could mingle in the yard or the work assignment but not in the chow hall. It wasn't done.

There were two white gangs, Northsiders[2] and Bikers. Gangs sat together in the chow hall. My job was to figure out which whites were independent. There weren't many.

Today, for the first time in my three weeks here, I'd planned my approach and plopped down at a table with what appeared to be white independents. One was a fortyish skinny guy with one front tooth, the second was a young muscle-bound man with plenty of tattoos, and the third was Henry Hillenbrand. Henry was doing most of the talking—inmates stopped by, food trays in hand, to greet him, and he had a joke or a quip for everyone.

He turned to me as I sat down.

"Hey, Big Stuff. Wasn't none of my business what I said about the color TV, but you got to be careful around here."

"Like I said, I'm new and I appreciate any nuggets of information I can glean."

"I got to tell you, down home we can make two sentences out of one of your words." He pointed at the skinny guy with one tooth. "This is Strickler." Then he turned toward the tattooed body builder. "And this is Lefty."

"Hi, guys."

Strickler, single tooth chomping furiously, said, "You really want advice, let me tell you, if a riot jumps off, take cover fast! Bury yourself in a group of bodies or get behind that counter there if you can, or better, under a table. But whatever you do, don't get under *this* table!"

"Why not?"

"Because that's where I'll be," he said as he broke into a grin.

While we were chuckling at this joke they'd all heard before, Lefty jumped up.

"Arm wrestle?"

"No thanks," I said. "I'm not really—."

---

2 The Northsiders were a gang so named because they came from the North Side of Chicago. In Menard, the Northsiders accepted almost any white gang-banger, even if they didn't "ride with them" on the street.

"Come on, Road Dog, I seen you on the handball court. You hit one so hard it stayed this high"—holding his hand flat and low, parallel to the floor—"all the way from behind the court to the wall."

"Yeah, but that's coordination more than strength."

"Come on, Dog. I'll use my right arm." From a guy called "Lefty," I took that as an attempt at fair play.

So this was it. If I turned down the invitation to arm wrestle in a chow hall full of hardened criminals searching for a weakness, I might as well stand up and shout, "Come get me, guys, I'm a pussy!"

If I accepted the challenge, I'd probably lose. Lefty was a body builder—you didn't have to see him lifting weights to know that. He was cut. Big shoulders. Well-defined biceps.

I figured losing had to beat refusing—at least I'd have tried—so I accepted the challenge. We sat in adjacent chairs and faced off, gripping each other's hand, getting ourselves pumped up.

"Okay," Lefty said. "One … two … three …"

I flexed my wrist and powered my arm forward. It was the split-second edge I needed. As Lefty said, "GO!" my arm started down and Lefty's arm slammed onto the table.

Whack!

Lefty looked surprised but immediately regained his composure and shot me a big grin.

"That won't happen if I use my left arm."

"I wouldn't have a *chance* if you used your left arm," I said, handing him back his pride.

∽

I was still living in an orientation cell. I hadn't yet been called to appear before the assignment committee to be given a job, but I'd been told they'd probably start me in the kitchen. Housing was by assignment, so for now I lived on Seven Gallery of the West House.

The West Cell House held five rows of fifty cells, called galleries, with Nine Gallery on the top and One Gallery on the bottom. One Gallery had a wide floor in front of the cells and the four galleries above it had much narrower aisles with wire mesh to keep inmates from jumping down—or being thrown—to the wider floor below.

One afternoon I was trudging up the stairs to my cell after lunch when I spotted a display of greeting cards on the wall of the first cell on Three Gallery. The cards were taped five high and three wide, cheery cartoon designs in bright colors on bold yellow card stock. The gate to Three Gallery was open, so I left the line climbing the stairs and stepped in front of the greeting card cell. A sign said, "Cards, 1 pack each."

"Hey, Hendricks!" a voice called out, startling me. It was Henry. I hadn't noticed him, lying on his bunk in the dark cell.

"Hi!" I said. "How'd you remember my name?"

"It's been plastered all over the news."

"Yeah, I forget how famous I am. Do you think I can bother you for a couple of those cards? They're really impressive. I can come back later if you—"

But Henry was already up and heading for the bars.

"I sleep in the day when I'm not in school, 'cause I stay awake at night to work on my cards."

"What do you use for light?" I saw a stool and a desk, solid welded iron but not bolted in like the bunks.

"This high intensity light, see? They sell them in the commissary."

"What I need right now is two birthday cards, one male, one female—and they're religious, so nothing risqué," I said. "My parents. Their birthdays are five days apart."

"Well, pick out what you want. They're one pack each, but that's just for the card. You want me to pick them for you, that's another pack."

I carried no cigarettes—didn't smoke—but I already knew Lifers coupons[3] would substitute for cigarettes, 90¢ roughly equaling one pack. Later I'd learn to keep some around for trading purposes.

"In that case I'll pick my own—and I'll pick two for your next customers so my two cards will be free."

That got me one of his grins and a quip.

"It didn't say in the paper you were Jewish."

I laughed. "How'd you get started making these cards anyway? You know, they're really good—great designs, well rendered. Is making greeting cards a prison cottage industry?"

---

3   The Lifers was a prison organization run by inmates. It sold food and clothing items. Its coupon books looked like Jaycees coupon books and were the only form of legal tender in the prison.

"Naw, it's something I do on my own," Henry said. "I get the yellow card stock and the colored pencils from the art supply store, and I have a bunch of patterns I trace. I drew most of the patterns, only I copied the first two. This one here was my first original." On the front a man's shirt was captioned "I was going to buy you a shirt for your birthday." On the inside beneath a message that read "but I didn't like the cuffs that came with it" was a drawing of a pair of handcuffs. "So I first made some cards to send to my boys down home."

"Where's down home?" I said. "Streator?"

"Oh, so you know something about me, too."

"I don't remember anything about the murders when they happened but I was living in Bloomington at the time you were recaptured and I remember reading about you then. You murdered your wife and her lover, right?"

Henry looked down for a moment then back up at me.

"Yeah, I'm not proud of it, but that's what I did." He was quiet for a second or two. "She wasn't legally my wife, but we did have a baby when we lived together in Joliet."

"Hey, man, I'm sorry I said that so bluntly," I said. "This place is a whole new world to me, with social rules I've never dealt with before."

"I've heard a lot worse, Hendricks, a heck of a lot worse. Don't worry about it. The truth is, I deserve it. I still can't believe it was me that did that."

That was when it hit me why I liked this guy. He was smart though probably not well educated, friendly, a joker who told good stories, but he was also honest. He said what he felt and he admitted when he was wrong—a rare quality, especially in prison.

"So you were saying you started making cards to send down home, and—"

"Yeah, except you ain't right about down home," he said. "I was raised in Streator, Illinois, but McDonald County in Missouri is my home. Lived there for thirteen years as Tom Elliot before I got caught. Anyway, after I started making cards for my boys, some guys here saw them and wanted some, and then after a while I made some for my friends back home to put in the Valley View truck stop, and when those sell, the money goes to my boys."

"It seems like you have a fascinating story. And if you don't mind another compliment, you're a natural storyteller."

"Well, I'm always talking and most of the time I'm telling some story. When I was in the jail in Ottawa, after I was captured—"

"Which time?" I said. "When you were captured after the murders or when you were captured after being a fugitive?"

"I wasn't captured after the murders, I turned myself in. I'm talking about when the FBI come out to where I was logging in the woods in Missouri. After that, when I was in the Greene County jail, a writer asked if I'd be interested in telling him my story for a book, and I wasn't sure about it at the time but then later on I thought, yeah, why not? But by then he wasn't asking no more."

"If a writer wanted to do a book about you now, would you be interested?"

"Now, yes. Back then it was so new, and I was still adjusting to the idea of being incarcerated—"

Just then a small guy with a big nose passed behind me.

"Hey, Al!" Henry called out. "Didn't you say you needed a clerk for the Voc School?"

"Yeah." He turned to me. "You don't have a job?"

"I'm still in orientation but it's been three weeks so they say I'm going to the assignment committee soon. I'll probably get a kitchen assignment."

"Man, you don't need to work in the kitchen! You want to be a school clerk? You get a desk and a typewriter, it's a real easy gig. It's just that not many guys here are qualified. You got to be able to read, write, file, you know, use a calculator—shit like that."

"Sounds good," I said.

"I'll take care of it. You'll have to move to Three Gallery, so find a cellmate you can live with. I'll put the paperwork in. You're Hendricks?"

"Yup, that's me. Thanks!"

With my new friend gone down the gallery, I turned back to Tom Henry.

"Do you think I could give you a list of my family and in-laws who—"

"In-laws?" he said. "You mean, like, relatives of your wife?"

"Right, my in-laws." He looked floored. I knew why, but I let him say it.

"Not my business, but ... you're still on good terms with your wife's family?"

"The only people who think I'm guilty are the 'people of the State of Illinois,' whoever they are," I said. "No one who knows me, including Susie's family, thinks I did it. It's just crazy, but—" I lost my train of thought, then snapped back. "Anyway, if I give you a list, can you make up the cards for me? I'll be glad to pay ahead."

"No, you'll pay me when you get them, just like anyone else. But sure, bring me a list and I'll have them cards ready for you."

"Thanks. One more thing. That desk you have. Do you know what they're worth in here? A guy said he'd sell me one for fifteen packs. Is that a fair price?"

"Okay, Big Stuff, listen up. Fifteen packs is way too cheap for a desk, and if anyone's offering you a desk for that price, his name is Jackson and that makes it way too expensive."

"I take it you're trying to tell me this won't be an honest transaction?"

"You catch on fast! Jackson's selling it half off to make it irresistible. When you buy it, he'll deliver it all right, and then you won't see him again. Who you will see is one of his buddies. He'll show up and say hey, you got Northsider property there. You say no, I bought and paid for this desk from a guy named Jackson. He says he doesn't know anyone named Jackson but the desk looks like one that belongs to his organization and will you turn it over just to be sure. When you do it'll have Northsider scratched on the bottom. He says give it up. And you will. And the next time you see Jackson he won't know you."

"Wow! Thanks, man. I barely know you and you've already helped me."

"Well, pay me back by keeping your mouth shut about it."

"Keep my mouth shut about what?"

"Right."

"So, what do you like to be called? Henry or Tom?"

"Well, people from down home call me Tom. My family from Streator calls me Henry, so does the prison. So I guess I'm Henry but I prefer Tom, 'cause Tom was a better guy!"

"What about Tom Henry?"

"I like that."

"Well, all right, then. Thanks for your help and your cards, Tom Henry."

As I turned to walk up the next two flights of stairs, a thought occurred to me. I'd been thinking of writing a book about myself but hadn't considered writing one about another convict. What a story, though! A double murderer pleads guilty, escapes from jail, lives as a fugitive, is recaptured, and tells his story to his cellmate in prison. *Tom Henry.* It had a good ring to it.

Tom Henry, still at his cell bars, seemed to sense my train of thought.

"Be careful what you wish for, Hendricks."

I stopped and turned. "What do you mean?"

"When I was a kid, I wanted bunk beds."

Three

"After you escaped from jail, how did you get your new identity?"

Tom Henry and I were talking over breakfast in the chow hall.

"Easy," he said. "I jammed a .357 magnum in some driver's face, so he was my taxi to Chicago. I went to a library, found a story in an old paper about a couple who died in a car crash and left a son about my age. I figure he got adopted with another name, so I sent in for a social security card. It come in the mail and now I'm Tom Elliott. Got my driver's license the same way."

"How'd you know to look up old newspaper articles?" I said.

"Asked a bunch of questions. Once I got to the library, the lady there showed me how to use that machine where you scroll through old newspapers. When I found some things I was interested in, she made copies for me."

I believed he felt terrible about the murders, but he was clearly pleased with himself for the escape and his cleverness in getting a new identity.

"I've got an interview today in Voc School for the clerk job," I said when we finished eating. "Thanks again for hooking me up with that guy."

Strickler, the neo-Nazi, glanced toward the black side of the chow hall. "What a waste, giving those guys milk. They can't even *digest* it!"

"Why don't you collect their cartons and explain how they can't digest it?" Tom Henry said, then turned back to me. "Just tell me if it's none of my business, but I saw news about your case on the TV—never thought you'd get convicted. Nobody here did. What happened?"

I took a second to compose my thoughts. I hadn't talked about my case, the pain was too raw. But my new friend had told me candidly about his. So I began with the crime-scene tape and the devastating news I got when I returned home from that trip.

"The cops thought I didn't show enough emotion—affect, they call it—so they suspected me immediately and arrested me soon after. At trial, the state hired a doctor who said my kids were killed before Susie came home, and I *was* at home then. My lawyers got doctors to say there's no way their doctor could know that, but the jury believed him."

"Can't be that simple," Strickler said. "Got to be more to it than that."

"Well, yes and no. The trial lasted ten weeks, so of course there's more. But really, that doctor's testimony was basically their case against me." I hesitated, then said, "There were models I worked with that testified I messed with them sexually."

"How many models did you sleep with?"

"None. I measured them for a back brace I was developing. I had several of them take off their tops and I touched the breasts of a couple of them."

"Did you need to do that?"

"Not really," I said. What a show it had been in the courtroom when the prosecution paraded model after model to testify I'd measured them, palpated for bony landmarks, then told them they needed to remove more clothing. The testimony—in front of my family, Susie's family, the whole world—convinced the jury that I'd used my position of trust to exploit those models.

"I was measuring them for a legitimate purpose, but having them disrobe wasn't legitimate. Of course, the models had nothing to do with the murders. They were just there to make me look bad. It's easier to convict a defendant you don't like."

"But they must of had some kind of proof," Strickler said.

"Only what I told you before. The doctor who looked at the children's stomach contents said my children died two hours after eating. But he was way wrong—I know, I was there. I didn't leave until after Susie came home, so I know they were alive until after eleven o'clock."

"What do you mean, the doc *looked at* the contents?" Tom Henry said.

"Used his eyes—period. He didn't use a microscope or a magnifying glass, didn't do a single test. He just looked at the jars they showed him.

"The thing is, the idea that our children were killed before my wife came home doesn't pass the common sense test. It goes against human nature. To believe it you have to believe she came home and went to bed without checking on her children two doors down the hall. Susie was in bed, peacefully asleep, when she was killed. No defensive wounds. But that's the prosecution's theory, and my lawyers weren't clever enough to show how unlikely it was."

"Man, you got screwed!" Strickler said.

Inelegant but accurate.

ᖬ

It was lunchtime, and Tom Henry was doing his thing.

"Old man Pitts had a dump with a great big Dutch elm tree right in the middle of it, with trash all around it. I used to shoot crows out of that tree.

Several times I saw this big old chicken hawk in it, but he'd spot me and fly away 'fore I could get in range with my .22 rifle.

"This time I snuck around real quiet till I was near enough to shoot. He was perched on a branch facing me and that spotted white breast with dark brown feathers around it made a good target. I shot him, he fell, then he spins around a few times in the trash. I walk up to get him, but my foot gets tangled in the hog wire and I can't find him—it's summertime and there was green briar bushes all around.

"I wanted to get a closer look—I was real proud I shot him. I did a little more hunting around before I finally saw him. He'd come up out of there and was standing on this board sticking out of the dump pile, so I went in after him. Well, he snaps his beak at me, real mad, and ruffles his feathers, and I see he's got a broken wing 'cause only one is stretched out.

"So I put my gun down—he couldn't go anywhere, just bounce around in there—and I reach for him, but he snaps his beak again and bristles like a cat and raises his wing but can't fly off. That chicken hawk is in one tight spot."

"So what'd you do?" I said.

"Took off my shirt, threw it over him, and carried him home. Most of the time you carry birds by putting their wings straight up above them—that way they can't peck you or claw you, and it don't hurt them. But I couldn't do that 'cause of his busted wing. I carried him behind the house with my shirt still over him, put rocks around the edge of the shirt to hold him in.

"I run up to the house with my gun and got an old cardboard box with holes in the side of it from the basement, put the box upside down over the hawk, set rocks on top of the box. The next morning I took some lunch meat out there to feed him but he wouldn't eat it. I took a bunch of clothes that weren't any good out there for bedding."

"I'm guessing you didn't have permission?" I said.

"Didn't have no permission for what I did the next morning, neither. When my mom went shopping, I got pieces of wood from the shed and nailed together a real nice box with slots and holes in it. I knew my dad couldn't find out about my hawk. He didn't want me to shoot things—didn't mind too bad if I shot a snake or a rat, but shoot a hawk and put it in a cage? No way.

"He always said, 'Don't cage up those little animals God meant to be free. How would you like someone to put you in a cage?'

"To patch up that wing I raided my dad's tool caddy for a roll of electrical tape and a small pair of wire cutters. I put a little piece of a rag over the wing and wrapped it up best I could. There's a real thick bone on top and I opened up the pinion feathers on the bottom to wrap the tape, had to bust one off with my dad's side cutters. He didn't like that one bit—the hawk, I mean—but I had to do it to open up the feathers wide enough to wrap the tape.

"Wasn't no easy thing, let me tell you. They're vicious, them chicken hawks. I put water out there in this little sardine can, and what he'd do is dump it over hopping around. So the second day I punched two holes in the sardine can and tied it with wire to the side of the cage.

"Third day I noticed the meat's gone. He started eating and drinking. I kept changing the meat each day, 'cause I didn't know hawks can eat any old spoiled meat. Nothing bothers them."

I felt as if I was right in that yard with the hawk. Could I get Tom Henry to tell me his life story like this? It would take forever to write it, but forever was what I had.

"So my hawk got to doing real good, peppy and all, but he never got over ruffling his feathers and snapping his beak at me. I peeked in at him through the holes, sweet-talked him, but he always remembered who I was and wouldn't never get friendly and I wanted to be his friend now, 'cause I really liked him. But even though I'm the one who bandaged him, no matter how much I feed him and take care of him, he knows I'm the one that shot him and we can't make friends.

"He stopped eating the lunch meat, so I took my mom's mousetraps out to the woods and brought him a dead mouse. He walks over to it real slow, gets it in his beak, shakes it, drops it, picks it up again. So I'm watching this, thinking he's used to killing his own stuff—this bird ain't no scavenger.

"So I stripped bark off old rotting logs to look for grub worms and I found me some pink baby mice and I put 'em in my cap to bring to him. And let me tell you, they're like dessert for my hawk. He clamps his talons on their little bodies and tears into them with his hook-shaped beak and never once stops to look up at me. Which I didn't expect, I just got a kick out of watching him gorge hisself.

"So after I've had him for maybe four weeks I go out there one morning to bring him some food and he's lying on his side. Of course I know he's dead. I could tell he'd been dead for some time, 'cause his wings and legs was stiff.

"What did he die of?" I said.

"I think he just died from a broken heart, corny as it sounds. I know he didn't die from my shot, 'cause I've shot birds in the wing and kept them alive a lot longer than him. I reckon he just gave up 'cause he couldn't be free."

∽

This guy could really tell a story. The question was, could I write one? With all the time on my hands during my year in jail awaiting trial, I'd read fiction, biography, history, textbooks, religious and philosophical works—and books on writing, from Joseph Trimmer's *Writing with a Purpose* to Strunk and White's *Elements of Style* to William Zinsser's classic *On Writing Well.*

The idea of writing Tom Henry's story was slowly taking root. I had a unique opportunity to write an amazing true crime story with a twist. *Tom Henry: A True Story of Murder, Jailbreak, and Life on the Lam, as Told to His Prison Cellmate, David Hendricks.* Could I do it? Could I complete such a work?

Could I at least make it longer than the title?

Four

Menard had two fenced recreation yards. Each yard had a baseball diamond, the outfield of which was used for football or soccer. Around the playing field was a track, and toward the rear of the yard were weight-lifting areas and handball courts. The Lifers ran a concession shack outside the track, and telephones were arrayed along the fence. Gangs ran the phones—if you didn't belong to a gang and wanted to make a call, you'd better have cigarettes ready.

That evening I was there to play handball, but mostly I wanted to talk to Tom Henry. He was already there as I approached the courts and saw that gang chiefs were using the handball courts for weight lifting, the gang soldiers standing in front of them, arms folded on their chests. Guards, probably alerted by the tower, were just now coming down to the yard to address the problem.

"Let's stroll around the track, Big Stuff," Tom Henry said. "If we're waiting for the handball courts when the screws chase them off, they might get the wrong idea."

"Good thinking. I wanted to talk to you anyway."

"Yeah, Al told me."

"I got the clerk job, but asking if I could cell with you was actually my number-two request. Al doesn't know about my first one."

"Does too. I told him you wanted to write a book telling my story."

"How the heck—"

"I saw your ears shoot up like the antennae on 'My Favorite Martian' when I said I might like to see my story in a book."

"Guess I shouldn't take up poker, then?"

"Guess not."

We came upon a group of weight lifters. I saw Lefty spotting for a guy with a huge tattoo and a long pony tail and even more muscles than Lefty.

"That's Spider, biker chief for the West House," Tom Henry said. "He's cool."

"How about Lefty? I'm having a hard time getting a read on him. He seems a little … volatile."

"When they moved Voc School down to Three Gallery," Tom Henry said, "I moved in with Lefty in West 3-15. Once I was snoring too loud to suit him, and I'm on the top bunk, so he pulls me off it right onto the concrete floor saying, 'Don't snore so damn loud next time.' His way of letting me know it was his cell, like a fox pisses on a tree to mark his territory."

"Well, if you let me cell with you I promise not to pull you off the top bunk."

"I know you won't, 'cause I got the bottom one."

"I can live with that, but take a look at my size—you really want to sleep below my bunk?"

"You seen my cellie?"

"Good point." Tom Henry's cellmate was only slightly taller but at least twice his weight.

"So yes," I said, "I'd like to write your story. What do you think?"

"I told you about that guy in Greene County. He was a writer. Can you write?"

I took a minute to think about it.

"The best answer I can give you is yes and no," I said. "Yes, I've been studying writing and I've been thinking about writing and I've always succeeded when I put my mind to something. So, no, I'm not a writer yet. But yes, I think I can do it."

"So why should I let you write my story when I told a real writer no?"

"Because I'm here."

"Lucky you."

We'd circled back to the handball courts.

"Really, what do you have to lose?" I said. "If we start and you don't like telling your story or don't like the way I'm writing it or I don't like writing it, we can stop. It's not like our time is limited."

"You never know. Yesterday I got a notice I'm eligible for two days of meritorious good time. They're going to take those two days off my three hundred and ninety years!"

"Look at the bright side," I said. "By the end of the twenty-first century your sentence will have shrunk to three hundred and eighty-nine years!"

"By the way, I forgot to ask. What'd you get? Natural Life?"

Natural Life in Illinois meant you never went to a parole board.

"I got four Natural Life sentences, consecutive!"

"Consecutive?" Tom Henry thought for a second. "Maybe you should see a jail-house lawyer and get him to file for a sentence reduction. He does it right, you might get those four consecutive Natural Life sentences broke down to four *concurrent* Natural Life sentences."

❧

Tom Henry's cellmate moved out the next day, as the clerk predicted, but it was three more days before I was approved to transfer. I got my transfer slip in the evening and first thing the next morning moved into my new home, the top bunk of Cell 3-50 of the West Cell House.

My trial transcripts hadn't arrived yet and I'd only been in prison three weeks, so all I had to move other than state-supplied clothes and bedding were my few legal papers, a couple of books, my color TV, and an oscillating fan. Oh, and I brought a board for a shelf.

It was a good thing I had so little to contribute, because Tom Henry had pretty much filled the cell himself. His four-foot-wide desk and stool sat in the cleared area next to the bunks along with boxes of card patterns, boxes of legal transcripts, and yet more boxes of clothes, food, and sundries. The space under the bottom bunk was the extent of our expansion possibilities.

Shelves were contraband, but everybody who could afford it had one. They could be suspended above the bars in the front of the cell, and a TV could be placed on this shelf and wired to the wall. That's how I had mine set up by the end of the first day.

Also prohibited was my fan. Fans were allowed, and almost every inmate had one, but you had to have a permit. Some had a bogus permit, which you could buy for two packs, but when a shakedown came and the guard checked it against his list, he took the fan and the bogus permit and gave you a ticket in return. The only way to get a real permit was to buy the fan from the commissary. This went for TVs, electric shavers, high intensity lights, radios, and almost any item of value. The only legitimate item I owned was my color TV.

❧

As I settled in to watch my first baseball game in my new home, a guy whose shaved head was tattooed with a spider-web on top and an eyeball in the back stopped at the door of our cell and waved Tom Henry over to him.

I was already getting used to the flow of card customers, but this conversation took place in hushed tones. The visitor looked at me, then left only to return a few minutes later with a book he handed to Tom Henry.

19

"It's true what they say," I said. "Never judge a book by its cover. I'd have bet anything that guy was no reader!"

Tom Henry thought this was hilarious. When he finally stopped guffawing he turned so his body was shielding the book and opened it about two thirds of the way through.

"Check it out, Big Stuff!"

Inset into its final pages was a shiny piece of steel, about five inches long and one inch wide—I couldn't tell exactly how thick it was, but it looked thin, maybe an eighth of an inch, no more than a quarter-inch—with one end taped and the other tapering to a sharp point. The book's pages were cut out as neatly as if it had been done with a router. Somebody had put hours into it. The shank didn't look all that lethal, but I supposed in experienced hands it could be plunged into a body to a depth of three, maybe three-and-a-half inches. Done in the right—or rather, wrong—place, it could be deadly.

Tom Henry shut the book and placed it in one of his boxes with the rest of his books.

"I'm not hooked up," he said. "When I first got here and they tried to recruit me, I didn't say yes, I was just friendly. They never send me on a mission but once in a while they ask me to carry or hold something. Old boy there told me he thinks he might of been snitched out, so I'm holding the book till they shake him down."

Just then a guard stepped up with a piece of paper.

"Chapel!" He unlocked the cell. Tom Henry grabbed his Bible and started out.

"Officer," I said from the bunk, "am I on the list?"

"No, just Hillenbrand. What's your name?"

"Hendricks. I just moved in today, so I'm probably still on the Seven Gallery list."

The ball game was over by the time Tom Henry returned. While he waited for the guard to lock him up, he ran up and down the gallery, talking to friends and passing out scripture wallet calendars for 1985. Even though it was late April, they went fast.

"You go to chapel for something to do, or are you serious about your faith?" I asked.

"Dead serious. I got saved at a place down home called Penitentiary Bend, believe it or not. I went there to kill myself by running my car off the road over a cliff. I was drunk at the time. But I skidded and got stuck in the ditch and I got saved. And I been saved ever since."

"Do you think it was God that got you stuck or you being drunk?"

Tom Henry took a minute to think.

"Let me put it this way. God did it, but it was one of his easiest jobs ever! Clarence from *It's a Wonderful Life* could of arranged it."

"Never saw it," I said. "I grew up in a house without television."

"You didn't have no TV?"

"No, our branch of the Plymouth Brethren was very devout and we believed we should keep our homes free from the influences of the world. Well, some of us had TVs. I'd say in a few years most will. Times change." I thought for a second about those good, sober, devout people. "But these aren't folks who change fast."

"Do you still consider yourself a member?"

"After I was convicted, I resigned. Some of them didn't want to accept my resignation, but it was for the best. You can't be a Biblical church and have a convicted murderer as a member."

"I heard it called a cult on the news."

"Well, if by cult you mean a small religious group that's a little bit unusual, yes. They take the Bible as the literal, inspired Word of God. They believe we're sinners in our natural state because of Adam and Eve's original sin, and only the sacrifice of Jesus on the cross can satisfy a righteous God as payment for our sins."

"That ain't unusual," Tom Henry said. "My church believes that."

"They also don't call their buildings churches. They're 'meeting rooms' or 'assembly halls.' And they don't have an ordained preacher, so it's pretty old fashioned. If you want a simple way to peg them, think of them as Baptists on steroids."

"So you're not a member, but are you still a believer?"

How to answer that one?

"After disaster struck my family—and me?" Big sigh. "I looked around and it seemed as if blind random luck, not divine guidance, drives human affairs. Bad luck, good luck, and you never know what's going to strike until it does. So that's a pretty humanistic belief. It's certainly not faith."

"Well, if you don't have faith anymore," Tom Henry said, "you're not a believer."

"I'm willing to get my faith back, but to be honest ..." Another sigh. "The truth is, I'm angry at God—which is a stupid thing to be, I know, because by definition God is good, but it makes my blood boil when people from my church group tell me things like, 'God must have some great work for you to do.'

"God had my family killed, just to make me into something useful, to form me to fit some job? They're talking about children who never had a chance to grow up. They're talking about a woman who was the sweetest, most selfless person I ever knew! And a good God had them savagely murdered so *I* could be prepared for some work? Are they *nuts*? Who would even *want* to work for such a God? That's no God, that's a monster!"

Five

I'd uttered the last three sentences with such vehemence I was trembling. Tom Henry sprang off his bunk.

"Man, I'm sorry! I wouldn't never—I didn't mean to get you like this!" He paused, searching for words. "You got a lot of anger in you." He started to sit back on the edge of his bunk, then before his butt hit the mattress he sprang right back up again. "But you can't call God a monster!"

"I know," I said. "I got carried away. For the last year and a half … I've had to take it and take it and take it, and I've never had a chance to talk it out with anyone. I can't talk to my family or Susie's family like this. It would just kill them. Just knowing I'm losing my faith is tearing them to pieces. So I'm really glad to have you to talk to. I hope you aren't sorry I moved in."

"No, Big Stuff, it's cool. When I get to telling you about how low I got before I found God, you'll understand. But anyway, I'm glad you're here and I'm glad to be here for you. I mean that, bro."

"All right. Let's just put this down as 'to be continued.'"

But we never did continue that conversation—we never needed to. I'd opened my heart to Tom Henry and he'd received what I had to say, despite his disagreement. A bond of understanding had formed between two guys about as different as two guys could be.

I went to sleep after that, but Tom Henry didn't—not because he was agitated by what I'd told him but because he didn't sleep much at night. That's when he colored his cards. Bored officers and night-shift sergeants would stop by to chat—Tom Henry would make coffee, and they'd usually bring along some treat from the officers' kitchen along with the latest prison gossip: which guard's wife was sleeping with which captain, who got arrested for bringing in drugs, which inmate got stabbed and what his condition was.

The next morning, I was heating up a cup of water when Tom Henry burst out laughing.

"You got coffee?" he said.

"You know I don't."

"So what are you going to do with that hot water?"

"Drink it—I've kind of gotten used to it. And it's cheaper than coffee."

"Never thought I'd see the day!" Tom Henry said. "A millionaire too cheap to buy coffee!"

"Not cheap—thrifty. And I'm no millionaire."

"Anyway, I should warn you. Sampson told me last night they're going to stop selling Magic Shave."

"So? *We* don't use Magic Shave." Black guys used it instead of razors—it dissolved the beard. White guys couldn't use it because it burned our skin.

"No, but the reason they're yanking it from the commissary is 'cause some idiot threw a boiling mixture of Magic Shave and baby oil in a nurse's face—put her in the hospital. Anything the commissary sells that can hurt anybody will be coming off the list. Anything sharp, like tweezers or toenail clippers. Anything guys can hurt themselves with, like extension cords or three-way plugs. Anything can be used as a weapon, like canned food.[4] What I'm worried about is what they'll take off next."

⁓

The following day I bought a typewriter and a high intensity lamp, four stingers, two six-foot extension cords, four toenail clippers, and two tweezers—just in case. I also got some Little Debbie cupcakes and instant coffee.

Little Debbie snacks sold well in the all-male prison, partly due to implied promise of the slogan on each package: "Little Debbie has a treat for you." But the commissary item I'd fallen in love with was the stinger, a small resister wire inside a coiled metal tube. You hooked it over the side of a coffee cup with the metal part immersed in water, then plugged it in. In a minute the water would be boiling and you could make coffee or tea.

When I brought it all back to the cell I told Tom Henry, "I want you to acknowledge that I bought coffee and paid for it out of my stash of millions."

"And what you going to do now, millionaire?"

"Now, if you don't mind, I'm going to turn on my millionaire color TV, brew myself a cup of millionaire coffee, and watch some millionaires play baseball."

It was the White Sox versus the Yankees, and it promised to be a good game. After the White Sox beat the Yankees in eleven innings, a victory shout reverberated throughout the cell house.

---

4 Soup socks were the same as soap socks, but more effective. You shoved a can of soup into the end of a sock, tied it off, and swung it vigorously.

"Of course," I said. "Most of these guys are from Chicago."

Then the yelling and the bar-banging started.

Debris flew through the air. Fires blazed on the gallery, choking smoke rolled in. Henry grabbed a sheet, pushed it into the toilet, then hung it on the inside of the bars in the front of the cell. It helped, but after a while the smoke started curling in around it. Inmates started yelling.

"I can't breathe!"

"Call the nurse!"

"Cell 5-41! My cellmate's got emphysema. He stopped breathing. Hurry!"

Guards streamed up the stairs and spread throughout the cell house, stomping out fires, yelling that anyone inciting anything was going straight to Seg.

Segregation, in a maximum security prison, was reserved for the baddest of the bad. A lot of the inmates were like Tom Henry and me, just trying to do their time and be left alone. But as for the rest, you couldn't appeal to "the better angels of their nature." You just threatened them with segregation.

⁂

The next morning the doors didn't roll. Breakfast came late, gelatinous oatmeal brought to the cell house by guards and left in the food slot.

We were on lockdown.

Lockdown meant no school, no chow hall, no yard, no chapel, no details, no assignments, no Lifers selling wares on the galleries. And come morning, the lockdown would turn into a shakedown.

It was the shakedowns that finalized a lockdown's dehumanization process. This was when they took away our few small comforts: curtains for privacy or to shield us from the cold, shelves to hold books or TVs, electric fans and TVs we'd bought cheap from inmates about to be released, a plastic clipboard or a 4H pencil, a homemade easel for painting—things that allowed us to occupy our minds. So we prepared for the worst, hid our treasures, and worried about what we couldn't conceal.

Since we didn't have to get up in the morning, I stayed up that night while Tom Henry worked on cards. I was reading his legal transcripts when Officer Alms showed up with fried chicken and cookies from the officer's kitchen.

"They're not sure when we'll be off deadlock," he said. "Some say Monday, some Tuesday, and I even heard there might be partial deadlock through next week." Partial deadlock meant you got out of your cell but only for meals.

"Two whites were badly beaten, one till his face is just pulp. That nurse who had hot Magic Shave and baby oil thrown in her face has permanent burns. They're bringing the Academy up from Springfield to do the shake-down."

"Well, you're a fountain of good news!" Tom Henry said.

I waited until Alms had moved on.

"Why is the Academy so bad?" I asked.

"Their guys are trainees," Tom Henry said. "They do the shakedowns by the book. Guys like us, we want guards who know us 'cause they know we're not doing nothing wrong so they don't mess with us. Academy guys, they don't know us. They're real assholes."

The shakedown crew made it to us the next day.

The door rolled and the guard said, "All right, up and out onto the gallery, just underclothes."

We were handcuffed to each other through the wire mesh across from the cell and stood out in the gallery in our undies. Our Academy guy took our fans and permits, a shelf, the clipboard, a curtain, a two-inch stack of Tom Henry's yellow cardstock—and threw it all onto the gallery floor.

He took so much time in our cell the rest of the crew had long since finished with our neighbors' cell and had moved down the gallery—which meant I was able to use my free hand to pass the shelf, the clipboard, the curtains, and the cardstock into the next cell while Tom Henry kept the young trainee busy with his chatter.

❧

Saturday morning brought a yell from downstairs at about nine.

"Hillenbrand! Visit!"

Tom Henry bird-bathed, shaved, and dressed in his best clothes. In Men-ard they issue you prison clothes at orientation but you can buy better clothes from the Lifers: blue jeans, a street-quality blue shirt with no stenciled letters, a denim jacket, and athletic shoes. Few inmates had Lifer clothes—they were a luxury item.

Tom Henry yelled downstairs to the Flag, the control box where guards were stationed.

"Hillenbrand. 3-50. Ready for my visit."

A guard materialized, unlocked our cell door, and Tom Henry was gone.

৩৯

Later that evening he told me about it. As soon as he got to the visiting table and hugged his sister, kissed his mother, and shook hands with his father, he gave them his big news.

"Guess who I'm celling with," he said. "David Hendricks from Bloomington! And he's going to write a book about my story!"

"Hendricks?" his father said. "Hendricks! How can you cell with him? You know what he did?"

"He says he's innocent, Dad, and I believe him. He's one of the nicest guys I ever met."

"I'll tell about your nice guy. A salesman from Bloomington who knew their family real well told me all about it. Hendricks belonged to a cult where the women were sex slaves and the men swapped them. The reason he had an airplane was he flew drugs across the border. That's where he got his money. And he had models stashed in apartments. One of them demanded he kill his family and marry her or she'd blow the whistle on him."

"Dad, don't you think that would've been on the news?"

"You can't trust the media, they cover everything up. Look at your case, the way they ..." He trailed off, shaking his head.

"Well, anyway, I'm celling with him," Tom Henry said. "You know, there's not a lot of Eagle Scouts in here to choose from."

"Sure, but Hendricks? Well, I could never control you when you were in my home and I sure can't control you now. I'll watch the newspaper for him killing you, maybe then they'll execute him like they should have done before."

A decade later, as I sat in the living room of the comfortable Hillenbrand home on the north edge of Streator, Tom Henry's dad told me how happy he was when he first heard his son was celling with me.

"I knew he'd be in good hands," he said.

I just nodded and scribbled on my legal pad.

৩৯

We were still discussing the visit when Dave, a West House enforcer for the Northsiders, interrupted from the gallery.

"I know the big guy just moved in and got settled and all," he said, "but I got bad news." Tom Henry hopped out of his bunk and went up to the cell door.

"What's up?"

"They're putting the gallery workers in the first cell of each gallery, and the Northsiders got Three Gallery. So me and Little Johnny need to move in here. You guys got to find somewhere else to live by day after tomorrow."

The cells with 50 in their number were adjacent to the stairs and right above the Flag—an administrative move to help the guards communicate more easily with the gang leaders, who were assigned as gallery workers, to give them freedom of movement and communication. It seemed a bad way to run a prison, letting gangs enforce the rules. It might be efficient, but the enforcement was capriciously violent.

"So what do we do?" Tom Henry asked after Dave moved on.

"We've got to get another cell together," I said. "It's the only way we can do your story."

"I know two white cells with one guy in each," Tom Henry said. "Lefty's alone down the gallery, and Rick's cellie just left. Rick can move in with Lefty."

"You think he'd do that?"

"I can talk to the Northsiders. They tell him to move, he'll move."

"Okay, if we have to. But you know what they say, you catch more flies with honey than with vinegar."

"Screw the honey, give me a big fly swatter!"

"Be that as it may," I said, "let me offer Rick some honey, okay?"

A few hours and a $20 book of Lifer's coupons later, we were making preparations to move into Cell 3-49, where we hoped to stay, uninterrupted, for at least a year. We had to dismantle everything we'd wired, glued, or hooked to the wall or ceiling, and Tom Henry had to take his card display off the wall.

Less than a week later another Northsider appeared at the bars of our new cell.

"I got bad news, homey," he said. "Looks like they screwed up and didn't open enough cells for all the organizations. So you're probably going to have to move out of this one too."

"When?"

"Not yet. I'm just giving you a heads up."

There were no more white openings on the gallery. Finding two anywhere would be tough, finding two in the same cell impossible. All we could hope for was that the rumor was just a rumor.

That night Tom Henry sat on his stool, cutting out a design for a card he planned to send his son, Thomas. His fingertips gripped the miniscule blade he'd acquired by smashing the plastic off a pencil sharpener.

"If I ever get out of here," he said, "I'm going to buy a knife three feet long, big as a sword, and a gigantic scissors, and hang them on the wall as ornaments—just because I can!"

"In the meanwhile, now's as good a time as any to start telling your story," I said. "Why don't you lie back on that bunk and tell the good shrink about your childhood?"

"Which reminds me," Tom Henry said. "You know who I saw the other day?"

"Give me a hint," I said.

"Well, what reminded me is this guy was examined by psychiatrists."

"Is Runner back from the Bug House?"

"Naw, Big Stuff, this is a guy from Death Row."

"The clown?" I said.

"John Wayne Gacy himself. He was in chains and four guards were taking him to the medical building."

"Now there's a psychiatric session where I'd have loved to be a fly on the wall."

"I'm sure he talked about his childhood," Tom Henry said.

"This guy had sex with young men, tortured them in this attic, killed them, buried them in his crawl space, and they have to examine him to see if he was sane?" I shook my head. "What I'd like to see them do is interview a hundred normal guys, then predict which one is going to go nuts. They get that right, they've got my respect. Like those talking heads on TV. The stock market dives and the next day they tell you why. Where were they the day before?"

"Are you going on a rant, or am I going to tell a story?" Tom Henry said.

"Good point, let's get to it." I grabbed my legal pad, clipboard, and pen.

"But first, while I'm on shrinks, let me tell you a cartoon I thought up. A psychiatrist is showing a patient some Rorschach ink blot cards, and the patient is throwing up his hands and backing away, saying, 'Don't show me that filth! My mind is pure!'"

"That's actually funny," Tom Henry said, laughing. He grabbed his coffee≈cup.

"So where you want me to start?"

"Anywhere you want," I said. "If you can't think of a good place, just start with the first thing you remember."

"All right, I'll start with my childhood. Early days."

"And keep in mind, I don't know shorthand. I'll write as fast as I can, but if I can't keep up I'm just going to let you rip, and what I don't get, we'll come back to. Okay?"

"Yeah, and if I get too excited, just tell me to slow down."

"It's a deal."

Six

Tom Henry

Earliest I can remember is living on Twelfth Street in Streator. That house had an old barn behind it that Dad kept locked. I wanted in, so I dug a hole like a ground hog under the edge of the barn by Mom's petunias—there wasn't no foundation.

I used to roam across the road and try to catch rabbits, snakes, little baby animals. I took my toy gun to the field and pretended to shoot Japs and Germans. This was before I went to school.

Grandma was religious, a real good woman, the kind you know will be in heaven if anyone gets there. She was always happy. She used to wear a black felt hat with a net on top and a great big long hatpin. I liked to stick flies with that hatpin.

Grandma would help anybody. She'd save her change from grocery shopping during the year and put five dollars in an envelope for me and Rosie. We couldn't expect much from Mom and Dad, they was so poor, but Grandma always got us Christmas presents.

I'd go grocery shopping with Mom and Grandma at S&S Supermarket. They had a toy rack, army men and cowboys. Grandma bought me a bag of those little hard-rubber army men and she gave me hairpins and I'd put the army men in the grass, bend the hairpins open, put a rubber band in between my thumb and index finger, then I'd pull back and shoot.

One Christmas Dad gave me money to buy Grandma a pair of nylons, the kind with the black line in the back. Grandma wore them with a long dress, and I could see them rolled up just above her knees when she bent over in the kitchen to pick something up.

"Grandma, you got my socks on?" I'd ask her when she came in from church.

"Yes, Henry, I sure do."

"You better take them off or you're going to get a run in them."

I used to put those nylons over my face and look in the mirror to see how funny I looked. When she sat at the table I liked to go under it and run my hand up and down the smoothness of the stockings. I'd roll the roll at her knee down to her ankle.

"Henry, you'd better quit that." And I'd start rolling them back up.

⁂

No one liked Grandpa, the mean old sucker. Grandma had to keep the presents she bought me and Rosie secret so he wouldn't complain about her spending the money. He wanted to use that money for whiskey, and he never gave her nothing.

Grandpa used to sit in the chicken house with my toy paddle, the kind that has the little ball and elastic string attached to it, and listen to the Cubs on his radio—that's the only good thing you can say about him, he was a Cubs fan. He used the paddle to kill sparrows that found their way in there—he'd smash them with it, get blood on the paddle. He liked that.

Dad and Mom's brothers Ronnie, Clarence, and Willie loved to play poker. I parked myself under the table, and any pennies that wound up on the floor they'd let me keep. The silver coins I had to give back. But most times Grandpa wouldn't even let me keep the pennies. He kept his money jar on top of the table—he'd put his winnings in it, then stick the jar under the table, and if I had any pennies he'd make me put them in it. I could get by with hiding two or three of them but that was about it.

I'll tell you how I stopped going under the table at the poker games. It was Halloween time, and Grandpa got up from the table to go into his room for some more tobacco and when he come out he turned off the light. When Uncle Ronnie got up and turned the light back on, Grandpa was under the table with a horrible ugly mask on. Scared me so bad I saw it in nightmares.

Once, while Grandpa was taking a nap, I got his pants from the hook in the closet and cut the threads that held his suspenders together in the back. He come out and hollered at me for it. I denied it, but who else could it of been?

So I just run to Grandma, and she scolds me real good. When my mom and dad come to pick me up, Grandpa tells them and *they* scold me about it. He liked that. Now, I didn't care if they got on my case at home but I didn't like them doing it in front of Grandpa, 'cause he stood there laughing at me.

I got him back, though. He kept his money jar, a peanut butter jar, in a little wooden chest he'd made, and while he was in the back yard one day I used Grandma's cheese slicer to unscrew the hinges and got the jar.

I was too little to hold the jar with one hand so I put it between my legs, but it slipped on my pants so I lifted up my pants legs and put the jar right on my skin. Then I took that rubber thing Grandma used to open jars and grabbed the lid with both hands to unscrew it. I took out a few pennies, figured he wouldn't miss just a few, and put them in Grandma's coin purse.

I got a big kick out of giving them to Grandma.

꙳

When we got new little chicks, I liked to go down to the basement and sit in the rocking chair and watch them in the incubator. The light was always on and they was always eating, drinking, or doing something. They'd sleep on one foot with the other tucked up underneath them, and when I tapped on the glass they'd open their eyes and the tucked-up leg would come down.

When the chickens started turning white, Grandma put them outside and they started laying eggs. It was my job to collect the eggs and take them in to her. She sold them to neighbors, that was how she got spending money.

When the chickens started molting, I got worried over Grandma not having any more money. I used to go out and talk to the chickens, told them to lay eggs for Grandma, she needs them.

But no eggs. So I went into Grandpa's jar again, and this time I filled my pockets with the silver coins and headed for Marx's grocery store on the corner. I plunked the change on the counter and told the lady I wanted it in eggs. She says how many and what size, and I tell her Grandma wants it all in eggs, the biggest you got. She gave me six dozen!

That afternoon I go into the chicken house and put one in each nest. I knew that wasn't the way the hens lay them, but that's how I put them. Then I went inside.

"Grandma! I seen some eggs through the screen in the chicken nest."

"No you didn't, Henry. They ain't laying."

But I kept it up, so she finally took me out there and I showed her the eggs. She didn't say nothing—she just looks at me, shakes her head, then flaps the bottom edge of her apron up and lets me load the eggs in.

Grandma knew what I done but she never told on me. It was our secret. I felt like a king, 'cause I was helping Grandma and getting Grandpa at the same time.

꙳

When Grandma was dying in St. Mary's Hospital, she asked for Mom to bring me in to see her the next morning, but she died that night. She left me her rosary. Grandma had a lot of friends, and after the funeral that house was so full all the people couldn't fit in, and so much food come we had to give it away.

But what made my dad mad was Grandpa and the other relations, them all just sitting and playing poker right in the kitchen at the table. Oh, boy, he told them all.

"Rose just passed away and here you are, playing cards. People here are mourning and you can't even let her get cold before you're sitting here drinking beer and gambling! Come on, Henry, we're going home."

I never cried when Grandpa died. I don't think nobody else did either.

∽

My earliest hunting was with spears. Bunches of milkweeds grew in the field across the road, long and hollow, perfect. You pull them up and shake the dirt off the roots, snap off the top, and you've got yourself a spear. How could my dad stop me? I jumped up[5] quail and threw my spears at them.

Later I made a homemade slingshot using the fork of a branch and some strips I cut off my dad's inner tubes from the shed. I used the tongue out of one of my dad's shoes for the pocket to hold the stone—or the marble. Marbles are better than stones, 'cause marbles shoot straighter.

My grandma used to buy me marbles. Right behind our house was a wishing well with a red pump and train tracks running behind it. I crouched behind the wishing well so my mom couldn't see me, and when a train carrying new cars came by, out came my slingshot—whoosh, plink! The window on a car would shatter when I made a direct hit, and when you hit that sheet metal it made a racket.

Grandma couldn't figure out how I could lose so many marbles.

Sometimes I walked to Oakland Park, the field by my school, to shoot squirrels. You can't miss in a park, they're so tame. Once I hit a squirrel in the head and thought he was dead, but he was just knocked out. A marble won't go through a squirrel, but sometimes I knocked them plumb out of the tree.

When I was seven, Grandma gave me a toy bow for Christmas. It was long as my arm, and the arrows had rubber tips. It wouldn't kill nothing, not even a bird. I'd lay down flat to shoot a sparrow along the ground and it'd knock him

---

5 "Jumped up" is a hunting term. You walk near them and they run from where they were hiding.

three feet, but he'd get up and fly away. So I took the rubber tips off and the arrows started sticking in them. I was a game hunter now.

When I got a BB gun, I felt like a big-time hunter. I'd stalk birds in the field across the road, shooting them and winging them. My dad didn't like that.

"God made them little birds for us to enjoy," he said, "not to maim and torture."

❧

My first experience with live trapping come from catching birds outside my window when Mom sent me for a nap. I had a string running through my bedroom window and an up-side down box outside with food under it. I propped one end of the box on a forked stick and tied the string to the bottom of the stick. I'd put the live birds in a dresser drawer, then take them out to the garage later to cage and feed them.

Here's what I done with some of the sparrows I caught. First I got my dad's drill and made a little bitty hole behind the tip of an arrow, then I put one end of a real long piece of kite string through that hole and tied a big knot to hold it, then I tied the other end of the string around a sparrow's leg. I stepped on the string near the sparrow so he couldn't fly off, wound the free string in a circle on the ground, then I shot the arrow. The string unwound real fast, and just before it was all out, I let my foot off.

I got a real bang out of watching them sparrows shoot off. When the arrow first lifts them off the ground, they go about thirty miles an hour! They fly around a while and when the arrow starts coming down they'll be way above the arrow, then it will bring them down slow. I'd reel them in like they was fish, talk to them, check them out.

❧

The first real gun my dad bought me was the bolt action .22 I ended up killing Patty with.[6] He bought it when I was twelve and showed it to me, then he tells me I can't have it yet, I'm too young! We didn't have no shells around the house, but when Dad was at work and Mom was at the neighbor's I used to get the gun out of the closet and look through the sights at the birds in the yard and pretend-shoot them—cock it and aim it and pull back the trigger and go

---

6 I tried to confirm this fact in an interview in Russell's home, but he vehemently denied giving Henry the gun he used for these murders.

"BOOM!" When I watched westerns on TV I'd shoot the Indians with it. Then I'd hear my mom coming and put it back quick. I never got caught.

I was thirteen when we moved to the Marilla Park house, and that November, when I turned fourteen, Dad finally gave me that gun. I took it into the woods all the time, burned that barrel up—I must of sent thousands of shells through that gun. And of all the .22s I ever had, that was the most accurate. I could just point the barrel without looking out the sights, like a BB gun.

☙

My dad was a TV repairman and at first I liked going with him on service calls, was always saying, "Dad, take me with you." But when I started dating Patty I come to hate service calls 'cause he made me go just to take me away from her. So we kind of compromised. He'd say, "Well, I got eight service calls tonight but I only need your help on three, so I'll do those first and drop you off back at home. What time was that dance, did you say?"

"Eight o'clock."

"Okay, I'll have you back in plenty of time." So we'd hit those three calls then he'd drop me off, take the tool caddy out of the station wagon and put it into my mom's car 'cause my mom wouldn't let me use hers, give me five dollars for helping him with the service calls, and he'd take right off. Long as he did that I didn't mind it, 'cause I had money and a car.

☙

My dad always wanted me to be more serious. He didn't like the way I was always joking. "Someday you're going to wake up and realize life isn't a big joke," he'd say.

When I look back, what I feel worst about, besides the murders, is disappointing my dad. He tried to raise me the best he knew how, but I rebelled against him.

Seven

Tom Henry

Old man Treawata let a bunch of guys hunt on his place. Now, his land was right next to our house by Marilla Park, and I considered those pheasants to be my pheasants. So I come up with a plan to trap them live before they could get shot.

I noticed that pheasants only push forward in the brush, never backwards. Even when I approached them from the front, when they're hiding in the brush, they'd just cower there until I was almost on them, then they'd rush out, trying to slip through my legs. Also, when I walked along a country road I'd see pheasants flying up out of a culvert.

So that gave me the idea. I took my dad's tin snips, hacksaw blades, cold chisels, and a hammer and I cut three slits in a culvert around fourteen inches back from the end, then I pounded the three sections together so it made a funnel with an opening about four inches across. I dropped some corn in there, went to the other end and threw a bunch of corn in far as I could, and dropped a little right at the opening.

A pheasant is a big bird, as big as a chicken. It could go in but it couldn't back out, so when I checked the trap, the pheasant would be cowering way at the end with his head pulled into his chest. I just lifted up the top flap, grabbed him with my hand, shoved the flap back in place with my foot, threw him in my game bag, and took him home.

I told Dad, "Don't buy me no shells if you don't want. I don't need shells to go pheasant hunting."

⌒⌒

Me and my friend George Wargo used to go after pheasants and rabbits. This one night we caught about twenty pigeons under the bridge. We caught them with a flashlight—pigeons won't fly if you shine a light in their eyes. We put them in a box and hid them in the woods. The next Saturday morning I got my dad's spray paint and we painted the bottom of their wings all different colors—red, blue, yellow, green, orange. Naturally when we turn them loose, they're going to fly back out to the bridge.

So we peddled our bikes into town to watch, 'cause when these pigeons flew, you could see these bright colors. But not enough were flying and not enough people were looking to suit me, so I went under the bridge and threw rocks at them. They flew up and circled around and gave the people a color show. As soon as I scared up a bunch, I ran back up and sat on the rail of the bridge to watch the people go by, looking out the windshield at the colors.

On our way home I stopped by Treawata's fence to take a leak. Now, sometimes a farmer will put a strand of electric wire inside his fence and energize it for two or three weeks so the new cows learn not to mess with the fence.

Treawata must have just got hisself some new cows. When my piss hit that electric wire, oh boy, that hurt! Way up inside me! That's one mistake I'll never make again. You do something that hurts enough, you only have to do it once to learn.

⁐

South of Streator, across the bridge on Highway 23, was Moon Creek Cemetery. There was an old lady lived right up the road from it, and folks said she went out in the cemetery as a ghost and chased people off. And it was partly true, 'cause she did take care of her husband's grave and the rest of the cemetery.

She was the type of woman that don't hold with partying and having sex with your girlfriend in the cemetery. She picked up the beer cans and kept the gates closed. But the road going down to Moon Creek Cemetery was a dead end dirt road, and a lot of kids parked there.

I didn't have nothing to do one Friday night so I decided to pull a prank. I got my mom's real long coat with the big brown wooden buttons, a scarf she called a babushka, then I put some flour into a bread wrapper. Well, I tied it all up with one of my belts, put it under the seat of my motorcycle, and drove to Norris's Dance Hall.

I told Jim Hogan I was headed out to Moon Creek Cemetery. "In about an hour and a half, tell everybody you just seen that old lady at the cemetery."

I rode down the railroad tracks to the cemetery so I could get in without nobody spotting me. When I got to the fence I climbed over, hid the gun and the coat in the grave. I knew what time Jim would start spreading the rumor, and soon after, three carloads showed up. I didn't know who was in the cars, 'cause kids from the Woodland and Streator high schools both went to Norris's. It was early yet or a bunch more would've come out, but I knew most wouldn't want to leave that soon—you park after dancing and it's hard to talk your girlfriend into going out to the cemetery to see an old lady ghost. But there are always some gutsy kids who'd want to check out a thing like that.

Well, here they came. I seen the headlights soon as they turned off the highway and crossed the railroad tracks. They turned right and drove down the dirt lane to the cemetery and into the gate I opened.

Now, I jury-rigged the gate so I can close it without being seen—attached enough fishing line to the gate so I can hide in the trees and pull the gate closed soon as they're inside the cemetery. They had their radios blasting and their windows open, laughing with their girls, so they probably wouldn't of seen me anyway. Screeeeetch! I drift further back in the cemetery, sneaking behind the trees and the tombstones.

All of a sudden I started worrying about what they might do to me if they catch me. I didn't know who they were—they might be from Woodland and beat the shit out of me if I embarrassed them in front of their girlfriends. So I figured I had to scare them off.

I step out right in front of them in the coat and babushka and call out with an old woman's real high-pitched voice, a shaky voice, "Hey! What you doin' here? Get out a here. Get out a here!" Then I took off running in that real long coat and all. It got real quiet, but after a while I heard talking again.

Now I'm scared, 'cause they was getting brave in front of their girlfriends, what with the beer they had in them.

"Where are you, Granny? We're going to bang bang you, Granny, when we catch you. Come on, Granny."

I had the babushka on 'cause I don't want them to recognize me, but I didn't have the flour on me yet. So I put the flour on my face and got in the grave and—damn!—I should of checked it out before. I couldn't lay down in it. Too little. So I'm sitting there with the sides about up to my shoulders, and I have to scrunch down to stay out of sight.

But I felt safe with that shotgun. Let them try something now, I'll get them going. So they kept coming and they was close enough I could hear them talking, mostly saying sexual things, what they planned to do with me if they caught me.

I took the babushka and wiped a bit of flour out of my eyes 'cause it was making a paste in there, then I put the babushka back on down to my eyebrows right as two of them looked into the grave.

One was looking in from behind me. When the second one looked in from my left side, I snapped my head up real fast. Soon as they saw me move, they took off running like bats out of hell! One of them hollered something. I jumped out of the grave and hid behind the trees. I could see them running toward their cars.

They started driving in between the roads on the grass of the cemetery, shining their lights and hollering crazy stuff. I stood out in the open and let the lights hit right on me. I've got flour all over my face plus the long coat plus the babushka plus the gun. I'm waving the coat back and forth with my shoulders hunched forward like an old lady.

They turned off their motors, then I heard a car door open and I knew they were coming out. I got out that shrill screechy voice again.

"I'm tired of you boys messing with me!" Soon as I said that, I go KA-BOOM, KA-BOOM, KA-BOOM! with the shotgun.

When they saw the fire come out of the shotgun, they took off fast! Now I'm scared one of them might plow through that gate. I closed the gate. What if they didn't see it? There are three guys that know it's me out here, and if someone gets hurt I'm in trouble.

But they hit the brakes at the last second. A guy got out and opened the gate, then the car drove on through and left him chasing after it, hollering.

I was cleaning up 'cause I was done for the night, getting this flour wiped off, still laughing, when I see the headlights of two of the three cars coming back! Then their lights went off.

They want more? I closed the gate and jammed it with a stick so they couldn't open it. If they think it's the old woman, I'll be all right—what are you going to do with an old woman? But if they think it's me, look out!

Now, there was a pillar on each side of the gate, probably five feet and made out of bricks. I climbed up there with the gun and waited for them, crouched down 'cause the pillar was crowned and I could only stand on it for a couple of seconds.

Their lights come back on and their cars creep forward.

I got two shots left—I fired three already—but I only ended up needing one. When they come a little closer, about 150 yards, I stood up real careful so

I didn't fall and I aimed right over the cars, about a 45-degree angle, BOOM! You can imagine what that fire looked like at night time.

You don't think they took off? The first car turned around and passed up the other car!

Now, I knew if they saw me on my motorcycle and caught me with the coat and babushka they'd beat the tar out of me, so I hid all that in the brush, figured I'd just come out tomorrow and get mom's coat. I went to the creek first and got into the water and washed, but that wasn't good enough, so I went to a gas station, looked in a mirror and really got cleaned up so no flour showed.

I went back up to Norris's, and it was tough to keep a straight face. I told Hogan and the other guys, "Don't say nothing about it." We went out into the alley and I started telling them about it and a couple of guys heard us laughing, so we split out of there. I told them again, "Don't tell nobody!"

We had a radio station, WIZZ, where the high school kids could talk on it for an hour or so. The reporter the next morning said, "We hear the old lady is on the prowl again at Moon Creek Cemetery. Or was that her? And would somebody please tell her new husband, Henry Hillenbrand, that last night wasn't Halloween?"

One of those guys snitched! Everybody at school asked me, but I just said, "Wasn't me." 'Course I wanted to admit it—I'd pulled off a really good one— but I still didn't know who I'd gotten. You know how ashamed they must of felt, scared like that in front of their girlfriends.

My mom never knew about that coat. By the time I got out there a couple days later the rain had soaked into it and the satin on the inside was ruined. So I just left it there, 'cause she didn't know I had it anyway.

She'll find out how she lost that coat when the book comes out.

Eight

Weeks had gone by since the Northsider chief had warned us we might have to move out of our cell. The good news was we'd probably stay in Cell 3-49, but our progress on the book was much slower than I'd anticipated.

"I've got to get a tape recorder or this will take forever," I said.

"Excuse me," Tom Henry said. "Maybe I misunderstood, but I thought you said you had four consecutive Natural Lives."

"You're forgetting about that sentence reduction. What are we going to do when I get it down to four *concurrent* Natural Lives?"

"You're right. We need a recorder."

We were still on his childhood. Tom Henry had paced and talked while I lay face down on my upper bunk, my paper clamped into my clipboard and my pen scribbling. But I couldn't keep up, so after I typed up what I had, we'd go back and fill in what was missing.

At first, I'd tried typing on my manual typewriter as Tom Henry dictated, but that was even worse. Writing, then typing it up at my leisure, turned out to be the most accurate way of capturing his story. But the process took hours for each small section.

"A tape recorder is serious contraband," Tom Henry said.

"Seg time, I know," I said, "but I need one. Maybe I'll ask in electronics class."

"Electronics class! Those guys don't know nothing! I heard the teacher told them to get a Fallopian tube and they looked in the cabinet!"

"I wouldn't mind going on a Fallopian tube search right now," I said.

"Settle down, Big Guy! You need to borrow a magazine, just let me know." Tom Henry always left out a few girlie magazines to distract the guards during shakedowns.

"So, a tape recorder," I said. "The commissary sells tape *players*. You think I can get away with special ordering a recorder? If they notice I could just say I didn't realize."

"I may have a better idea. Let me talk to Al."

৩৽৹

A few days later Tom Henry said, "I talked to a teacher's aide. He's not too good with electronics but he has a skill that might help us."

"What's that?"

"He knows how to steal."

"You found a recorder?"

"Better than that! I found one they only use as a player. All you have to do is buy a tape player from commissary. My guy can switch them and you'll have a tape recorder *with a permit*. But it has to be a Panasonic."

"But when the teacher goes to record something—"

"That's the beauty of it, Big Stuff. It's only used to play an orientation tape once per semester."

I bought the cassette tape player from commissary, paid the teacher's aide to make the switch, and within a month I had a working, nearly new cassette recorder—with a permit.

"Let's try it tonight," Tom Henry said.

"We don't have tapes," I said.

They were on the way, eight of them. I'd ordered them from a recent Bible conference held by the Christian group I used to belong to, the Tunbridge Wells branch of the Plymouth Brethren. They were recordings of gospel messages. They would come in through the chapel, where the staff would verify their religious nature.

෴

They arrived not long after by means of the chaplain himself.

"I listened to considerably more of these tapes than I needed to because I enjoyed them," he said. "If you don't mind, tell me how someone with a taste for this type of Bible teaching wound up in here?"

I gave Chaplain Bouma the short version. I liked him right away but didn't reveal the cassette tapes' true purpose. Later, as he became my counselor, confidant, and friend, I let him in on the secret. Over the years, this man of God suffered through my loss of faith with a consistently non-judgmental approachability.

Now that we had some tapes, we couldn't wait to get started.

"I might not be a believer anymore," I said, "but I still don't feel right erasing these until I've listened to them. On the other hand, I can't wait. So one of these lambs is going to be sacrificed on the altar. Which one will it be? Eeny, meeny, miny, moe." I popped one into the machine.

"You're up, Tom Henry."

He began to dictate and pace. In what seemed like no time, the tape was full. Now, instead of scribbling, I lay back, eyes closed, head on the pillow, and let the story wash over me. I didn't worry about missing parts, didn't worry about pieces that didn't make sense or events that were out of order—I had it all on tape!

∽

Now we were on a roll. About twice a week Tom Henry would record a tape and over the next couple of days, I'd transcribe it. Then he'd read it and make corrections. He might add a thought, delete an error or, most often, reorganize the chronology. It's not easy to keep A before B and five before six when you're telling your life's story.

We were surprised, now that we had the tape recorder and things were easier, how little extra time we had in a day. We were in prison, we should have oceans of time! But between meals and assignments and recreation and sports on TV—even before the NFL season—it was tough to carve out enough time for the book project.

Lockdowns gave us more time to work, but who would ever wish for a lockdown? Welcome or not, they did come. And with the lockdown came the shakedown, when our cell would be disrupted, our possessions confiscated— and our tape recorder put at risk.

∽

"Hendricks! Hillenbrand! You guys want phone calls?"

Phone calls were rare in Menard. A gang member with a clipboard and a telephone on a very long cord would hand the phone through the food slot.

"Ten minutes," he'd say, then start the timer. You had to call someone collect, and if they were home and accepted the charges, you talked to them. If not, you just dialed someone else. If it took three tries to get someone who was at home and who would accept your call, you had about five minutes left to talk.

Tom Henry called his boys, I used my ten minutes to call my mother, then the phone man left our cell.

"Those ten-minute phone calls are the fastest time we'll ever do." Tom Henry said.

∽

About one thirty in the morning one Saturday night, we were still up recording. Tom Henry was pacing and speed-talking, coffee in hand. I was sitting on my stool in the front of the cell but turned around backwards to face him. All of a sudden Sergeant Sampson appeared at the bars.

"Hey guys," he said, "What's up?"

We both spun around. Had our tape recorder been snitched out?

Tom Henry sashayed up to the cell bars. "Hey."

"You interested in some peach pie?" He had half a pie with him in a tin. "Got this from the officer's kitchen. Don't tell no one."

"Thanks," Tom Henry said. "Let me make you some coffee."

"Not tonight, got to be going." Sergeant Sampson looked back at the tape recorder. "Your radio's still got the light on but I don't hear anything."

Tom Henry punched the off button. "It's not a radio," he said. "It's a tape player. It don't always shut off when the tape ends."

"Looks like we're going to be on lockdown—if not tomorrow then the day after tomorrow," Sampson said. "They'll be taking desks and stools. Way too many shanks are coming from them."

"I'll hate like heck to lose my desk," Tom Henry said. "It's what I do my cards on."

"That's how it always is," Sampson said. "You're using your desk like a desk, the assholes are cutting them up into shanks, and you'll lose yours and they'll keep theirs!"

"Man, I thought we were busted," I said when he'd left.

"Me too. He brought us this pie but he'd bust us in a second."

"The way he appeared so suddenly, I was sure we'd been snitched out."

"He's sneaky," Tom Henry said. "Let's put the recorder away for a while."

Sure enough, ten minutes later Sampson popped up again.

"I'll send the machine down the gallery tomorrow morning," Tom Henry said.

"So you not trusting him, does that apply to the pie too?"

"Heck no."

It was delicious.

◌

The shakedown Sergeant Sampson predicted didn't materialize the following day, so we thought we might have dodged it, but that night he was back with chicken and information.

"They're planning a good shakedown this time," he said. "All electrical appliances are going to need a permit. Your radio I saw the other night, that thing have a permit?"

"Yeah, my cellie bought it from the commissary, but we got a coffee pot they'll probably take," Tom Henry said.

We were going to have to be careful—Sampson had the scent.

What Tom Henry hadn't told Sampson was that besides our illegal tape recorder, the metal desk, and the two metal stools, we had a Coke bottle, a knife, a stapler, two clipboards, and two Styrofoam shelves—all contraband.

The next morning we woke up to cold breakfasts and a shakedown starting at the far end of our gallery. Tom Henry extended his mirror past the bars and peered out.

"Looks like a thorough one," he said.

"What's being thrown out?" I asked.

"Stools and desks. Sampson was right."

This news cast a pall over us. If we lost our desk that would leave us only the built-in desk at the front of the cell, less than a foot deep and two feet wide. You could hardly do anything on it. The desk we were about to lose was luxuriously large by comparison. In the outside world no one would bother with it, but to Tom Henry, it was gold. As was the stool, because there was nothing else in the cell to sit on except the toilet.

We could take turns on the mini-desk in the front of the cell, I with my typing, he making greeting-cards—but without a stool, we couldn't use that either. It was too tall for kneeling and too short for standing. That we were doing something positive meant nothing to the monkeys who ran the place. I wanted to scream.

The shakedown crew got to us around three o'clock in the afternoon. Our door slid open and we were handcuffed to each other through the wire mesh at the far side of the gallery. Tom Henry brought a tall plastic coffee mug with him and sipped it slowly, so as not to let the level of the coffee go below the top of the item the Northsider gang had told him to hold through this shakedown.

In front of the cell next to us was our friend Strickler, standing in his underwear. He was handcuffed through the gallery mesh to his cellie, just like every other inmate all day long as the shakedown had worked its way toward our cell. But Strickler presented an additional spectacle.

The leg holes of the tall neo-Nazi's white briefs were about four sizes too large for his skinny legs. Hanging down through one of the hugely oversized leg holes was his scrotum, about twice as low as the end of his pecker.

It was all we could do not to laugh, which we wanted to avoid—not only to spare Strickler's feelings but also to not give our shakedown guards the idea we might be pulling something over on them.

In the end, we lost our stools and Tom Henry's desk as well as some bleach and our second shelf, but we kept our clipboards, Tom Henry's art supplies, my books, and our trial transcripts.

∽

"So what are we going to do now?" I asked after we'd put things away as best we could. The loss of the desk was a blow and the loss of the stools devastating.

"The good news is they didn't sign us up for the twice-daily beatings."

"Yeah, it can always be worse," I said. "We still have our clipboards. I can type standing at the end of my bunk if I just fold my mattress back here—like this." I stuck my manual typewriter onto the upper bunk's frame and fed a piece of paper into it and typed as I stood. "My arms are a little high, so I'm going to gain some new muscles, but I can do this."

"And now that we don't have a desk, we have more room for books and files. Man, we got a lot of shit."

"Wait! I have an idea." I said.

"I thought I smelled something burning."

"Do you think I could slide my mattress under your bunk and sleep on the floor? Then I can put my books and files on top of my bunk and leave my typewriter set up full time. I'll put my TV on a box where your desk was and we'll make another shelf there." I pointed at the wall.

It seemed a little crazy, me sleeping under the bottom bunk, and it was possible we'd be told it was against the rules, something any guard might assert at any time. I had a suspicion there was a Catch-22 rule: "Whatever an inmate wants is against the rules, but what he doesn't want is allowed."

In any case, we rearranged our cell. Tom Henry had sole use of the tiny desk in the front of the cell, which he used while seated on a homemade stool he'd fashioned from two boxes, folded and glued in a corrugated pattern for strength. I had a huge desk and working surface, for which I needed no stool since I had to stand to reach it. I arranged my transcripts in boxes. I kept incoming letters in one box, by date, and I bought three-ring binders—still available because no one had yet been stabbed with a curved metal ring—in which I began storing my handwritten journal and my *Tom Henry* notes and manuscript.

∽

"Hillenbrand! You got mail," the guard at our bars said.

Men in prison live and die from letter to letter. A wife's "I love you and I'll wait for you" can make a guy float on cloud nine. A wife's "I've got a new guy and your kids call him Daddy" can drive an easygoing guy bonkers.

Tom Henry got two letters of the good kind. One was from his ex-wife, Faith, which warmed his heart—not because she wrote that she loved him and would wait for him but because she wrote about his seven-year-old son, Thomas, who was playing baseball. He'd been offered a dollar for each home run he hit.

"Thomas hit two home runs in one game," she wrote, "and after he got paid he asked me how many more he'd have to hit so he could go see Daddy."

The other was a card from Tom Henry's daughter, Winkie. It was a pink and yellow thinking-of-you card with a scripture verse. He read it to me.

"She says, 'This might not be as special as one of your glorious cards that I have kept close to my heart, but I just thought I would say hello and that I think more about you than you must think. Things just take a little time, some things more than others. Hang in there with me!'"

"Sounds like she's starting to come around," I said.

"Yeah," he said with a sigh. "But she's back and forth a lot." He shrugged his shoulders.

He glanced back at the card, then broke into a smile.

"She signs it, 'Your daughter, Winkie.'"

∽

At the Christian Fellowship that night, we sat with a guy I knew from the university economics class. Frank looked like—and was—the kind of guy you'd want as a neighbor. He'd held the same job for years, had an enduring marriage, and had recently built a new home with his wife.

Then it all went wrong. His wife found a lover but didn't move out. Instead she called the police and had Frank kicked out. He was beside himself, and in a suicidal fog he broke into her house—their house—intending to shoot himself in front of her. But while the shotgun was pointed at his face, she taunted him one too many times. He turned the gun around and pulled the trigger.

Back in the cell after the Christian Fellowship, I said, "I'm developing a theory."

Tom Henry rolled his eyes, then said "Let's hear it."

"My theory is, the best guys to associate with in prison are murderers. Now, I know that sounds a little counter-intuitive—"

"It sounds more than a *little*," Tom Henry said, "but I'll bite, professor. Why do murderers make the best buddies?"

"Because they're not criminals. Here, I'll prove it. Think of the top five guys in here you'd choose to cell with but don't tell me who they are."

After a few seconds, Tom Henry said, "Okay."

"I'll bet you four of them are here for murder."

Tom Henry thought for a bit, then said, "All five are."

"So here's my theory. Most murders are crimes of passion. Frank, from the fellowship, is a good example. He flipped out and did something crazy. But what he did isn't what he normally does—that is, he's not a criminal by nature. He's just an ordinary guy—a worker, a homeowner, a neighbor—then things go bad and he goes nuts. And the thing is, with a bullet, once you start it on its way, there's no taking it back. You know that better than anybody."

"I've thought about that many times."

"All the other guys here are thieves, rapists, burglars, pedophiles, and so on. But in each of these cases, this isn't something they did once. It's what they do, it's who they are. They were criminals before they got caught. So I'm saying the reason you and I tend to associate with murderers here is they're not really criminals. They're actually the best guys here."

"I think you're right. Murderers, huh?" Tom Henry looked pensive. "A word of advice, Big Stuff."

"I'm all ears."

"If your appeal works out and you get a retrial, don't tell the judge your theory. He'll send you right back here, no further evidence needed."

"I wasn't planning on it," I said. "What do you say we do some recording?"

Sampson had never returned to check on the tape recorder, so Tom Henry's fears, if prudent, seemed unfounded. Still, ever since that incident we'd been placing the recorder inside a folded blanket.

"Go nuts!" I said as I loaded a tape and pushed a button.

It was a 120-minute cassette tape and Tom Henry was up to the challenge. He dictated for two hours straight, not even pausing for coffee.

I moved the recorder to the top of the bed and loaded a fresh page into my typewriter. I turned the tape player on.

Music played.

I looked at it, fiddled with it for a while, then said, "I don't understand this. How do I get it to play?"

Tom Henry examined it for about two seconds. "It *is* playing," he said.

"You recorded two hours of music!"

"Oh, man, I'm sorry!"

"Don't worry about it. Shit happens. Let's do it again, right now, or we'll feel bad about it for days."

"Okay, if you're up to it. I'm the one who screwed up, but you're the one who has to do the work."

Later, after I transcribed it, I said, "You actually did it better the second time. I think we've hit upon a new recording technique. The first time I'll just pretend to record it, then I'll tell you all I've got is music and can you do it over."

"You got any free space on that tape?"

"Yeah, why?"

"Cause I'd like to record my response, so you can listen to *it* over and over."

⌒⌒

A week after that visit, Tom Henry got a call pass.

"It says here I'm going to go on the bus tonight."

"Nice notice by your lawyer!" I said.

"Court is scheduled Thursday morning, so he'll probably talk to me tomorrow."

"I think I'll stay in from work today and type," I said, "so I can clear some of the tapes."

We spent the late afternoon, evening, and what we had of the night filling five tapes.

With Tom Henry gone, I started to worry. What if we got permanently split up before I could get his story recorded? We were nowhere near done. Anything could happen at any time. One of us could be stabbed, God forbid, or go to the infirmary, or be put in Seg—not impossible since the Northsiders made Tom Henry hold shanks from time to time.

Or what if the appellate court decided my case favorably and I was released? That sounded like a good problem, but I wanted to finish this book now that I'd begun it.

And so the day he returned from court, out came the tape recorder and Tom Henry started talking.

Nine

Tom Henry

Ifirst met Patty when I was in eighth grade. For a while it wasn't no boyfriend-girlfriend thing. Patty was a tomboy, I just got to knowing her from hanging around some with her brother. She used to ride bicycles in the streets with us and she worked at the Salvation Army gym where I used to shoot hoops. I liked to joke with her and tease her.

I was a sophomore before things really changed. I never gave her no ring, never said, "Hey, now we're going together," but everybody just assumed we were boyfriend-girlfriend 'cause we was always together. You can't put a date on it, but I was never with no other girl and she was never with no other boy.

In my high school days, it wasn't so much my hunting and fishing that kept me away from my schoolwork as it was Patty. I still did some hunting with my friends but not as much. I spent all my time with her and what we loved to do was dance.

After Dad built the new house, I'd bring Patty on my BSA 125 motorcycle through Marilla Park, drop her off and say, "Meet you down at the bridge in a little bit." Then drive home on my motorcycle, come in and say, "I don't want no supper," grab a sandwich, and head out with my fishing pole.

My folks thought I was down there by myself, and me and Patty would do a little fishing, a little of this, a little of that. Soon as I knew my dad was out on TV service calls, I'd come back, tell my mom I'm going to ride my motorcycle around Marilla Park, and sneak Patty home.

I used to skip school and take my motorcycle over to Woodland School, pick Patty up, and take her to a roadside table where we'd make out during lunch hour. I skipped a lot of school.

Sometimes when my dad went on service calls I'd sneak out of the house, ride the motorcycle to Patty's, meet her in the alley, and take her for a ride. Or if no one but her baby stepbrother was home—he was only one or two—I'd come inside while she babysat until June or Junior come home from the restaurant, then I'd slip out the window and be gone.

I bought Patty a hope chest when I was a sophomore. She used to tell her folks that was the only nice piece of furniture in the house. It was the best one at

Applegate's and it took me six months to work it off. And I kept buying charms for Patty's charm bracelet. Every time a new charm came into Frank's Jewelry, Patty got it. She had the most charms in school and she was real proud of it.

∞

When I started driving, we wouldn't like to stay in Streator—my dad knew everyone in town and they was all his spies. I'd be minding my own business when all of a sudden he'd jump down my throat for something I did two weeks ago across town. So and so said they seen you revving it up, speeding. Stool pigeons.

See, on the side of my dad's station wagon in big letters it said, "Don't Fuss. Call Russ." Everybody knew whose car that was. One of the stool pigeons was a TV man named Sullivan. I went over to his house one time and told him I didn't appreciate him snitching on me to my dad.

"Hey, your dad's a friend of mine," he said. "When I see his son speeding with his car, I'm going to tell him. I'd want to know." So I took off, cussing him, and a few days later I heard about *that*.

Even if it wasn't a snitch, somebody would spot me in my dad's car and ask him, "What were you doing on a service call at eleven-thirty?" Well, he knew right away it was me. So I couldn't stay around Streator, I had to go out of town. I used to take Patty to high school dances all around, Oglesby, Ottawa, everywhere. We just cruised around.

∞

I can't remember the first time I kissed Patty, felt her up, or made love to her. We just started playing around and it gradually progressed. She was my first and I was her first too.

Even before Patty and I were screwing, we'd be in the back of my dad's car—see, he had a big RCA tube caddy back then, but we used to put the rear seat down flat, and there was still enough room—and we'd take our clothes off and I'd be on her, humping, and I'd come, and shoot all over her stomach, and she'd giggle, and I'd wipe it off with my shirt. Then I'd take my tee shirt and shove it under the driver's seat.

One time my dad said, "Big plans you had of cleaning up the car. You left the rag under the seat!" But it was my tee shirt.

One time, after a date, my dad found footprints on the ceiling of the back of the station wagon. Boy, I heard about that!

Patty didn't have periods until about fifteen, and her stepsister told her if she wasn't having periods yet she couldn't get pregnant, so we had a great time. When her periods did start we got scared and laid off for a while.

∾

Patty went to Woodland High her freshman year 'cause she lived in the south side of Streator. I went to Streator High School and shared lockers with Patty's stepsister, Debbie, who passed along our love notes. We'd fold them into little triangles. On top of each note we wrote, "Suck man what ails ya?"[7]

My prom was coming up and I was all set to take Patty, but June and Junior said she was too young to go—she was a sophomore—so I had to ask another girl. Well, at the last minute they said Patty could go, so I paid my friend Gary to ask this girl to the prom. She was hurt, but it worked out okay. They started going steady and I think they ended up married.

One Friday during my senior year me and Patty was on a date, just riding around by the Santa Fe train station, and she had to go to the bathroom. While she's in there, I see on the schedules that the next train for Chicago is at seven forty-five that evening.

So I say, "Patty, I know what we can do that's different. Let's take the train up to Chicago and—see here? We can go up, goof around a while, and come back by eleven-fifteen."

When we got to Chicago, we started roaming around the station. We went into the restaurant, I got coffee and she got cherry Coke, then we went upstairs and outside. We started walking along sidewalks as big as streets, holding hands, looking in windows, up skyscrapers, until we got close to the Loop, where things were busier and there was more to look at, and we got lost.

We asked for directions—"Over to Wabash, to Michigan, south …"—but we got more and more confused. We made it to the depot past eleven-fifteen, too late to get our train back to Streator. The next one left in the morning, at six forty-five.

---

7 Burt Bayer said, "I remember Henry, whenever he went by me in the hall at school, he'd pump his fists back and forth by his side and say, 'Suck man what ails ya?' When this becomes a movie, you have to have the actor do that."

We were scared, strangers in the city, so we got a room for the night. Eight dollars and fifty cents for a single. Patty waited outside while I checked in. I didn't want to come right back with Patty, so we went for another walk. We got about nine blocks away when two cops in a station wagon pull up. One of them gets out and asks what we're doing out so late.

"Me and my sister here came up on the train to see our aunt, and we're lost, sir."

"Where does your aunt live?" I give him the address where I rented the room, and he tells me it's about nine blocks that way.

"Thanks, officer."

The room was on the third floor. We walked up the steps instead of taking the elevator. The room had a sink but no toilet. That was down the hall. We stayed there all night, giggling and playing. She didn't want to undress in front of me, so I went down the hall to the bathroom. When I got back she tried to hide and said, "Turn that light off." I turned it off, then turned it back on about ten seconds later. She screamed.

I said, "Patty, you know what's going to happen to us when we get back? We're going to get grounded for months, so let's make the best of it." We were laughing about it, giggling, saying crazy things. We pulled the mattress off the bed and onto the floor and wrestled around buck naked with the lights off. I wanted to call Dad but I couldn't think of what to say, so I didn't. We got in bed in our underwear and I played with Patty's body. We finally went to sleep about four.

We slept right through the six forty-five train the next morning but we had to check out by eleven. I called Dad about six and told him we'd come home on the next train—figured he'd be home from work by then but I could of gotten him any time that day. He didn't go to work, he was so worried about me. And he didn't say much of anything, he was so mad.

We went to the depot and bought the tickets. We had good intentions.

We sat on the wooden benches waiting for our train, which was due to arrive in Streator at eight-thirty. I told Patty, "We're both in for it, so let's make it worthwhile." So we left the train station and walked around holding hands, walking through Central Park, by the Field Museum, lying in the grass near the bushes—we didn't stay there too long, though, 'cause we thought the cops might come around looking for us. We finally walked back to the train station too late to catch our train, so we got on the one scheduled to get to Streator at eleven-fifteen.

We rode in the two-decker car with the glass bubble. It said, "Super Chief, Pullman" and had a picture of an Indian. We went to the upper deck, still giggling, and since we was all alone up there and since we knew it'd be a while before we'd be all alone again, we didn't waste the time. Of course, we had to be ready to suddenly get respectable in case somebody come up them stairs, but that just made what we were doing more exciting.

The train rolled in.

Sure enough, they were there, my dad and Junior, the only time I ever saw our dads together. We saw their heads latch onto each window and rotate, slower and slower as the train slowed down. When our window went by them, their heads stayed with us. We're the last to get off the train, and before we even get down the steps, my dad grabs me and Junior grabs Patty.

Dad lectured me all the way home, then sat me in the chair and pointed his finger at my chest and thumped it with each word.

"You're grounded from now until I say you ain't. How could you do this to us? Me and your mom we're worried sick! You're grounded, son, and you ain't going to see Patty, and you're taking the bus to school, and you're going with me to service calls...."

It lasted about two and a half months, but Patty and me managed to see each other about two weeks later on the sly.

⚘

After we was allowed to see each other again, me and Patty worked out a system. I parked the station wagon in front of Junior's restaurant so when my dad rode by he'd think I was in the restaurant working, but really we were out riding around in Junior's car. Junior let us use his car as long as we promised to try to catch June with her boyfriend. He even paid for the gas.

Junior liked having me around the restaurant 'cause he ran a poker game upstairs, and whenever a cop come in I'd press one of the buttons—one under the cash register and the other by the dishwashing sink in the kitchen—and a bell would ring upstairs.

Patty worked in the restaurant every day after school and on Saturdays. Junior was upstairs gambling and June was running around, so Patty ran the place. Her brother started dipping into the cash register and Junior blamed it on Patty. Now, stealing was something Patty would never do. She got so mad she left to go work in Ida's cafe, which Junior didn't like 'cause Patty took a lot of business with her. You know how a particular waitress will stick out in your mind? Patty was that kind. She made people want to come back, always smiling and friendly.

Junior was so mad he kicked Patty out of the house.

∽

About that time, my dad paid the $75 fee to sign me up at Allied Institute of Technology in Chicago to learn heating and air conditioning. Seeing as Patty was only a junior and had been kicked out of her home—and I was just about ready to move up to Chicago to go to school—Dad decided to take her in.

Dad really didn't have nothing against Patty except she took all my devotion. He'd tried for two, three years to break up Patty and me, lecturing me, grounding me, but it didn't work.[8] So he finally figured he'd put her in the house so I wouldn't worry about her and I could concentrate on school.

All through high school Dad pushed me to get good grades, but by the end I'd lowered his standards so much he was happy just to see me graduate. I was number 481 out of 487 (and 482 through 487 were my buddies). But Dad still had big plans for me. He was going to build a service building out by our house so the two of us could go into business in Streator, repairing appliances, furnaces, and air conditioners.

He'd built the Marilla Park house up high. The blocks ran six or seven feet above ground level, then we pushed dirt up to the blocks, sloping it away from the house with a shallow grade. So me and Patty had to be real careful what we did in the basement, 'cause you could see right in. We did our dance routines and played ping-pong down there.

We'd have the record going for dancing, but a lot of times we'd just be on the sofa smooching. If Dad stood on the hill outside he could see in without stooping down or looking like he was spying. I'd see his legs go by the window on the way out, though, and by the time he looked in, we'd be dancing.

Mostly, we did rock and roll routines. Jitterbug, Charleston, rock and roll— we liked Chubby Checker's "Peppermint Twist." Our favorite slow dance song was "Moon River," by Andy Williams. Fast dance was "My Love," by Petula

---

8 Russell Hillenbrand said, "You could put a sack over Henry's head, take him to California, and he'd find his way back to Patty."

Clark. And another we liked, that starts out slow and gets real fast, was an instrumental by Sandy Nelson, "Let There Be Drums." This was in the early sixties. We hit all the school dances around the area, and if no school dances were going on, we hit Norris's downtown.

Patty was really pretty. When I first started running around with her, she was a skinny kid with pimples and stringy hair, but by now she had shiny blond hair and an hourglass figure and long legs—and it wasn't just her looks, she was friendly with a big smile and great personality. All the guys was jealous of me.

In Chicago I got a room at the Crillon Hotel, about five blocks from Allied Institute of Technology. Since the classes were at night, I found a day job at Blommer's Chocolates. I came home on weekends in my 1960 Oldsmobile. I had a job, so I had money to spend on Patty. We made all the dances. One Saturday night the Streator High School held an elimination dance for tickets to The Hop, a TV dance show in Champaign, Illinois. Patty and I won—we had the liveliest routines and I liked to show off, flipping Patty over my head, sliding her between my legs, spinning, bobbing, and acting like a fool. The kids called for an encore after we won, so we danced in the center of the circle, just me and Patty.[9]

I wanted Patty to have the nicest things, which took money. It seemed stupid to keep going to Allied—I already knew how to fix furnaces and air conditioners, so what good was that diploma going to do me? I quit school and got me a full-time job at Sears making signs, but I stayed in Chicago and went home on the weekends like I was still in school. Dad never guessed I dropped out 'cause he seen my first report cards, which were good, and he didn't ask to see no more.

One weekend Dad took me for a walk. I could tell he wanted to talk but he just asked about school and stuff for the longest time before he finally come around to the point.

---

9 Bert Bayer said, "Once I went to Norris's and thought there was a fight. About 100 kids were crowded in a circle on the dance floor, clapping and cheering. Turned out it was Henry and Patty dancing. He threw her over his shoulder, under his legs, all around. They looked really good together."

"You're serious with Patty?" He knew I was. "Henry, I'm afraid she's not the girl you think she is."

I gave him a real hard look. But his face looked upset, not mad.

"She's been running around with other guys, son. I'm just reporting what I hear from good sources. I don't want to see you get hurt."

I didn't know why Dad would say that, but I knew Patty. Hadn't we been together since we were kids? And look at all we'd been through together!

That night I asked Rosie, 'cause I knew Rosie wouldn't never lie to me. When I asked her, though, she just kind of looked down at the ground and didn't say nothing. Which was saying something.

I couldn't believe it. What did they have against Patty? Couldn't they see how much I loved her? Dad had always tried to keep me from her but that was more about Junior, the bum, than really about Patty. She was so good. And I loved her so much! But Rosie—there's no way Rosie would lie to me. Then again, there's no way Patty would do what they was saying.

I couldn't figure it out so I just tried to stop thinking about it. I didn't say a word to Patty. It would hurt her too much.

༺∽༻

It was time to move back to Streator, now that my Allied Institute course would of ended. Dad and Patty weren't getting along, so when I told him I was coming back home, that was his chance to get rid of her.

Patty moved to a girl's boarding house, where I could visit her but I couldn't come inside. If the girls got caught with a guy, they got kicked out. We could sit on the front porch swing, but that was all.

Applegate's, where Dad worked, gave me a job. We all knew each other, so they just assumed I had my certificate. I delivered appliances and furniture, installed antennas, assembled riding mowers, hooked up 100-amp services for farmers, stuff like that. With my income—less than I made in Chicago, but more after expenses—I paid for Patty's rent and clothes and food. She waitressed part-time but she was starting her senior year in high school and couldn't work much.

We couldn't get together at her place or my place, so our dates usually ended in my car's back seat. One night, we'd just left a New-Year's Eve party and parked in a dark spot in the woods. I was planning a little party of our own, but Patty wanted to talk.

"Henry, I think …" Her face looked real serious, and I sort of knew what was coming.

"What?"

"Well, I ain't had a period since before your birthday!" My birthday was back November the 23rd.

"You're pregnant? Are you sure?"

"Pretty sure."

Oh boy!

"It's going to be great, Patty!"

"I'm still in high school!" She giggled. "What are my friends going to say?"

"We'll have to get us an apartment. And we'll have to get out of Streator."

౷

When we left, we didn't tell a soul—not my folks, not Patty's folks, not even her step-sister, Debbie. We just took off in the middle of the day in my 1960 Olds with $280 between us. We pulled off onto a country road and slept in the car that first night. The next morning, we drove into Joliet, went to this cafe, cleaned up in their restroom, and started looking for apartments.

We rented an upstairs apartment from a nice couple, where we had to go through their house to get there. I got a job at Home Juice Company, driving a route on commission. I liked it 'cause the pay was based on how good I did.

No one was looking over our shoulders in Joliet. Patty stayed home and I worked. She always had a home-cooked meal ready when I come in from work and she was always happy to see me. After a while we got an upstairs apartment closer to my job and we bought a pool table from Sears, the best one they had, and stuck it in the middle of our kitchen.

Those were the best days of my life.

౷

How Dad found me is, I started working at a Sunoco gas station and a guy who knew him saw me there. A few nights later, he showed up at our apartment. He talked nice, so I let him in. He said he just stopped to see how us kids was getting along. I told him we never were happier. That was the truth, too.

"Your mom's been worried about you." He said she was fine and we're welcome to come home any time. He stayed about twenty minutes. Before he left he looked outside to where I had the 1960 Olds sitting up on blocks with a bad transmission.

"So that's the car I been paying insurance on," he said.

༺❦༻

Winkie was born in St. Joseph's Hospital in Joliet. Patty had a short labor while I waited outside, nervouser than I ever been in my whole life. I watched through the glass while our baby was getting born but I didn't see her actually come out. I just saw this tiny baby being held up, crying. I watched them wipe her off.

A nurse come out and told me I was a father, and a man overheard and congratulated me, asking what kind, boy or girl, but I was so excited I didn't remember. Patty wanted to name her Jean and I wanted to name her Winkie,[10] so we named her Winkie Jean Hillenbrand.

When Winkie was born I wasn't thinking about my parents and Patty wasn't thinking about hers. We three had each other. Winkie slept between me and Patty. We didn't mind getting up at nights, and even as young as we were, sex didn't seem so important with a little baby between us. The love we had for Winkie only made our love for each other deeper, which is what makes what happened later so hard for me to understand.

༺❦༻

By now everybody knew where we lived and Winkie wasn't no secret, so me and Patty started talking about going back to Streator. We didn't really want to, and I wish to heck we hadn't of done it. Our life was so good in Joliet, and for a while we stayed.

Junior stopped by for a visit and this time he wasn't asking for money. His friend Tommy Canale had a big building where he stored pool tables, pinball machines, jukeboxes. He thought the place would make a good restaurant and he wanted us to manage it for him. I wanted to work for myself, so we ended up with a deal where Tommy would rent us the building and we could live upstairs, but we had to put Tommy's machines in our back room.

---

10 Not her real name, which has been changed for her privacy.

Dad liked the idea of us moving back to town and he said he'd help but on one condition—Junior couldn't be involved in it.[11] We signed the contract with Tommy Canale's lawyer, Ed Rashid, who was also Junior's lawyer.

We moved into the apartment above the restaurant and started up with the remodeling. Dad helped me build counters and countertops. He made really nice cabinets. We replaced broken tiles, installed a grill, put in a copper gas line, and bought used restaurant equipment—coffee makers, fryers, steamers, dishes, tables. Illinois Fruit and Produce gave us $1,800 credit on our first order, and BAM! We were in business.

We didn't know what to put on our menu or what to charge, so me and Patty checked out all the cafes in town. We ended up serving simple stuff—hamburgers, fries, soft drinks—and our specials were cheap things everybody likes, spaghetti and hot roast beef sandwiches and so on.

We called it the El Camino to save money, 'cause the sign was already there. Once, just on a lark, I put "hillbilly spaghetti" instead of just "spaghetti" on the menu and sold about half again as much, so I started making up fun names for all the specials.

We stayed open 24 hours, seven days a week. Me and Patty didn't get much social time together, but we were having fun. Patty had all the latest clothes and I got her a sharp '67 red Chevy convertible with white interior and spinners on the spoke wheel covers.

૭૭

Patty started going dancing out at Indian Acres, the hot night spot in the area. And my waitresses started telling me Patty was in the back room or out in cars with guys while I was asleep upstairs.

Then Dad started in.

"Henry, are you blind? Don't you listen when your friends tell you what Patty's doing? Darlene told me Patty's out there at Indian Acres making out with guys out back, getting into their cars and leaving with them. I told you what she's been doing and now your employees are telling you—when are you going to listen?"

---

11 Russell Hillenbrand: "In spite of that agreement, Junior would hang out there. One time I saw Junior walk up to the register and pull some money out of it. I told him to stay the hell out of there. 'But these kids need help,' he said. 'Like taking money out of the register?' I said. 'I'll bet they can do that by themselves.'"

I fired that waitress for talking to Dad. But I did confront Patty.

"What the heck are you doing out at Indian Acres?"

"Just having fun," she said. "With all the hours I put in around here, I deserve some time away."

"It's not right, Patty. We live together and we have a baby and you're out there behind the place with guys, and—"

"Henry, it's nothing. Quit acting so jealous. You know you're the one I love."

❦

It all boiled over when Patty bought a cocktail dress with all this lace and embroidered designs on the puffed arms and it was so sheer you could see right through it everywhere except for the tiny bra and panties built into it. She wore it one Friday night out to Indian Acres and when my drunk crowd rolled in after midnight they told me Patty was a big hit on the dance floor, "dancing with almost nothing on."

I met her coming up the stairs. "I heard about your new dress tonight," I said.

"Oh, it's nothing."

"That's what they told me! They're DRUNKS, Patty!" I'm screaming at her. "You showed yourself off to DRUNKS!"

"I didn't show myself off! I just feel like I'm in a cage, that's all. I need some freedom."

"You want freedom? I'll give you freedom!" I grabbed her sheer dress and ripped it right off her and she stood there completely naked. "Feel free now?"

❦

A few days later someone taped a Polaroid photo to the outside of our kitchen window, facing in. It was a picture of Patty, in a strange house, drunk as a skunk—and naked! I didn't say anything to Patty. Who took that picture? I swore I'd find out, and when I did, he'd pay.

I didn't care about the restaurant anymore. I started giving away strawberry shortcakes mounded with ice cream. The waitress I fired spread rumors that one of my other waitresses had a venereal disease. An OSHA man ordered me to install a $1,400 exhaust fan. So I hung out a "closed" sign and me and Patty and Winkie moved to an apartment.

Patty got work as a waitress again and I babysat Winkie and looked for a job. Dad couldn't understand why I was looking for a job when he could get me one at Applegate's.

I got a job at the Smith Douglas Fertilizer Plant.

∽

One morning my car wouldn't start. It cranked but it wouldn't fire. I missed work that day. My landlord told me later a guy had pulled up that morning in a Dodge station wagon and fiddled around under my hood. I knew it was Dad. The second evening my friend Porky came over, and just as I was hooking up the jumper cables Dad pulled up.

"Car trouble?"

I cussed him out.

"How stupid can you be, son? I can fix the problem."

"You caused it!"

He snickered. "That's the trouble with you—you never listened to what I taught you. All I did is push the coil wire up inside the distributor. I wanted to get you still long enough to talk to you. You got your life all messed up, you lost the restaurant—"

"I'm working at—"

"Patty's running around."

"—Smith Douglas."

"You want to load fertilizer the rest of your life?"

I ran at him, swearing and swinging. He caught my right hand with his left, then just as I swung *my* left Porky caught me from behind and pulled me to the ground. Dad was still lecturing me, pointing his finger, and I was trying to kick him but my arms were pinned. Porky held me down as Dad drove off.

I got a warning for missing two days at my job, so I quit. I sent Patty in to pick up my last check, 'cause I was ashamed. But if Dad thought he was going to force me to Applegate's he was wrong.

So I started hanging out with Junior in bars and pool halls, and it wasn't long before he suggested the burglary. Up till then I'd hadn't never broke the law, unless you count shooting squirrels in the park.

Ten

Tom Henry

Patty was working at Jim and Letty's café, and since I didn't have a job I was there helping her out when Junior comes in to get a cup of coffee. He's mad at June, says he's going to get back at her by robbing the Germosik house.

Mrs. Germosik was June's mother. Alex Germosik, the old man, was in the hospital. Junior tells me Alex owes him money "and if I don't take it now, I won't get it after he's gone." Alex had antique Russian swords and a valuable coin collection and guns. Our deal was I'd get the guns, Junior would get everything else.

Now, Junior was a bum, no car, and my Chevy didn't have license plates on it. But Patty had a pink 1960 Rambler wagon, so Junior borrowed it.

The Germosik place was an old house just north of Ottawa. About eleven-thirty we drove by it twice real slow, parked and walked back to it. We tried the front door, which had a new padlock, and the windows, which were locked. Then we drove to Ida's café, 'cause Patty would still be at Jim and Letty's, and we sat at a booth and talked about it over coffee. Junior was worried.

"I'll do it," I said. "It's your relatives. You need an alibi." So he went to Rokey's go-go bar and I drove back to Ottawa about three in the morning. I parked the Rambler wagon in a wooded area about half a mile away and walked to the house. I put masking tape on a window and broke the window with my fist.

I cut my hand as I pulled it out, had to tie my hanky around it to stop the bleeding. I reached in to turn the window catch and in ten seconds I'm in, walking through the house with my Ronson lighter. I take the swords off the walls and the guns out from under the bed and I find another gun in the closet and take that too. I wrapped them all up together in a bedspread and carried them to the window.

I found the safe in a bedroom. It looked like an end table because it had a cover over it hanging down to the floor and a lamp on top. I never would of found it if Junior hadn't told me it was there. It was way too heavy to carry, so I dragged it through the house to the window on a rug and used an ironing board to get it up to the window sill and through the window onto the ground outside.

I threw the bedspread bundle with the guns and swords through the window and climbed out. I left the safe by the window, carried the bundle of guns past the mowed part of the lawn and left it in the brush, then walked to Patty's car. I cranked the tailgate window down—it made too much noise to do it at the house—unhooked the taillight wire, and drove to the house with my headlights off. I parked by the road and got my package from the woods, then went back to the safe.

I could roll it across the lawn but no way could I lift it. I backed Patty's car up so the back wheels were in the ditch and the tailgate was level with the ground, then I rolled the safe into the back of the car. A light lit up in a house not far off. I eased the tailgate closed while holding in the handle, then I took off.

I got home about four in the morning. I took the swords and guns out and put them under the bed. Then I drove to a vacant farmhouse, backed the car up as far into the woods as I could, and rolled the safe out of the car. I went to a car wash and cleaned the grass and mud out of the tailgate, then I drove down a dirt road to get dirt back on the car. I went back to our apartment, lifted the cold air return cover, and stuffed the swords and guns in there.

I had the car back to Patty before she got off work in the morning. After she was asleep, I pulled the swords out and inspected them. I took off about ten that morning and met Junior in Leo's Café, the horse-betting place. We talked in the booth, and Junior was real nervous, so we left together for a walk.

"Let me see the swords," he said. He was all excited.

"I hid them in the apartment—Patty's asleep there."

"Well, let's go see the safe," he said.

"Wait till it gets dark."

That night we went out there and looked at the safe, but we couldn't figure out how to get it open, so we carried it further into the brush and went back to town.

The next evening, when I figured Dad had left for service calls, I went over to the house and talked to Mom for a while, then I got me a three-pound hammer, a screwdriver, a tire tool bar, and a cold chisel from the garage. I picked Junior up and we drove out to the house in the country. We spent at least two hours trying to open the safe with the tools.

I knew the owner of the vacant farmhouse, so the next day I rented it for $45. That night we carried the safe into the house but we still couldn't figure out how to get it open.

The next night we took it back out to the yard and tried again with the tools. We fiddled with it for a couple hours—we had it sideways, tilted, upside down—and when it was upside down we noticed something written on the bottom of it, scratched into the metal.

The combination!

The safe had savings bonds, coins, insurance papers, and letters in it. Junior burned all the papers except the bonds. I couldn't see the sense of that—we could of at least given them back those papers. But that's how Junior was.

All I wanted was the guns. There was a Savage .22 over-under—a .22 on top and a .410 under—and a .38 pistol with a holster. The rest was Junior's.

◡

A couple days later, Officers Don Haage and Kenneth Jackson showed up at my apartment.

"We need to ask you some questions."

"About what?" I said.

"Let's go for a ride."

They drove me to the Streator Police Station. We didn't go to an interrogation room and I wasn't handcuffed. We just sat down by Don Haage's desk.

"What do you know about the burglary of the Germosik residence in Ottawa?"

"Nothing."

"Come on, Henry. She's June's mother. We know you've been hanging with Junior. Did he put you up to it?"

I denied everything.

◡

The next day, Bill Dummett took me to the Ottawa Police Station, and this time I was put in the interrogation room. I still denied everything. He apologized for bothering me and offered to drive me back. So I'm in his car when just past Grand Ridge a call comes in on the radio from the Streator Police that they found a safe in a farmhouse rented by a guy named Henry Hillenbrand. We turn around and drive right back to the Ottawa interrogation room.

"We know you did it, Henry." Bill ticks off the points on his fingers. "One, a neighbor saw you and Junior case the house. Two, June says Junior was in on it. Three, Junior has an alibi. He was seen at Rokey's. Four, the tire tracks came from Patty's car. Five, you rented the house where the safe was found."

"You got me," I said.

The next day I took them to the old farmhouse and showed them where the rest of the stuff was. They'd only found the safe. Then we went back to Ottawa, where they booked me and I signed the confession.

I said Junior didn't have nothing to do with it.

∽

Bond was set at $3,000. I had to put up $300. They had Sunday-only visiting, and the first Sunday Dad and Mom showed up for a twenty-minute visit and a first class butt-chewing job. It was set up so you stood at these bars with wire mesh between you. My dad didn't even offer to bond me out. He just said for me to think things over.

Ed Rashid come up one night with Patty, sent by Junior. I told him to tell Junior to get me out of there. Rashid said I'd get probation. I waited, but I didn't hear from Junior.

Dad come the second Sunday and told me he'd get me out on bond on three conditions. First, I couldn't see Patty, Second, I had to live at home, And third, I had to work at Applegate's with him. I said no, no, and no.

I sent three more letters to Junior. I didn't want to tell on him, or it would be all over with me and Patty, so I worded my letters real careful: "Junior, you know I wasn't the only one involved." He didn't answer.

So the third Sunday I accepted Dad's offer. He come first thing Monday morning and bonded me out. I didn't go to work that first day, I was so happy just to be out of jail. Patty quit at Jim and Letty's 'cause they told the police about Junior borrowing the car that night. She went to work for the Libby Owens glass factory as a packer.

I saw Patty a couple times, but it was hard 'cause my dad was like a watch-dog. I treated him real bad, wouldn't talk to him the whole two weeks I was home. He had to drive me to work, but I tried to get on jobs with other guys.

The only one Dad didn't mind me being out with was Porky. He come out and drove me around and we hung out together. One day he told me he seen Patty with one of the Evans brothers, said he thought it was Harry.

I found out where Harry lived and talked my mom into letting me use her car. I drove out to the trailer court, walked up onto Harry's porch, and looked through the little window on the door.

I saw Patty laying on the sofa bed, which was pulled out. She was in her waitress uniform and her uniform skirt was drawn up to her hips.

I started pounding on the door and hollering. Harry opened the door— I pushed him and flung a lamp down and told him to stay out of my way. I grabbed Patty and told her to get in the car and wait for me and she went out. Harry just stood there.

I got in the car and started yelling at Patty.

"What the heck are you doing here?"

"Nobody told you to come and get me."

"Harry don't love you, Patty. He ain't going to take care of you."

"Like you're taking care of me? Breaking into June's mom's house and going to jail? Turn here. I got to get Winkie."

So I dropped her off at her sister's, then I took Mom's car back. Tell you the truth I didn't know what to do I was so mad and hurt.

∽

I lived at home for a couple more weeks, then one day after work I rented an apartment across from the hospital from a guy we'd delivered a stove to a few days before.

That's where I was living when I killed Patty.

Dad got on me about breaking my promise but he didn't mind too bad 'cause I still didn't have a car and I still wasn't living with Patty. I started spending time with her again, but she seemed different. She was happy to see me and we even was intimate, but she told me she wanted to keep seeing other guys.

"We were going to get married," I said.

"And we are. I just ain't ready yet, Henry."

"I don't like you hanging around them Evans brothers," I said.

"George was there for me when I didn't have no one. You was in jail, June was mad 'cause I let you borrow my car, and I wasn't even talking to my dad."

What could I say? At least Patty said she still loved me, and with Winkie, no one else could ever take my place. I didn't like it, but what could I do? We saw each other sometimes at my place and sometimes at hers, and I was painting and fixing up my place so Patty would move back in with me.

⚬⚬

A few days later I came downstairs and another Polaroid was stuck under my door. It was Patty, drunk, sitting on a sink she'd just thrown up into and a bit of drool was on her lips and her feet dangled limp. And she was naked.

All I could think of was a bunch of guys laughing and carrying on with my Patty! I couldn't work all day. That night I told Porky all about it and we began putting the puzzle together. He figured she was dating two of the Evans brothers, George and Harry, but she was hot and heavy with George, the one just home from Vietnam.

I surprised Patty that night by being in her apartment when she came home from work a little after eleven. I showed her the photo.

"Oh my God!" she said.

"Who took this?"

"I don't know, Henry, really I don't!"

"You DO know! Patty, those guys don't care about you. They're using you! Would I take a picture like this and spread it around town?"

She just stared at the photo.

"Would I? You know I'd never! Was it Harry or George?"

"I told you, Henry, I don't know."

I felt like screaming but I decided to try another approach. I put my arms around her.

"Patty, I love you. You're my wife, and Winkie is our baby."

"I'm not your wife. We just been saying that."

"Let's make it true. We can get our blood tests at the hospital and get married at the courthouse. Then you really will be my wife."

She started crying. I held her and she said she'd move into my place. We slept together that night, and the next day me and Porky moved her hope chest and some clothes to my apartment. She'd just paid the rent, so she told me she'd move as soon as the month was over.

A couple nights later Porky was helping me paint my apartment and he found two more photos. Patty was on a bed and everything was showing.

෧

I started drinking. I bought liquor from Pic-a-Pak Liquors—Bali Hai wine, Boone's Farm apple wine, Southern Comfort.

Patty was working the three-to-eleven shift at Libby Owens and she usually went to Jim and Letty's cafe when she got off, so me and Porky waited there for her. When she didn't show we drove to her apartment, then back to the cafe where some guys said they seen her with George up at Rokey's.

I hopped in the car and zipped over there. George and Patty was sitting at the bar, which was in the shape of a square horseshoe, and I grabbed a stool right across from them and stared at them. Pretty soon they moved down to the end of the bar where I couldn't see them without standing up, so I stood up.

George finally come over. He was over six feet tall and muscular. He tells me to get the hell out of there. I start talking smart with him in a real loud voice, then I tell him to meet me out back if he's man enough. I left and a minute later he steps out with half the bar on his tail. Patty come out too. We're cussing each other when George takes a step toward me.

"Don't, George, don't hurt him!" Patty says.

"I ain't scared of you, you big-ass Marine!" I said. But George wouldn't fight me 'cause of Patty.

"Don't worry about him hurting me!" I yelled. "You hurt me a heck of a lot more than that big son of a bitch ever could."

Patty got George to stay away and we sat in her car while she tried to calm me down. She told me to go back to her place, she'd get rid of George and come over. I waited for over two hours and was boiling mad when she come in—until she said the reason she took so long. "I told him it's you I love and we're going to get married. I broke it off with him."

I was so happy! And I believed her, not a speck of doubt in my mind.

To celebrate, we made a dinner date for the following night.

෧

I picked Patty up at her apartment for our date. She had on a white dress and her blond hair was curled and soft and it smelled so nice.

I kissed her. "Want to see my new car?"

Driving off in my '57 Chevy listening to the radio, it felt like it used to be in Joliet, with Patty snuggled up by my side and my arm around her. Soon as we were seated in the restaurant, I went out to the car and I got two roses and put them in a water glass on our table. Patty ordered fried chicken with French fries and a Coke and I ordered the catfish special and coffee.

"I got my blood test this morning," I said. "It's easy. You can go in Monday. Nothing to it, you just—"

"Let's talk about something else," she said. "We're eating."

"You're going to get your blood test, aren't you?"

"Henry, let's talk about something else."

"You told me just last night—*just last night!*—you told me we're getting married!"

I stormed out of the restaurant and Patty came out to calm me down.

"You think those guys love you?" I said. "Patty, they're just using you. I love you!"

"I love you too, Henry, you know I do." Patty kissed me and tugged on my arm and said she loved me again, she didn't love George. "Come on, Henry, let's go back in."

The rest of the evening went good. We drove home, me and Patty made love at my apartment, then I drove her home. By the time I got back to my car, though, I was getting mad again. Why should me and Patty be living apart? And if she loves me so much, why won't she get her blood test? She's making me feel good but she don't really want to be with me.

By the time I got to my place I was so worked up I needed a drink. It was after midnight, so I went to Rokey's. I don't remember how long I drank or how I got home that night, but I do remember puke in my car the next morning.

I rode to work with my windows down.

Leon, a guy I worked with, come over to look at my car when I pulled up.

"Nice." Then he looked in through the open window. "What's that smell?"

"Hey, Leon, want to buy a pistol? I got this Ruger Bearcat .22 I'll sell you for twenty-five bucks, holster and all."

"I don't use guns, Henry. You know that."

"Yeah, but it's a great deal," I said. "It's worth more than that. You trust me, don't you?"

"Sure, I trust you. Now why don't you trust me and tell me why?"

I told him about George and the fight I almost had and how George was so much bigger than me and how I'd been drinking the last couple weeks because of it all.

"I'm afraid I might—I mean, I just don't want to own no pistol in case ..."

"I'll buy it and hold it." Leon said. "You ever want it back, I got it."

☙

That day I made a delivery to a guy in Wenona who was just burglarized.

"Damn thieves," he said. "I work my butt off to get nice things, they steal 'em and sell 'em for a fraction of what they're worth. They took my wife's ring! They'll sell it to some fence for ten bucks."

What could I say? I was out on bond for a burglary. I thought about Junior burning the insurance papers, then I thought about George. That's what he was doing—taking something valuable to me and just throwing it away.

By the time I got home I was so worked up I went straight to Pic-a-Pak for a bottle of Southern Comfort, then I walked to the Pence house to pick up Winkie. I always babysat her after work. I watched her play while I cleaned up and thought about me and Patty in Joliet and how happy we was there.

I took Winkie back about six, then headed straight for Rokey's. The beer's cheaper before the girls start dancing. A few minutes after I got there, Porky showed up.

"What's the matter?" he said.

"Patty ain't getting her blood test."

"Don't she want to get married?"

"She wants to see other guys."

"I'm sorry, man." He was, too. Porky was the kind of friend who cared.

☙

Porky had to work the next day, so he went home about ten. I cruised around town looking for Patty and George. Nobody knew where they was, so I finally went home, drank some more, and slept until noon on Sunday.

I got up and had me some more Southern Comfort and by three o'clock I went over to spend a little time with Winkie, who was real happy, jabbering away and walking around in her little diapers. I played with her about a half-hour, then I went over to Rokey's for a few beers.

Porky come in around six o'clock. We talked and drank more beer. By midnight my head was slumped onto the bar. Porky tried to wake me but it wasn't no use. Porky drove my car and Ed followed in his car and they got me upstairs and onto my sofa.

I kind of drifted in and out of sleep for a while, finally got up and drove to Rokey's but the building was dark. I started driving around and I was thinking about Patty not getting her blood test at St. Mary's, so I drove to the hospital and parked in front of it and sat in the car for I don't know how long and walked across the street to my apartment and passed out on the sofa.

Eleven

Tom Henry

I woke up a little after six in the morning and went down to get my car, but it was gone. I tried to think where it might be—couldn't remember when I drove it last. I walked to the front of the house and saw it parked on Spring Street in front of the hospital. Why would I put my car there?

George! He was playing games. Taking Patty isn't enough, he has to torment me with pictures and pranks. Well, I'll fix him! He might be bigger and stronger but with my gun in my hands I'll get Patty away from him, and he better not try to stop me.

I opened my trunk and got my .22 rifle and started walking up Bloomington Street, through downtown, across Main Street, past two sets of train tracks, then turned left two blocks to where George lived.

I saw a broken window and crawled in. As I come into the bedroom I see Patty and George—in bed. George looks up, surprised.

"Hey, what the—"

"Get up, Patty!" Then I turn to George. "I'm taking her home."

George lunges up out of the bed at me like he don't even notice my rifle's already up.

BOOM! I shoot him in the head. Seems like his body keeps coming at me, but he's dead. I push him back onto the bed. Patty's yelling at me.

"You shot him, Henry! You'll pay for this!"

His head is starting to bleed. She looks at him on the bed, as if—as if she loves him. What I just done, shooting him to death, ain't registered with me yet, but the look on Patty's face, *that* registers. She's looking at me with pure horror in her eyes.

She tries to run by me out the door and I swing the rifle butt and hit her in the head. Makes a hollow-sounding thunk. Blood spurts from her head and she slumps down the wall to the floor. I help her to the bathroom and try to stop the bleeding, wrap a white bath towel around her head but it turns red real fast. She's moaning and her head's bleeding something terrible, so I help her into the back seat of her car and drive to the hospital.

In the car Patty keeps saying, "Where's Winkie? Where's Winkie? Don't hurt Winkie!" I pull into the emergency entrance to the hospital and jump out, but Patty won't move.

"Where's Winkie?" she says again. Winkie was at her sister's place, but my mind's not straight—I jump back in the car and drive to my apartment to take her to Winkie.

I help Patty out and we make it to my door but I don't have my key. I run back to the car—hold on, these aren't my keys because it ain't my car. I notice my broken rifle on the front seat. The stock is gone, snapped loose off the forearm, which is still attached to the barrel. I pick it up.

When Patty sees me with the broken rifle she staggers across the lawn, screaming. I yell "Stop!" She's bleeding and bleeding but she starts *running*. I have to stop her.

I shoot her with my broken gun. She falls and I run to her

"Henry, you *shot* me!"

I try to stop the blood from flowing out of her stomach. She rolls and somehow gets up and runs again, across one yard and through another, and I'm chasing her, yelling and shooting. She finally collapses on a back porch.

I hit her again with my gun.

Loud voices shout at me and I see a face in a window. I throw the gun in some bushes, run, and drive to my dad's house.

ᘒ

My sister Gloria answered the front door.

"Henry! Oh, no! Daaaaaad!" I walked past her into the house. Dad come down the hall.

"What the hell happened?" he said. "Where'd that blood come from?"

"I need help." I walked into the kitchen.

"Does this have to do with Patty? Henry, what did you do?"

"I think I killed someone."

"Who did you kill?"

"I shot Kennedy."

"Where?"

"308 West Stanton,"[12] I said.

---

12 From the police report of Russell's phone call. What Henry meant is unknown. It appears his mind combined the assassination of President Kennedy eight years earlier with his grandmother's address.

Dad called the police. I walked into the kitchen and got a knife out of the drawer to stab myself, but Gloria grabbed the knife and I ran out the back door, through the woods and into the creek.

The cold water cleared my head and I realized I needed to clean up, so I splashed around a little before I crossed to the other side and followed the creek to the Highway 23 Bridge and went under it. I saw a farmhouse with a silo on the other side of the creek, so I swam back across, ran to the silo, climbed up the welded wire on the side, and went into the auger hole at the top.

From there I could see a police car south of the bridge sitting at the shoulder with two policemen. Another came from the north and stopped by it, then it turned around and shot back toward the north. After a while, one of the two policemen got out and the car headed south.

It was so hot I near suffocated in that silo, but by now my head was clearer and I was thinking. I could continue by the creek all the way to Sandy Ford Bridge where there are thousands of acres of woods ... but I wanted to find out about Patty.

There was blood on my shirt. Was it Patty's?

I climbed down, crossed the highway, and headed for the house. A man was in the greenhouse watering his tomato plants. I asked him could I use a phone and I called the hospital.

"Do you have Patty Hillenbrand there?" I said. "I need to know how she is."

"Who is this?"

"Just tell me, is Patty Hillenbrand all right?" There was no answer, so I hung up. I called again but I couldn't find out nothing. I turned around and the farmer was staring at me.

"Can you take me to the police station?" I said.

"Come with me." He got in his Jeep and I climb in next to him. He kept eyeballing me while he drove.

We ran into the police roadblock at the corner of Rudy's market. I got out of the Jeep and walked toward a policeman but got jumped from behind and slammed against the car. They put me in the back seat with my hands cuffed behind my back and Don Haage climbed in beside me. He knew me and Patty from eating in our restaurant.

"Don, tell me one thing. How's Patty?"

He just looked at me.

"How is she?"

"The worst," he said.

⟡

Once we got to the police station, they put me in this little room and left me alone with one policeman to guard me. I knew all the Streator police from the restaurant and I could hear them talking.

"Russell—boy, I don't know how Russell's going to take this." Nothing about my mom, just all about Russell. "I don't believe it." They all knew me and knew how I felt about Patty.

Four of them finally came in and sat down. Chief Gene Robertson read me my rights and asked if I understood them. I said I did and signed the paper.

"Do you have or want an attorney?" he asked me.

"I ain't got one and I can't afford one," I said.

"If you want, the court will appoint one for you."

"Don't see what good it will do me, do you?"

"No, but you can have one if you want, is what we're saying."

"I don't," I said. "No one can help me now."

"Henry," Gene said. "Want to talk about it?"

"I ain't going to answer no questions unless you tell me how's Patty," I said.

They looked at each other, then Don Haage spoke up.

"She dead, Henry. I told you that in the car."

I started crying. I kind of knew it all along, but to have someone say it to you so you know for sure makes it real. He started talking in a soft voice to me about it all and asking me questions.

"Where was your gun? Did you carry it up the street? Where's your car?"

"I don't know," I said. "I walked to George's house."

"George who?"

"George Evans. That's where it happened."

"No, let's back up a little bit. It happened in back of your apartment." He was talking real nice.

"Yeah, that's where I shot her, but that ain't where I first hurt her," I said. They thought I'd just killed Patty. They didn't know nothing about George.

After they asked me everything they could think of, Ed Rashid popped in and told me not to answer any questions, he was going to represent me and he'd get back with me later that day. Since I wouldn't talk any more, they put me in a cell.

The bars of my cell window faced the sidewalk in front of the park. Now, this was the old city jail, just five steel bars and a wire mesh, and I could hear everything outside. Junior was out there hollering about how he's going to kill me, he's going to do this and that, and all his sidekicks are out there with him.

The police were afraid for my safety there and worried about Junior and his buddies causing a ruckus, so they took me to Ottawa, but they did it kind of sneaky. They had a deputy go out front and tell Junior and his guys they had to leave. Junior starts shouting and arguing with the deputy. While that's happening out front, two squad cars pull up in back, load me in, and off we go. They let Junior win the argument—after all, his daughter was just killed—and he and his buddies stayed there a while longer, thinking I was still in the jail.

When I got to Ottawa they locked me in the padded cell downstairs because my dad was worried about me since I tried to stab myself with a knife in his kitchen. I was glad to be in that cell 'cause I didn't want to be around nobody. They brought me something to eat and a few guards squatted down to talk to me through the flap in the door.

The next morning William Dummett brought me out to interrogate me some more. I told him I couldn't say nothing to him till I heard from my lawyer.

"We just want to know one thing, Henry, for our investigation," he said. "We found Patty's blood on the floor and on the wall and George's blood mostly in the bed but some of it out of the bed, so we figure he wasn't killed in bed. Why'd you put him back in bed?"

"I don't remember about that," I told him.

"Were they sleeping when you found them? Were they nude? Did you put clothes on him?" When I didn't answer, he went on. "There was powder in George's hair. Based on the angle of the bullet, my theory is you must have shot upwards. George pressing you against the wall must have made the gun go off. But what I want to know is, why did you put him back in the bed?"

"I didn't," I said. "I shot him in the bed."

&

I got a visit from Mom, Rosie, and Dad. Mom was crying and Rosie just stared at me. We had to talk through these flat, square, two-inch metal bars with wire mesh between them. There was a guard on the inmate side and one on the visitor side. Dad talked about getting me a lawyer and I told him about Ed Rashid.

"He's no criminal lawyer, Henry." Dad wanted to get me a good lawyer. "I'll do all I can for you," he said. Then he gave me one of those lectures. "I tried to raise you right, I told you, how many times—"

"Dad, don't start."

"—to stay away from the Pences. And to get a good education and work hard, but by golly, how come you have to keep snapping at me like a junkyard dog?"

I felt like getting up and walking out, but I stayed there. Rosie just stared at me. Mom, all she did was cry.

"They say you'll do twenty years," Dad said. "I won't be around by the time you get out, but I want you to remember I did everything I could for you. You know how hard I worked to build the house. You helped me. You know how long we saved and I'm still paying it off. But if I have to I'll take a second mortgage out on it.

"I'm going to keep you from getting the death penalty. By the time you get out I want you to always remember the love your father and mother had for you, even after all you've done to us. But I pray"—he didn't say to God—"that someday you have a boy. Then you'll know the love I have for you, in spite of what you've done."

We just had ten minutes to visit. Afterward I went upstairs and wrote a letter.

&

Dear Mom and Dad, what I committed is the worst sin imaginable taking ones life away but I do believe in God dad and he will take Patty in and help her. It says in the Bible we are all God's children. Like Im your son and you watch over me. God has Pattys sole now because shes Gods child and some day he will want me. This is how come I never had the courage to take my own life because God never wanted it that way. As long as I'm alive Dad Patty and Winkie will always be with me and if I have any control afterwards they will be with me. Believe me, I never wanted to hurt Patty just all of a sudden everything inside me exploded.

Ive always said I wanted to be alone but no one really does. You have to have something or someone that is part of you.

Like you are still trying your best to help me and I keep asking myself why. You have got to believe this Dad, theres not going to be anyway that your going into debt or loose your house and everything all the years you work for those things that are part of you there not going to be taken away from you. help me yes Dad but don't go to any extremes because theres a way I could stop it all.

But I want to keep living Dad till I hear some how that Winkie will be taken care of until she can take care of herself. Her and Patty is part of me so don't hurt them Dad and let me carry there image inside me. Just take care of Rosie and Diane especially Mom. I know it will be hard but you can do it. I keep asking myself why, but even I don't know. Theres got to be some reason why Ive always hurt the ones I love. Ive got to have some help Dad some one to talk to. I know how I feel but I cant express it. If anything does happen to me I wish to be buried next to Patty because shes all I have. I doubt if this letter reaches you they probably won't let it go out. But I had to try.

Love Always
Henry[13]

෴

Dad and Mom first learned of that letter when the prosecutor made me read it from the witness stand thirteen years later.

---

13 Word for word this is Henry's actual letter, which would later become a court exhibit.

Twelve

Tom Henry

I figured Dummett's investigation was all done, but one day a jailer hollered my name like I had a visit and he took me to the interrogation room and there was Bill Dummett.

"Let me ask you, Henry," he said. "What do you know about the Monts murder?"

"I didn't have nothing to do with it, if that's what you mean," I said.

Old Man Monts ran an old country store on Highway 23 just blocks from our El Camino Restaurant. He had gas pumps out front and chickens in his yard and I used to buy eggs from him for my restaurant.

One day a customer pulled in to get some gas and when he went inside he saw Old Man Monts shot to death with his own double-barreled shotgun. It was big in the papers.

"Weren't you a customer of his?" Bill Dummett asked.

"Everyone traded with him," I said. "Why would I hurt a nice old man like him?"

"I don't know, Henry. You tell me."

"I'm telling you, I didn't have nothing to do with Monts's murder."

"Henry, we know you bought eggs for your restaurant from him. We know you got into money troubles. Was this a way of getting out of debt?"

"You're barking up the wrong tree," I said.

"Would you be willing to take a polygraph test?"

"Why should I? I ain't guilty."

Dad brought it up on his next visit.

"Bill Dummett tells me you won't cooperate with his investigation of the Monts murder," he said. "And it's been in the paper, 'Hillenbrand suspected in Monts Killing.'"

"Do you think I'd kill an old man, Dad?"

I wish I could forget my dad's answer.

"I never thought you'd kill Patty, either."

"I was out of my mind when I killed Patty," I said. "You really think I'd shoot an old man? For money?"

He didn't say anything.

I agreed to the lie detector test because of that.

They handcuffed me and drove me to another city for it. The paper said I was going up to take a polygraph, but they never printed that I passed it.

⁓

Ed Rashid didn't show up the day I got to the Ottawa jail, but the next day he had to see another client, so he called me up to talk. He asked me was I drinking that night. He asked me to write out everything that happened in detail and keep it where no one could see it, and he gave me a few days to do it.

I wrote the statement out, six pages, and it's the same statement Rashid gave to another lawyer for his Dram Shop Act suit. And we don't have the statement to this day. It ain't in Rashid's files.[14]

I was in that solitary padded cell for about six days, nothing there but rubber matting. I needed at least three of those days in there. It's dark, no one to talk to, nothing to do, so all you do is think—and I needed to think. Think and cry. I was thinking about what I did, about Patty, and also about that comment I overheard, "I don't know how Russell's going to take this."

This padded cell didn't have nothing in there. No toilet, just a plastic bucket in the corner. No sink—when you wanted water you had to ask and they'd bring it to you. For food they gave me a big spoon and a round metal bowl with everything all together.

The first day they didn't give me no clothes and they checked on me all the time. After that I got a jumpsuit to wear and they knew I was going to be all right, so they didn't bother me. Through the slot where they push your food they can see in but you can't see out. But you can hear the footsteps coming and going.

I was lying on the floor when I heard the food slot door. I looked in it and Tom Tibb's face was there. He was the night jailor.

"How you doing, Henry?"

"Can't you get me out of here, man? I ain't going to hurt myself. I can't stand it, laying on this cold floor and my stomach growling and I ain't got no one to talk to."

---

14 Rashid has died and his secretary couldn't find the statement in his papers. There is a court record of its being lent to Craig Armstrong, an attorney who was preparing a dram shop act lawsuit in connection with the murders. Mr. Armstrong testified he read but did not copy the statement before returning it to Mr. Rashid.

A few minutes later he was back. He slid a bologna sandwich through my food slot.

"Here's something I picked up from the kitchen."

"Thanks." I took a huge bite. He didn't say nothing but he stayed. "How's Winkie?" I asked him.

"Who?"

"Our little girl. Is she okay?"

"I don't know, Henry. I didn't hear anything about her. I'm sure she's in good hands."

What's going to happen to Winkie? *Oh God, I don't deserve nothing but take care of Winkie. Don't let her be raised by Junior.* It was my first prayer.

"Why'd you do it, Henry?"

"I don't know," I said. "What would you do if you caught your wife in bed with another man?"

"I suppose—well, I guess I'd do well to remember what happened to you, Henry, 'cause I know what I'd feel like doing."

"I sure wish I could do it over. But I can't," I said. "I sure am sorry."

"Are you sorry you killed George or just Patty?" he asked.

The question was a surprise. I hadn't even thought of George until then, and now I did, I didn't feel a thing.

"No, I ain't sorry I shot George," I said. "I sure am sorry I shot Patty, though."[15]

இ

I didn't get recreation or no other activities in there. One day, after about a week, they asked if I'd like to go to a cell with others.

"You bet I would!"

Cellblock Six was on the third floor. The floor was made of sheet metal and it made a wumba-wumba sound when you walked across it. The guys downstairs would yell for us to quit pacing. After breakfast each morning we mopped it and half an hour later it dried and the rust was back, so we put our mattresses on the floor during the day to keep our clothes clean.

Jail is boring. You sit and don't do anything but think about being free. But on Friday July 17th I thought about Winkie. It was her second birthday, and I didn't know if I'd ever see her again. On her first birthday Patty baked a

---

15 Tom Tibb would later recall this conversation almost to the word.

cake with one candle and me and Patty and Winkie kissed all at once and I got smeared with Winkie's frosting and Patty laughed and laughed.

I gave the guys my day-old doughnuts and went to my bunk and cried into my blanket.

⁓

The next Monday was my first time in court. The judge read the grand jury indictment, denied me bond, and I was back in my cell in fifteen minutes. A week and a half later I was in court again. The judge set a date to hear the pre-trial motions. This time Rashid talked to me for a few minutes. He said there were matters that needed to be decided on before trial. Three weeks later, I'm back in court and the judge asks me how I plead. Rashid said my plea is not guilty and that I demand a jury trial.

It was October before Rashid came to the jail to see me.

"The state has all kinds of evidence, Henry. They say if we go to trial they'll ask for the death penalty. And they'll probably get it. If you plead guilty, they won't ask for it. You'll have a chance to get out of prison in fifteen, twenty years, maybe less. We go to court in a few days. The reason I'm talking to you now is you're going to have to satisfy the judge that you know what you're doing when you plead guilty. I can't do it for you. He'll ask a bunch of questions. He has to. Just keep saying you understand, even if you don't."

He was in a hurry to go and I was taken back to my cell. So that was it. I was going to prison. Fifteen to twenty years! All the guys had been telling me about prison. Stabbings, beatings, gangs, and for a small guy like me, rape.

⁓

I decided to cut my wrist. I told the trusty who swept the hall I needed a spoon. I had one in less than two hours. That night after everyone was asleep I started scraping it against the mortar between the cement blocks in the hallway, kept at it till it was sharp enough to do the job. I really tried, holding the spoon in my right hand with my left wrist pinned against the mattress. I knew to cut your wrist you had to slice the long way. Well, I couldn't do it.

So if I can't kill myself I figured I got to escape the other way. I looked at the mortar where I sharpened my spoon. It was indented between the blocks about half an inch. If I scraped away at it for two or three nights, I could get that block loose and get to the hall. The window across the hall from our cellblock had a big fan in it, but the one across from Cellblock Five only had bars.

There was cement dust on the floor. I scraped it onto a paper and flushed it down the toilet. Then I mashed some Ivory soap to fill in the mortar where I dug it out, but it was too white, so I mixed in cigarette ashes till I got it just right.

I figured it would take three nights to get the whole block loose and all the cement down the toilet. But shoot—there's no way I'll fit through that size opening. To crawl through the wall I got to remove four blocks, two by two, and that I can't hide. I got to get a better plan.

∾

On Dad's next visit he told me to do what Rashid told me.

"You should be paroled by about forty," he said. "That's young. You can still have a good life."

"I'll survive all right," I said. "Just make sure you get that bail money back from the burglary, 'cause I don't need it now." How could I tell him I planned to escape? Dad was so honest he'd turn me in.

"Don't you worry about no three hundred dollars," he said. "You got bigger problems than that."

I reminded him again the next Sunday, but I couldn't make him understand he needed to get that money.[16]

∾

On Monday I pled guilty in court.

On Tuesday Tom Garrett moved from Cellblock Five into our cellblock. Garrett was always escaping—out of county jails, police cars, a house the cops had surrounded. He got to be so well known they called him "Garrett the rabbit" in the newspaper. He had a big scar right by his heart from a cop shooting him with a .38 special. He escaped five times in three years and was shot three times. He was in this time for trying to dynamite his mother and father-in-law's house 'cause his wife and kids lived there.

---

16 Russell Hillenbrand said, "When Henry told me to get my bond money back, I knew what he was saying, but can you imagine the heat on me if I got my bond money back just before he escaped?"

86

Now, Garrett was a big bossy guy, always fighting. He got kicked out of two cellblocks before coming to ours, but me and him got along good. The sheriff thought he'd finally hit on a good combination.

So did me and Garrett, 'cause we decided to escape together.

His idea was to pull the stainless steel elbow out from under the sink and fill it with soap. When the guard took us for a shower, we'd hit him over the head with it and take his keys. Then we'd surprise the other guard and make him open the front door. We'd grab his pistol and tie him up. I wasn't real impressed with this plan.

"You could kill someone, man. They'll give you the death penalty."

"Have to catch me first," he said.

"I ain't going to hurt nobody. There's got to be a better way."

"Not unless we can get a stick of dynamite in here."

Within a few days we had a plan we both liked. Get hold of some hacksaw blades—we didn't know how yet but we were sure we could do it. Use them to cut the cell bars to get into the hall, then to cut the window bar to get outside, then we'd let ourselves down to the ground with a rope made from strips of our sheets.

❧

Sometimes when we flushed our toilets and so did the guys downstairs, they got our shit in their toilets. We worked it out so we could send messages and tobacco from the third floor to the second. Here's how it would go.

I wrap some Bugler tobacco or whatever in a plastic bag so it's sealed and drop it in the toilet. Say it's nine o'clock. On the fourth chime of the church clock across the street I push my flush button and on the fifth chime the guy downstairs pushes his and on the sixth chime I let my button out. Blurp! Into the downstairs toilet it pops. That system worked good, 'cause the trusties could carry things up but they was pat-searched after they finished on the top floor.

Don Owens on the second floor was always needing a smoke or a snack, so I kept him supplied through our third-floor toilet. Once he asked for a deck of playing cards and for a joke I sent them down the toilet. They made it.

Then one day he sent me a note saying he's bonding out of jail soon, so I sent a note back into his toilet.

"Hey, man, we need some hacksaw blades."

He sent a note back: "How many?"

∾

We made a string from the edging of our mattresses—it was so fine it took a few nights to braid it together. We tied it to a pencil right where the metal joins the wood and threw it point forward, trying to get it through the fan across the hall, about six feet away. Now, if you get it there but you so much as nick the screen, it won't have enough force to make it through. It'll just fall inside the fan opening, and that's a foot and a half wide. So we got to hit nothing but air.

We finally got it through and we sent a note down: "It works!"

Don wanted to go for a trial run and get some drugs, but I sent him a note, "No way! You'll get your drugs soon enough."

When we heard Don got bonded out, we waited up at night and listened. He said it'd be a couple days before he could take care of us, but we were ready. The signal was a guy whistling at a girl in the street. Soon as we hear that, we drop a string down the wall.

The third night we heard a whistle. I threw the pencil through the fan and lowered the string down till I felt a tug. Now, we'd made that string long enough to reach to the garage roof—the sheriff's garage was right under our window—and still have about six feet extra for insurance.

All of a sudden the string was jerked real hard! I had to let it go 'cause I was scared it would break. About three feet shot through my fingers before I could stop it. Boy, was I glad for the extra length I figured in!

As I pulled it up, it felt like a two-pound bass was on it. I figured Don would of gave us one, maybe two hacksaw blades. What did he do, put a pound of dope in with them?

I pulled it up until it stopped at the window, and I was trying to pull it through but whatever was on it was so heavy it just hung down straight. The only way it was going to go through was for the back end to come up and for it to slide in straight. So I fished the string around at all different angles, up, down, to the side, and all this time the string is across the hall and if the deputy comes through we're caught. If I let the string all the way down, it'll still be on the floor and he'll see it. So I'm frantic, jerking it around.

Garrett is saying, "Let me do it, damn it!" He's all hyper, but I wasn't going to let go now. I almost had it.

I climbed up on the bars real high and held on with one hand and reached up with the other while Garrett pushed on my butt to hold me up, and finally, with my hand stretched way up in the air and wiggling it as much as I could, the package came loose and slid through. Cleared the fan and clanked down against the bars in the hall.

We pulled it in, took it to my cell, and started unwinding the tape. Instead of going all the way around, winding it off slow, as soon as we got enough unwrapped to see the red paint of the blades we just wiggled them back and forth until the teeth cut through.

Wasn't dope that made it so heavy. There was eight blades wrapped with masking tape. Oh boy! These were the *good* kind of hacksaw blades, not them cheap ones that wear out before you get done sawing your first piece of aluminum. We couldn't wait to use them—we went over in the corner and tried them out on the bunk.

∽

We stayed up all that night thinking about where to cut. We both had to go back to court and we was both going to be shipped out,[17] so we had to get a move on. I slept through the next day, then that night I started cutting. The bars of our cellblock weren't round like the window bars—they were flat, about two inches wide and two inches apart. The up-and-down bars were on the inside and the side-to-side bars were outside and they were riveted where they crossed.

If I cut through three bars on each side of a square I'd have me a fourteen-inch opening. That would have to be enough.

The first night I cut through one bar. It wasn't easy—the bar vibrated and the blade handle cut into my hand and made a blister. And cutting the steel bars made a lot of noise, so I had to do it real slow. Since the bars was painted the same gray color as the cement blocks, I mixed Ivory soap and cigarette ashes to fill in where I'd cut.

"I'll stay in the cellblock," I told Garrett the next day. "When you go by the cellblock below here, rap on the bars. Do it on the first floor too. I want to see how loud the vibration is."

It was loud! All three floors of cellblocks were welded together, so the sound really carried. I was going to have to be careful.

---

17 Jail is for misdemeanor convicts and for not-yet-convicted felons. As soon as felons are convicted, they're transferred to prison.

That night I used my socks as mittens because of my blisters. I found when I held the bar below the point where I was sawing, it vibrated a lot less—this made cutting slower, but it was worth it. I cut two bars that night, one on the left side and one on the bottom of the square opening I planned. I didn't want to cut all the bars on one side or it wouldn't be as strong. I filled in the cuts with my soap-ash putty.

I worked the next few nights cutting through all the bars. 'Course I quit whenever Tom Tibb came by—he'd gotten used to seeing me up at night and he liked to stop on his rounds and talk. Garrett slept while I worked. By Sunday morning when my folks and Gloria come to visit, there was only four bars left to cut, one on each side, and the blister on my hand was starting to harden into a callous.

This might be the last time I'd ever see my family, but they didn't know that. Mom said I looked tired. Gloria told me she got straight A's on her report card. When I told her she was following in my footsteps Dad rolled his eyes.

"I wish I could bring you a cake for your birthday," Mom said.

"Don't forget some hacksaw blades to slice it," I said. "And a cutting torch so I can light the candles."

"She can share your cell," Dad said. "I can just see you climbing into the top bunk, Martha."

And that was it. I wanted to say goodbye better, but how could I?

∾

That night, instead of cutting completely through two bars I cut halfway through all four bars that were left so there was something solid on each side of my square. The next night I cut through three of the four bars left, so that only about half of the top bar was still connected. I filled in the cuts with my homemade putty.

"Next time I saw I ain't filling in none," I told Garrett, 'cause we're going!"

"Tomorrow?"

"Tomorrow. Soon as old Tibb makes his eleven-o'clock rounds." Tom Tibb always made his rounds when he first came on his night shift and after that we usually didn't see him for hours. Sometimes he'd be right back around, but we just had to take our chances. Well, he come through at eleven and then

I got to sawing, cut through that quarter-inch I left on top. The square of bars was completely free, but the soap and ashes was still holding it in. I was just about to take it out when Garrett says "Somebody's coming!" It was Tom Tibb with a state trooper.

We was busted! Somebody snitched, I didn't know who, but anyone could have. The whole jail knew what we was up to.

Turns out Tom Tibb just wanted to talk. The trooper was there bringing in a drunk driver. He knew about my case and he wanted to meet me.

I jabbered a mile a minute trying to keep his eyes from the fresh cut in the bars until finally the trooper said he'd best get going.

When they were gone I pulled out the square and went into the hall to work on the window bars. They was about five inches apart, so I only had to cut one big round bar. I didn't have to worry about vibrations, so it should of been easy, but once I cut into it about an eighth of an inch, the hacksaw blade wouldn't cut no further—there was no cutting feel and no cutting sound. Why not? And then it dawned on me the bar wasn't solid. It was hollow and there was a solid bar inside it that rolled with the saw blades.

Holy moly! What am I going to do now? Weeks of planning, nights of work, just about out and now this! And worse, I'm in the hall. I'm busted—I'll never get that square of the bars put back in.

Then I had an idea.

I got another hacksaw blade and put it with the teeth going the other way. It was kind of hard to hold, and it took a while, but it worked.

"Let's go," I told Garrett. He tried to get through the opening I made in the cell-block bars, but he was too big. He was mad as heck!

"Just get going!" he says. "I can't make it."

I'm five-foot-nine and 135 pounds and Garrett was six-foot and 200 pounds. There's no way we'd of had time to make the opening any bigger. We had to go now.

"I got an idea," I said. "Take your shirt off and soap your body real good."

I pulled from the outside while a kid named Tim Stanton helped ease Garrett's soaped fat through from behind, and this time he made it. But he got him some ugly gashes on his back and on the outside of his hips.

When we were done, Stanton said, "I'm going with you guys."

"Are you crazy?" I said. "You're only in here for stealing a motor-cycle!" But he was already climbing through. "Well, come on then, we got to hurry!"

We already had the rope we'd made from sheets ready, twice as long as we needed to reach the roof so we could pull it out after we got down. We put it around the bar next to the one I cut out.

We helped Garrett's big body go through the window bars feet first. He grabbed the rope and down he went. I came out next and climbed down hand over hand.

Thirteen

Tom Henry

Soon as I cleared the second-floor window my feet hit the roof of the sheriff's garage. Stanton's skinny body slid down quick behind me. I looked over the edge of the garage roof and saw a free spot, so I jumped. Stanton hung from the edge and dropped.

Garrett was long gone. We zigzagged through the alleys till we come to the river. Anytime we saw a car or a house with lights on, we stayed out of sight.

On the way there, I set up a decoy. I had a coat with me and some Bugler tobacco and a little food in a package we put together for the escape. I knew they'd be going up and down the river looking for us and I knew they'd never think I'd throw away my coat and my tobacco and my food when it was this cold outside, so I wrapped the food and tobacco up in a bread wrapper, put it in the sleeve of the coat, and threw it in to float down the river.

We get to the old bridge and we're set to cross the bridge, but there's too many cars with their lights on, and at the other end is a car just sitting there. Could be a cop car. No way we can cross the bridge, so we decide to walk down the bank until we come to a boat.

We walked along the river, through yards, trying to keep dogs from barking. That's all the police would need, someone calling in because their dog's going nuts. We was moving right along the edge in the shallow water so when a barge came along the waves would wash out our tracks and our scent. It was still pitch dark and the barges had lights on them, but we knew they couldn't see us. They came down the river every forty-five minutes or so all night long.

There was a bunch of jagged rocks along the water, and I was afraid one of us would sprain an ankle in the dark. Imagine escaping by cutting through bars and shimmying down a homemade rope and dropping to the ground from a roof and then getting caught because of a sprained ankle from tripping on a rock. We also had to get across the river before it got light—it was getting too populated on this side.

So we swam across that river. Talk about cold! We planned to swim straight over, but the current carried us way downstream to the west. It was still dark when we crossed the river and started walking along the edge just like we done on the other side, but it was much easier on this side 'cause there weren't no houses. We saw a couple mercury lights in the distance and thought there must be houses close so we started heading towards them, but no matter how far we walked, they didn't get any closer.

By now I'm thinking the law knows we're gone and they're looking for us and I'm not worried long as it stays dark, but time's running out on us.

"I knew I shouldn't of went with you guys," Stanton said.

"I told you not to come!" I said.

"I'm hungry."

"It ain't even breakfast time."

I'm really mad at him but I can't do anything about it now—if I leave him and he gets caught, they'll know where I'm at. So I got to put up with him.

It was still dark when we came to a house, but there was a truck there so we didn't go up to it. We walked around the edge of this field on the grass till we come to an open shed with a tractor in it. There was plastic over the distributor cap, so I made a depression in the ground and put the plastic there. I wiggled the battery cables off the battery, undid the caps, poured some acid into the plastic, then tied it off to make a bag. I put the battery back and forced the cables back on the posts. I kept the screwdriver I found there.

"If the dogs come after us," I said, "we can spread this battery acid on our trail and they can't smell us."

We kept walking down the river till it started getting light. We come to the edge of this steep bank and there was this hollow going down to the river that was full of leaves. Now I get to thinking. We can't walk along the river in the daylight, they'll have boats and airplanes up and down it. And we can't walk in the woods, because the dogs will track us. If we're on the steep slope of this hillside by the river, they won't see us. They'll walk on top of the hill 'cause they can see the river fine from there.

I figured the dirt would be soft what with the water level coming above it every year and if we hide in the side of the slope no one would notice us. So I used the screwdriver to scratch the dirt out and we started digging with our hands and throwing the dirt out of the hole. We put battery acid all around, more on top than on the bottom, so if the dogs came sniffing they wouldn't pick up our scent.

We now had a shallow bed on the steep bank. We got a bunch of leaves and put them in the hole for comfort and we lay in it on our backs, feet toward the river. We could see the river but not behind us up the slope. We used our hands to rake enough leaves in to cover ourselves up. We spent all day in that hole. It was cold at first 'cause we was all wet, but we snuggled up together and after a while it got bearable.

We watched the boats going up and down the river and the plane flying back and forth trying to spot us. There wasn't no boats with "Police" written on them but we saw some with guys in civilian clothes and carrying guns, looking all around, not fishing. They had to be after us, 'cause by now news of our escape would be out.

Several times that day we heard the searchers walking by over our heads. We couldn't turn to look up at them but we could hear them talking and calling on their radios, and by golly we was scared. This one time someone stopped right above us, just a few feet away, then they walked off slow, then stopped and walked back. Then they left. For an hour afterward, I thought they was just waiting for help.

A lot of times we heard squirrels. False alarms. A squirrel darts and a man walks, so after you listen a while you can tell which is which. All my life I been the hunter—I got the gun and the animals run from me. Now I'm the hunted and a squirrel makes a noise and I'm scared.

We stayed in that shallow grave under the leaves till late afternoon, hungry and cold and scared. We hadn't heard a noise for a long time then so we come out. We'd passed through Mother Goose Gardens before we dug in—I knew it from exploring when I was a kid—and we were on the west edge of it. Now we headed toward Starved Rock.

Stanton complained all day. If he can't last one day I know he's going to do something stupid and get us caught, so I better get us some food. I tried flipping up rocks looking for crawdads—you can pinch off a crawdad's tail, take the top shell off, and eat that little piece of meat. But then I saw this fence and I had me a better idea. I got to thinking we could get us a squirrel.

When a farmer makes a barbed-wire fence, he usually wraps some extra wire around the corner post a few times before he staples it. So I went to a corner post, pried off the staple with my screwdriver, and got me a piece of wire about four feet long. I folded it in half so there'd be twice as many barbs and smashed the folded end flat on a rock. Then I bent the last few inches of the free ends and made a handle. Now I had me a squirrel-hunting tool.

In the summer squirrels live in their leaf nests, but now that it was cold they were in their tree holes. Usually a squirrel will be a couple feet into a hole.

The red-headed woodpeckers make the holes for their nests, but they'll only be down about six inches. The squirrel will use the woodpecker's hole, then dig the bottom out deeper 'cause squirrels usually have two to six babies.

Soon as I saw a squirrel go into a hole, I climbed the tree and stuck the wire in the hole and kept turning it. Pretty soon it started to get tighter and I could hear the squirrel barking. They make this odd little noise when they're hurt. I kept twisting till it got real tight. His rear end came out first and he latched onto the inside of the hole with his back legs to keep me from pulling him out. And believe me, he was strong. I couldn't pull him out. So I put my finger in the top of the hole where his tail was and grabbed a few hairs and pulled his tail out.

Then I got a tight hold on his tail and with that and the wire I was able to wiggle him up and down. I eased up a bit and let him turn around to bite the wire, then I grabbed his tail and jerked him out of the hole. Soon as he popped out I let go of his tail—a squirrel's teeth can bite all the way through your bone—and I swung the barbed wire he was still tangled in to smash his head into the tree.

I used one of the barbs to pull the skin off from the thighs down to the ankles. I wiggled the legs until I busted the joint at the top and I had meat from four legs. I didn't fool with the guts or meat off the body.

"That's gross!" Stanton said. Now he wasn't hungry.

So I ate all four legs raw, then I buried the carcass, 'cause dogs would sniff it out quick. Stanton thought that was ridiculous. To him, this was a game. He's just in for stealing a motorcycle, don't seem to realize he could get shot. This is serious business.

I threw the barbed wire in the river. It was evening now and starting to get dark. We saw one house with smoke coming out of the chimney and we veered away from it. I'm thinking, we got to get the heck out of here. We need clothes, food, and money if we're going to make it.

After a while we come to a house.

"You stay by this trash barrel," I tell Stanton. "Something happens, we'll meet down there by the Utica Bridge."

I walked around the house and peeked in all the windows. It didn't look like anyone's home so I climbed in the bathroom window and looked around. The first thing I took was the cigarette lighter.

I went out and said, "It's okay. Come on in."

∽

While Stanton ate I took two pillowcases from the bedroom. Stanton filled one of them with food while I searched around the house. I found a .20-guage Remington semi-automatic shotgun with grip handles and a box of shells in the bedroom. Then, just like all those shows on TV, I found a pistol in the top dresser drawer, a Colt .357 magnum, already loaded. I took both guns and filled my pockets with shells.

We took some clothes and a quilt. I found a bunch of coins in little books and popped them out, then I found a jar full of silver dollars and eight dollar bills. We shaved so we wouldn't look like bums and we took a razor and a little bar of soap. We drank the six cold beers from the fridge. By golly, they tasted good after five months in jail!

"We got to get out of here quick," I said. "When these people get home the cops will swarm."

I didn't know how much more of this stress I could handle. You hear about convicts escaping, being out for a few days, then giving up. Well, if you've ever been in that position you'll know why. It takes all your willpower to concentrate on the long-term benefits and not give up just to stop the tension and the hunger and the shivering.

We left the house and started walking by the road towards the Utica Bridge. Up ahead was a T intersection with a stop sign. The first headlights I saw I ducked into the woods 'cause I wasn't ready to try anything yet. I didn't know how to go about it—should I take the driver out and tie him up and leave him in the woods? Should I put him in the trunk? What if it's a woman?

So I'm a ways down from the stop sign, watching that first car stop and take off again. I watched a few and every car looked like a cop car to me. Even if it's not, by now everyone knows about our escape and our pictures are in the paper. I told Stanton to wait in the woods while I paced up and down the road, checking things out, thinking, then I sat cross-legged to think better. I can't run up to a car with that shotgun. If it's a private person they'll be scared and take off, and if it's a cop, he'll have a gun.

So I have to leave the shotgun with Stanton, but I don't trust him. He might be feeling like giving up by now and I can't have him pointing a shotgun and saying, "I'm going in and you can't stop me."

So I took the shells out of the gun and gave it to Stanton but I didn't tell him it was empty.

"I don't care what the next car is," I told him. "We're taking it to Chicago. We got to get out of here tonight." I gave him half the coins. "You hear any shooting up there, take off. If everything's okay, I'll have the guy drive down here and we'll pick you up."

I walked to the intersection and hid in the woods. I was scared to death. I was going to hold a gun on someone, but if they took off, no way was I going to shoot them. Sure, I'm a murderer, but there's a difference between a crime of passion and a cold-blooded killing. And if my bluff don't work they'll drive straight to Ottawa and the cops.

So this is a one-shot deal.

∽

I see the lights, then hear the car slowing for the stop sign. I crouch-crawl behind brush near it so the driver can't see me. As soon as it stops I yank the door open—good thing it wasn't locked!—and point my gun at the guy. The car starts moving forward, so I jump in and push the gearshift up into park. The driver is shaking.

"Don't move!" I say. I got the gun right up to his head. I look into the back seat and no one's there. "I don't want to hurt you, but I need to get to Chicago. This magnum will put a hole in your head the size of a quarter but it'll leave a dollar's worth of change on the window."

I'm just putting a scare into him so he won't do anything brave.

"All I need is a ride to Chicago," I say. He nods his head like there ain't nothing in the world he'd rather do.

"Sure, I'll take you to Chicago. Take my car, anything."

"I can't let you go. You'll tell." I say I escaped from jail and my buddy's down the road.

When I got in on the passenger side he seemed like he was in a trance. I had to nudge him to get him going.

"Okay, now turn left and don't do nothing dumb.... Now stop here." I opened the passenger door. "And turn the dome light on so I can see you better."

Stanton come out with the shotgun and we put it and the clothes and food in the trunk. Stanton got in the front seat and I climbed in back. The driver looked like he was relaxing a little, so I asked him if he heard anything about us on the news.

"They just said you killed your wife and another guy and now you escaped."

"What would do if you caught another guy with your wife?" I said.

"Well, I ain't married, so –"

"I'll tell you what I did. I cut off his balls and stuffed them in his mouth." I wanted him to think I was a real psycho.

He laughed, but it was a nervous laugh.

I turned on the radio but we only heard ourselves mentioned once and it wasn't even a big deal. We're still looking for them, we think they're in the area, we don't know if all three are together, consider them armed and dangerous—just normal stuff. Nothing about the burglary yet.

After a while I noticed the driver has this death grip on the wheel.

"Hey listen, man!" I said. "What's your name?"

"Michael Little."

"You got to be calm, Michael. I ain't going to hurt you, I just want to get to Chicago safe. You keep driving like that, you'll kill us all. I can't drive and watch you at the same time, so if you can't calm down I got to put you in the trunk and that ain't too safe 'cause if shooting starts, they won't know you're there."

"We got a problem," he said. "I'm just about out of gas." I looked at his gauge. It was almost on empty. I knew where a big station was, but it was busy with cars and lights. We pulled into a small gas station back from the road.

The guy come out and Michael tells him to fill it up. The guy leaves the nozzle in the side and goes to clean the windshield.

Michael gets out and walks into the station!

Stupid! I trusted him too much, should of kept my gun on him. But I can't pull it out now with the guy washing the windshield. I thought about climbing over, starting the car up and taking off. But the gas only shows one quarter and we need about half a tank, so I decide to get behind the wheel and take off when it's a little past that.

It sure was filling slow!

When the gas gauge got to just about half full, Michael comes strolling out with a couple packs of cigarettes and three pops! Right then I knew he was going to be all right.

Those Pall Mall cigarettes tasted real good, by golly. You don't know how many times I wished I hadn't thrown my Bugler away. I kept the car lighter glowing while we drove to Chicago.

We talked the whole way.

∽

We pulled into this two-story motel right next to the Crillon Hotel where I stayed when I was going to Allied. I was grubbier than heck, so I sent Stanton in to rent a room for one person. He come out with the key. I didn't want the desk lady to see us all go in, so I had Stanton take a pillowcase of stuff from the trunk up to the room.

I was talking to Michael in the car about how scared Stanton was.

"He wasn't half as scared as I was," he said. We laughed about it. After twenty minutes me and him went upstairs to the room.

"You got to tell on us," I told him, "or how can you explain where you were? Only thing I ask, wait till you get back to Streator. That'll give us time to clean up and get the heck out of here."

"I will," he said. "But I don't even know how to get home."

"Tell you what," I said. "I know a burger place near the highway. I'll take you there, then I'll catch me a bus back."

Just then, Stanton picks up the shotgun and points it at Michael. Remember, he don't know it ain't loaded.

"We should kill him."

I walk right up to him and take the shotgun.

"Don't even talk like that. Take a shower. Me and Michael's going out."

So we left to go get some food. Michael pulled into this hamburger place and he walked in to order the food. He could of gone out either side door or told the counter girl to call the cops, but he came back out with the food and we ate in the car and talked.

"I'd better get going," he said finally.

I drove with him to show him the entrance to Route 66, then he dropped me off at the nearest bus stop. I said I was sorry for scaring him so bad. He wished me good luck and left to drive home.

I bought a CTA bus ticket with a transfer, then walked the last few blocks to the room. Stanton wanted to know what I done with Michael.

"I won't tell you so you won't know," I said. "For your own good."

While I cleaned up, Stanton ate and went to sleep. I was exhausted but I was afraid to sleep. At any time they could bust through this door 'cause Michael could of told. I wrote Stanton a note that I was going to see a friend and I'd be back.

I stayed away from that room all night. It was hard to stay awake, but it helped that I was so cold. By morning I knew Michael hadn't told the cops on us, so I went back into the room and me and Stanton got out of there. The shotgun we left behind. The pistol I took to sell.

The first thing we needed was money. Our coins was worth a lot more if we sold them than if we spent them, so I went to a bookstore and looked at coin books. But they had a bunch of different categories—fine, mint, and a couple others—and I got confused. So I got to talking to a guy and he took my friendliness for an opening to ask me for a cigarette. A Junior Pence type. Perfect.

I gave him a few coins.

"I ain't got my ID on me," I said. "If you'll take these in there and sell them you get a meal out of it."

I did this at different pawn shops in different areas with different bums. By doing it in small amounts, if anything looked suspicious I could get out of there and not lose all my coins. But it worked each time. They never asked for ID, so I started doing it myself. I sold everything except a few old coins and some silver dollars. I gave $50 to Stanton and kept $100 for myself.

"Let's visit my aunt in Cicero," Stanton said.

"They'll check who visited you in jail."

"She ain't never visited me in jail, so they won't know her."

"They'll check out all your relatives," I said.

But I couldn't talk him out of it. I agreed to take the subway with him to visit her, but really I figured it was time to part ways.

Then he wanted to call his aunt to say we were coming so she'd be sure to be home. Holy moly!

I don't get rid of him now, he'll get me caught.

We walked down the subway stairs and the train come in and Stanton wants to jump right on. I say, "Let's go down to the last car." We walk to the end of the train and Stanton steps in. I stall until the door's closing behind him, then just as the car starts to move I walk up the stairs and out the station.

☙

I paid three dollars for a tiny room in a flophouse with only a bed in it. No sheets or blankets. It had a sink in the room but you had to go down the hall to the bathroom.

The next day I was walking by one of those red newspaper dispensers and see the headline, right through the glass: "Jail Escapee Apprehended!" I had to buy it.

Sure enough, Stanton got caught at his aunt's place. Fortunately there weren't any pictures.

I carried a picture of Patty with short hair in my billfold. It was unraveling 'cause of getting wet when I escaped, so I went into this place where you put in a quarter and got it coated in plastic. I hid it under the linoleum by the bed in my room, 'cause it had "To Henry, Love Patty" written on the back. Even though the ink was faded I knew it could get me caught, so I couldn't carry it on me.

I never planned on leaving it there, but here's what happened. I read the want ads in the newspapers, trying to get an idea of where I could work. I didn't have no ID and I didn't have enough money to get no fake ID. I looked for an ad where I might be able to get a job without an ID and I saw one at Idle Hour Stables. I could get there on a bus. I had enough money for that so I figured it was worth a shot.

The place was in Northbrook, Illinois. The boss's name was Fat Cat. When he asked if I knew anything about horses I lied and said I did. They paid in cash plus room and board, so when he asked when could I start I said, "Right away!"

I never expected to get hired on my first job interview. And this was a perfect set-up. No more rooms or restaurants where people could recognize me. I was safe at the horse stables and I didn't want to go back, not even to get Patty's picture. I'd already took enough chances.

I'd have to keep her image in my heart.

Fourteen

"You planning to let me read that diary sometime?" Tom Henry asked me. I kept a journal of my prison experience, wrote in it on a legal pad nearly every day.

"Better yet, I'll read it to you," I said. "Want to check out what I just wrote? It's not too long but it's making me think."

I picked up the legal pad.

"'Today is December 7, 1985. Three years ago today Susie and I lived on Carl Drive, CASH Manufacturing Company was booming, and the kids were happy in school. Two years ago today I had no family and was waking up to my second day in jail. One year ago today I'd just been convicted of killing my own family and was awaiting a probable death sentence. Today I'm in prison with Natural Life, but I have hope. In fact, except for a short while two years ago, I've never lost that hope.'"

"Wow!" Tom Henry said. "By the way, you not losing hope reminds me. What's happening with your appeal?"

"It's still in the Appellate Court. They'll probably have it six months to a year more. If they decide in my favor, they'll probably reverse with a remand, which means my case gets wiped clean and sent back for the prosecutor to retry me. If they decide against me, the appeal will go to the Illinois Supreme Court—but I really don't want to think about that."

"If you get another trial, what would be different?" Tom Henry asked.

"Depends on the reason. Basically they only reverse when they find an error by the judge, like if he let the jury witness something they shouldn't have."

"Well, what would that be in your trial?"

"Probably those models they paraded in front of the jury. You're not supposed to let the jury hear something if its prejudicial value outweighs its probative value."

"Now you're using them big words again, College Boy."

"Say you killed a dog."

"I've killed lots of dogs."

"So let's say you're on trial for stealing a car. To a juror who loves animals, hearing you killed a dog would make them more likely to think you're guilty of stealing a car, but killing a dog's got nothing to do with stealing a car."

"So if your next trial don't have the models, what's left? How did they convict you?"

"They showed jars of my children's stomach contents to a doctor who said those children died within two to four hours after eating."

"How sure was he?"

"Positive."

"Is the science that good?"

I guffawed.

"So what are your chances of winning your appeal?"

"They've got to be good. The appellate court has to realize what happened in court when they read the transcripts."

"You think they really read the transcripts?"

That question arrived like a blow to the gut. What if the appellate judges just read a summary? What if they're busy that day? What if they don't care?

"They've *got* to!" I said. "Some sick bastard's out there walking around, ready to do it again, and I'm stuck in here!"

I relaxed my white-knuckle grip from the edge of the bed.

"Now that you've got me all worked up, why don't you tell me about the people you left behind in Streator?"

"Well, there's a lot I don't know," Tom Henry said. "I've learned some on visits and some from letters and newspapers."

"I notice you get the Pineville paper," I said, "but not the one from Streator."

"Streator's my past," Tom Henry said, "Menard is my present." He gave me a smile. "I'm afraid it's also my future."

"That makes two of us." I turned on the tape recorder.

"I'll start with my friend Porky," Tom Henry said, "because I figure he was the first one they questioned."

He grabbed his coffee and started pacing.

"The very morning of my escape, the cops showed up at Porky's door, asked him where he was during the early morning hours the night before.

"'Come on, guys!' Porky told them. 'I didn't have a thing to do with Henry's escape. When I heard it on the radio was the first I knew about it.'

"'Give us exactly where you were from last evening up until now. We need times, people, places.'

"Porky did it, then he told them, 'Henry was my friend—is my friend, but I wouldn't help him escape. And he wouldn't ask me to.'"

༺༻

When I interviewed Raymond "Porky" Boyles at his home in Streator years later, he told me, "Henry was a good enough friend never to contact me while he was gone."

He also told me that seven years after the escape, the FBI visited him again.

"'Do you know where Henry is?' they asked.

"I said I didn't.

"'You know the statute of limitations has run out,' they said. 'You can tell us now.' I said I had nothing to do with Henry's escape.

"'You'll tell us if Henry ever contacts you, won't you?'

"I said if I ever got a call from Henry the first thing I'd do is ask him not to tell me where he is."

I won't forget the last thing Porky told me during that 1997 interview.

"Since Henry, I've had friends—but never a really close friend again."

༺༻

"George Evans left behind two brothers, Harry and Jeffrey," Tom Henry said, "and one sister. Jeffrey's a prison guard at the Pontiac Prison. You ask me, he's a little lulu. He claims he and a bunch of army buddies conducted a revenge raid on the Ottawa Jail to break me out."

"He claims *what*?"

"Hey, there's no need for me to *tell* you about it. You can read it." Tom Henry was rummaging in one of his boxes of papers. "Here it is. Check it out, Big Stuff."

He handed me an article from the *Streator Times Press*.

Brother Says Friends Joined in Raid on Jail
By Rod Perlmutter

Streator Fugitive Henry Hillenbrand doesn't know how lucky he was when he escaped from the LaSalle County Jail in 1970, a brother of one of his murder victims said Tuesday.

"Hillenbrand didn't know how close he came to being extinct," Jeffrey[18] Evans said.

Evans said the convicted murderer was almost the victim of what Evans called a "guerrilla warfare" takeover of the LaSalle County Jail.

"It never happened, absolutely not," LaSalle County Deputy Herb Klein said. "If it did, it would've made headlines in every newspaper in the country. Somebody's smoking you."

But Evans said it did happen, in late November or early December of 1970, though without arrest or report.

Evans said he and 14 fellow army veterans drove across the country with automatic weapons to take Hillenbrand by force out of the LaSalle County Jail.

"We were so mad, we didn't care who we'd take on," Evans said.

Evans, who is now a prison guard at the Pontiac Correctional Center, said the plot began when he and 14 other Vietnam veterans had coinciding 15-day leaves at Ft. Hood, Texas.

Evans said it took at least three days to drive across the country, but they were resolved to get Hillenbrand.

"We just wanted him," Evans said. "One of the guys wanted to execute him right off the bat, 'cause he killed a woman.'"

At about 2 a.m., the 15 soldiers appeared at the station, wearing army fatigues, combat badges, and carrying M-16s, and .60-caliber and .45-caliber guns and hand grenades, Evans said.

Evans said he and others entered the police station and told the desk officer they wanted Hillenbrand. If the officers resisted, the soldiers were prepared to tie them up.

"They said, 'Sorry, he's gone.'" Evans said. Hillenbrand escaped from jail on November 17, 1970.

The sheriff came out and talked to the group of armed men for about 45 minutes, Evans said.

---

18   Not his real name. I've called him Jeffrey throughout this book, so I've changed his name in this news article to that as well.

"They were scared out of their wits," Evans said. "When you're facing 15 heavily armed guys, and all you've got is a service revolver, what are you going to do?"

"He said, 'I know you're mad, and I know how you feel. If I was in your position, I'd feel the same way,'" Evans said.

After that, the sheriff offered them coffee, Evans said.

"It would've been a hell of a fight," Evans said. "We knew what we were getting into."

"I don't think they'd have prosecuted us, either," Evans said.

∽

"I'm not a betting man," I said when I finished the article, "but I'd wager this'll find its way into the book."

"Moving on to the Pences," Tom Henry said, "I can't blame Junior for Patty's death—I shot her, not him. But he's the one who suggested the burglary to me, and it was while I was in jail that Patty started with George. And since Junior didn't bail me out, I had to accept Dad's terms of not seeing Patty, which allowed that relationship to grow."

"So you do blame Junior," I said.

"Well, I killed her. I'm the one to blame. But by him being the crook who put me up to the burglary and the weasel who wouldn't bail me out, he started the chain of events that led up to the death of his daughter."

"I wonder if he ever thinks of that as he grieves for her," I said.[19]

"That's why he never testified at my sentencing," Tom Henry said. "He'd of had to admit about the burglary. But if you want to talk about the main victim of what I did, it's my daughter, Winkie. She was just two years old when I murdered her mother—which made her an orphan after I escaped."

"Even if you hadn't escaped," I said. "Because you were headed for prison."

"She got adopted by Norman and Sally Pence," he said, "so God answered my first prayer, one I made long before I knew Him, which was not to let Junior raise Winkie.

---

19 Streator Police Chief Gene Robertson said, "I couldn't understand the way Junior carried on. He never cared about his kids one bit."

From what she writes me, the main thing they did wrong was to try to erase her past. They changed her name to Pence, they never talked about Patty or the murders, they told her I was a drunk who ran away and Patty died in a car crash.

"That story left Winkie with an empty feeling, like there was something people were hiding from her. Keeping the truth from her was unrealistic anyway, 'cause she grew up in the same town where I killed her mom, where Patty was buried, where her friends' parents were our friends."

Tom Henry stopped talking but kept walking, and I could see his eyes were moist.

"I thought about Winkie a lot down home when I was a fugitive," he said. "I knew I couldn't never contact her, but I sure would of liked to know she wasn't being raised by Junior."

I waited while the tape player recorded empty air.

"And then there's my family," he said finally. "They got hurt too. My dad had a dream of one day starting Hillenbrand & Son Heating and Air Conditioning. He was proud of his reputation and the 'Don't Fuss, Call Russ' on the side of his car. He held his head up high in Streator.

"And then I murder two people and suddenly his pride is turned to shame. Every time my family heard the Hillenbrand name on the news, it burned through them. As time went on they tried to put their lives back together, but it wasn't easy.

"I wound up being sentenced to prison, but they were sentenced to shame.

"My folks got ugly calls saying things you wouldn't believe. My dad had to install a switch on the phone to turn it off so they could sleep. His business went way down, he had to rebuild it in other towns around Streator.

"Dad said his phone was tapped the whole time I was a fugitive. 'The FBI never heard nothing but your mom's recipes,' he told me. Every month the FBI come up from Bloomington to Applegate's in Blackstone to talk to Dad. 'We want to bring our file up to date. Have you heard from Henry?'

"Once he gave a ride to a kid from Dwight who was about my build, and he got stopped at an intersection and the cop said, 'I need to see your IDs.' 'You don't know me?' my dad says. 'I know you, Russell, but who's this riding with you?'

"Dad told me that all the years I was a fugitive, he was on one side of the bed praying I could live my life out in peace and Mom was on the other side praying I'd get caught so she could see me again."

Fifteen

Tom Henry

Idle Hour Stables was a perfect setup for me.[20] When I first got there I said my name was Charles. One boarder's name was Henry, and whenever someone said his name I flinched. Good thing I was just a flunky with a wheelbarrow who mucked out horse shit and no one paid me no notice.

About a month after I got to the stables, I went to the public library in Skokie to look in the papers for information about me. I found some stories, but looking them up got me to thinking there might be a way to check out old obituaries, find someone who got killed, and use his identity. So I asked this librarian how I could look something up in an old newspaper. She showed me these little TVs with green screens and a knob. I never knew nothing about microfilm, but she showed me how to look through old newspapers.

It took three trips to the library before I come across what I wanted: a mother and father and this little baby got killed in a car crash, but a two-year-old son, Thomas Elliott, survived. I got the notion that, with him being that young, whoever adopted him would likely give him their name, so there's probably a birth certificate sitting somewhere with the original name.

So I got a form to send in for the certificate, then read all the fine print. I had to do this right. I rented a post office box in Skokie, and that's the address I gave for the birth certificate to be sent to.

Soon as I'd sent off for my new identity I told the guys at the stables, "Call me Tom. That's my real name, Charlie's just a nickname." So by the time I met Frankie I was Tom, and he always knew me as Tom. Which was good, 'cause Frankie's the guy I went to Missouri with later on.

After enough time had passed that my birth certificate should be in, I went into a pool hall in Skokie near the Post Office and offered a kid five dollars plus a hot meal to get my mail.

---

20 The young fugitive Henry Hillenbrand had no idea how suited Idle Hour Stables was for him. The owner, Silas Jayne, was infamous in Chicago for burning horses alive for insurance money, killing his own brother, hiring a man who had raped and murdered three teenage boys, and having criminal dealings with Richard Bailey, a fellow stable owner who was suspected in the murder and disappearance of candy heiress Helen Brach and sentenced to 30 years for defrauding her.

I didn't want to open it in front of him, so while he ate I dodged into the rest room. Hello, Tom Elliot.

I got my social security card the exact same way but I never bothered with a passport. I didn't get a driver's license until I got down to Missouri, though I bought a car in Chicago and drove it all the way to Missouri. The people that sold me the car left the plates on it, and I drove around Missouri a long time with them.

Once I had my ID, I sure felt good. Before, there was probably a 90 percent chance a cop would run me in if he stopped me. Now it was more like 10 percent.

I got a horse rider's license and an insurance card—that came in Fat Cat's mail one day. It was perforated, and it said, "Fill in your name if you want insurance," because he was in the higher-up class. When he threw it in the trash, I picked it out and filled it in and put it in my billfold to look like I had some insurance. And I put in pictures of some of the kids of guys around the racetrack.

I wasn't figuring to stay put for long. I didn't want to muck out stalls all my life, and Illinois was dangerous territory for me. I remembered how in Joliet someone noticed me and mentioned it to my dad. So I kept to the Idle Hour premises as much as I could.

ᠻᢇᠯ

One of the stable hands had a Remington .22 semi-automatic rifle he wanted to sell. I gave him $65 for it. I started buying shells and going up along the creek early mornings or late evening, shooting water moccasins, blackbirds, crows, animals in the forest preserves. People heard me shooting and called the cops, but they never caught me. They were city cops. I was much more experienced in the woods.

One time while I was out in the woods I saw a cop car at the stables. My heart went nuts. Did they know I was here? I waited until they left before I snuck back. The other stable hands told me the cops were after the guy who was shooting out in the woods. I cooled it for a few days, but a week later I was out there again. It happened so many times the police must have started ignoring the calls—or maybe people just got used to the noise.

ᠻᢇᠯ

One time Jake, the foreman, was arguing with a customer in the big arena. The customer came into the office mad and complained to Fat Cat, who chewed Jake out right in front of the customer. Jake got cocky and Fat Cat fired him.

"You guys know what to do out there," he said. "Just do it until we get someone." All the older guys were doing a real good job, trying to impress him. On the third day, he made me temporary foreman. All these guys had been working a lot longer than me—I'd only been there about five or six weeks at the time—but they accepted me 'cause I was just temporary.

Now, the night watchman was Italian, about forty-five, didn't talk to no one and you hardly ever saw him around the stables. All of a sudden, one day he's gone. I got his room and now I'm the watchman too.

I was in my room one evening and it was warm, so my door was open, when a guy hollered up at me to come down quick. I see Frankie on a bottom bunk kicking at Willie, who's got a chair in his hand—he's knocked Frankie down and now he's waving that chair around like nobody's business.

"What's the matter, Willie?" I'm careful to say it in a normal voice. Willie's drunk, and I know not to throw gasoline on a fire.

"Damn you, damn Fat Cat, damn this whole damn place!"

When I get close to him he comes at me with the chair and backs me into the corner. I start walking toward him, talking low, trying to soothe him. Finally, he throws the chair down.

Everything's cool then, but Willie don't stop drinking.

ᶜ∿ᵔ

Later that night I'm up in my room when I hear a big crash. I go through the hayloft and head downstairs. Just as I'm coming down the ladder—before I even get in the room—I hear another big crash.

The first one I had heard was the Hinkley and Schmidt water bottle. It was smashed and water was running out. The second crash was when Willie busted up the glass in the showcase that holds the horse trophies.

Now, trophies are real important to a horse stable, 'cause they prove you know what you're doing. Soon as I come in, I see Willie smashing up the whole room with this twitch. It's like a bat but with a loop of chain through one end. You put a twitch on a horse's bottom lip when they get wild or start to jump up, and with just one hand you can bring him to his knees.

When he saw me Willie looked madder than heck, so this time *I* pick up the chair. He comes at me with that wild look in his eyes, and the closer I get, the louder he gets.

"STAY AWAY FROM ME DAMN IT!"

"Willie," I said, "you really messed up now."

"Stay the hell away from me!" he screams.

Fat Cat had left me with a gun I always carried around 'cause I was the night watchman. But I couldn't shoot the guy!

So as soon as he raised the twitch up at me, I ran at him with the chair held high in front of me and smashed the chair on him and he falls backward, out cold. I sit him up in the chair—the same one I hit him with—and I take the twitch and get some rope and tape from the tack room. I'm back as he's coming to and tie him good to the chair, then to stop him from hollering and cussing at me I wrap tape around the bottom of his face, his mouth, his ears, everywhere except for his nose, so he can breathe.

I'm afraid to call the law so I call Fat Cat. I figure if Fat Cat wants to call the law or if things don't sound right, I might have to take off in the middle of the night, especially if Willie wants to press charges on me. If I need to, I can get money from the machines 'cause I got the keys.

Fat Cat came right over. You could hear his car—one of those Ranchero pickups—tearing down the lane, skidding to a stop. When he come in, he ripped poor Willie's tape right off.

"Don't even think of moving or I'll blow your damn brains out!" he said. "I ought to beat you half to death, I ought to—you're going to pay for every-thing broken, you're going to work until it's all paid off!"

Then he turns to me.

"Untie him!" Now, Fat Cat always carried a gun, unless he was on a horse. Willie was scared to death.

I told Fat Cat, "I'm afraid I might get in trouble with the law, but you told me to protect the place. I couldn't let him tear everything up!"

Fat Cat had been so mad when he come in and seen the room tore up he didn't quite register what Willie looked like: strapped into a chair, taped up like a mummy, wriggling and rocking. Now he looks at me. "What'd you do, run him over with the damn dozer?"

Then he got to laughing. It would've been comical if poor old drunk Willie hadn't of been hurt so bad.

"Come on, Willie!" Fat Cat said. "We got to get you to the hospital."

I had to tell the guys what happened, 'cause I needed them to clean the place up before the morning. This incident was the butt of jokes for the next few days. Top Cat started it the next day with a comment about me teaching the rodeo guys how to tie up cows.

But about three and a half weeks later, it wasn't no joke. Some kids were riding motor scooters around on the property in the forest preserve, spooking the horses. I got a lead on them and I took the car to see what I could find out.

While I was gone, here comes Willie just out of the hospital with his head all bandaged up and a patch over his eye. He's there with two cops and a warrant for my arrest. But I wasn't there. They said they'd wait for me and sat down in the office and Fat Cat told Linda to go into the back room and call Top Cat, who came right up there.

When I walked in Willie said, "That's him there." Boy, let me tell you, when I saw two cops in the room and Willie pointing me out, I wanted to bolt. I knew the forest preserve and I could get away. But seeing Willie with them, I knew they wasn't there for the murders.

"Are you Tom Elliott?" they said. "We've got a warrant for your arrest." They started reading me my rights.

Top Cat stepped right in there.

"Hey, this man"—he pointed to Willie—"was tearing up my place, broke all my trophies, and this man right here"—pointing to me—"works for me. I had a licensed watchman and he quit on me, and until I get another one I asked this man to fill in. He lives here, he's responsible for what happens here, and he did what he had to do to protect himself from a drunken fool with a baseball bat."

The cops and Fat Cat talked to Willie in the corner, then the cops took him away.

୶

My plan was to go to Colorado, and what happened with Willie and the cops made me think about leaving while I had the chance. I got to be pretty good friends with Frankie, and he talked about McDonald County in Missouri, where he had a wife and a new baby.

"Well, I'm thinking of driving that '62 Chrysler I just bought to Colorado," I said. "Looks like McDonald County's on the way. You want a ride home when I go?"

∽

This is how I ended up leaving the Idle Hour Stables.

One morning I saw Jam-Boogie, a black stable hand, sprinkling this white stuff in his Doberman's food.

"Feed a dog gunpowder, you can make him real mean," he said. "You'll be the only one who can handle him. The gunpowder goes to his brain and makes him like a person with a migraine headache all the time."

While he was mixing the food, I noticed the pistol on his side.

"How come you carry a pistol?" I asked, just to be friendly.

"If it was any of your business I'd of told you." That was a typical remark for him. He lived in a room upstairs by himself and always kept it locked, even when he was in it.

Not long after that, this boarder come over to my aisle and told me he wasn't happy with the way Jam was taking care of his horse. I knew how Jam was, so instead of confronting him I asked the boarder to show me what he needed, and I started taking care of his horse.

Jam saw me and started cussing me, right in front of the boarder.

"Get the hell away from my horses! This is my aisle."

Who's that little sawed-off runt think he is, telling me what to do? I'm the foreman. So I go over to him and he pulls out this gravity knife and says he's going to use it. I backed up slow, grabbed a twitch, and moved in.

"You son of a bitch, you want to stab me? I'll hit a home run with your head. You been nothing but trouble ever since you got here."

I acted like I was going to hit him in the head but I really wanted to get rid of his knife, so I started swinging at his head then smashed the twitch down on his arm. The knife flew out of his hand. Then I raised up with my twitch and charged him, snapped his jaw.

Soon as I saw Fat Cat coming I backed up. I knew I was in the right—but Fat Cat come diving out and swung at me! I dodged and he swung again, and this time I barely ducked out of the way in time.

"Get the hell out of here, Elliott!" he said. "You need to calm down."

"You don't have to worry," I said. "I quit!"

Frankie quit with me and we drove to Missouri. When we showed up, Frankie got a real cool reception. He was Edd and Ada's son-in-law and he hadn't sent one penny down there, didn't have no money on him, and Frankie's wife, their daughter, had a seven-month-old baby.

Frankie just moved in and flopped down like a bum.

Me, I had around $800.

Sixteen

Tom Henry

S taying at Edd and Ada's I had this .22 Remington, and I couldn't believe you could just go out in the yard and shoot all you wanted. Before I always snuck around. Now I could go out whenever I liked.

I took off into these woods around their house and I'd been in there for over two hours when these little seedling ticks got on me. I felt this movement all over my body, biting me and itching—in my hair, on my legs, everywhere.

When I looked close I could see all these tiny bugs. I tried to brush them off but they bit me faster than I could clear them away. If you ever get into them, you'll know what I mean. I took my clothes off and shook them out, but by golly it seemed like there was a gazillion of them.

I finally got them mostly off after a while, so I put my clothes back on and headed back toward Edd and Ada's. Then the ticks started getting at me again. I went through the same routine, throwing away my socks this time, banging my boots, trying to pick them out of my clothes.

No wonder I didn't see nobody hunting in these woods.

By the time I got back to Edd's they're biting me again! I ran up there, not knowing if they bite you with poison or what. I couldn't run into the house with them on me, so I went out to the barn and took off my clothes. I could see them real good against my underwear, little brown specks crawling all around. I figured if I could see them on my white underwear, they were on the rest of my clothes too.

Edd comes ambling out, about six foot four, tall and skinny. He seen me run in there.

"Something get your clothes?"

"Edd, I got a whole bunch of bugs biting the heck out of me." I was trying to reach back and get this persistent one wedged between my buttocks. It was right in there, digging in deeper and deeper.

Edd snickered like crazy, but he got me a rag and put some acetylene from the tractor's acetylene bulb on it.

I couldn't ask him to get the tick out of my butt, but I told him about it, 'cause it was really getting to me. So he gave me this mirror and I put it on the ground, squatting down, trying to see back there, spreading my cheeks, determined to get that critter. Edd was just about rolling on the floor laughing. Old Edd never let me live that down.

❦

So I wound up staying at Edd and Ada's a while—they was good to me and I was getting home-cooked food and I liked going in the woods once I learned how to keep off the ticks.

I felt safe in Missouri. In order for the law to find me, someone would have to say they saw me at Idle Hour Stables. Then the law would have to find out I left with Frankie, and then they'd have to figure out who Frankie was and where he come from. But Idle Hour Stables paid in cash and didn't care who you were, plus they didn't like the law.

I was already being accepted by McDonald County people because I came there with one of their own, so I rented a little rundown house and started looking for work. At first I was doing odd jobs for farmers, work with animals, and mechanical work. And I spent all my spare time in the woods.

Staying in McDonald County turned out to be a good decision for me. There were woods and creeks and it was a low-income rural area, so a young guy with an old car and a few dollars who loved to hunt could fit right in. It's a tri-state area, with Missouri, Oklahoma, and Arkansas meeting at a point near South West City. And Kansas ain't far to the north.

Plus, McDonald County was used to fugitives—not that they knew I was one. The James brothers spent a lot of time around there, so did Pretty Boy Floyd and the Dalton brothers. In Pineville they celebrate Jesse James Days in July. There's even a sign in the courthouse that says, "Jesse James was shot here in 1936." But that's a joke—the sign is referring to the movie.

❦

I pulled quite a few pranks down home in Missouri. I'll tell you about a couple.

A farmer had just spread chicken litter up in his field. That's chicken shit, and some of the feed passes through the chickens, and the vultures come out there and pick out the corn. Talk about stinking!

I'd seen some turkeys in the field next to the farmer's a couple times, but I was never fast enough to stop the car and shoot them—they was either running into the thick brush or flying too high. Wild turkeys are smart birds, almost as clever as crows. Then one day I'm driving through there and I see this turkey going through the brush. I stop the car and steady my 30-06 on the hood and take my sweet time to get the best possible shot. I see his head come up and BANG! But that's a heck of a shot from 120 or so yards away, so I just nicked his wing and knocked him down. I run out there to get him, and darned if he doesn't turn out to be a vulture.

I was going to step on his head but I didn't think the farmer would appreciate someone leaving a vulture dead in his field. So I took him home.

At first I kept him in the wood shed. Then I thought of a trick to play on Dean, the old man that ran the little store just down the road from where I lived.

I took one of these fluorescent orange gloves I had for handling ice at the chicken plant and cut a finger out of it along with a strip the length of the glove on each side, then I wrote out a note:

Hi Dean. I'm Goober.
I come from above
and I need your love.
If you give me care
God's blessings you'll share.

I put that note in an eye-dropper bottle and stuffed it into the finger and tied the two bands so it wouldn't hang on the ground when the vulture walked. I already clipped his wings so he couldn't fly.

Soon as the mailman put the mail in Dean's mailbox, I set Goober on the ground by it and went into the brush to watch. Dean saw Goober and noticed the fluorescent orange on his leg. He snuck up on him and started herding him with his feet, like you do ducks. Dean just wanted to know what was on his leg.

I was in the brush, trying to stay out of sight.

Dean got a box and put it over Goober's head, slid a piece of cardboard under him, took him in, and took this capsule off of him.

Of course he told everybody. I went up there to talk to him about it and tried to buy Goober off him. Normally Dean would sell anything he had if he could make a nickel, but he wouldn't sell Goober.

"If I take good care of him, God's going to take care of me."

He acted like Goober flew down direct delivery from God. Of course I wasn't one bit religious back then, I was making fun of Christians. But Dean was scared of what God would do to him if he sold me Goober.

❧

Chuck King had some exotic hens that laid pale-green eggs. I asked him to let me have all of them, said I had a good joke to pull on old Dean. I was catching loose White Rock chickens at the chicken plant and selling them to Dean for a quarter each. He'd sell them for 60¢ at the Goodman sale once they feathered out, and while he was feeding them, he was getting eggs to sell at his store.

I went up there at night and put pale green eggs next to the white ones. Dean wanted to find out which chicken laid the green eggs, so he separated his chickens. When he finally thought he had it narrowed down, I quit taking them up there. Two weeks later he put the chickens all back together.

So I put the pale green eggs back. I drove old Dean nuts.

❧

I'll never forget the first big buck I shot. I was walking home with my 30-30 rifle, the first deer rifle I bought. I was on top of a ridge when all of a sudden this big buck trots out of a brush pile and runs up the hillside. I wasn't thinking of seeing no deer and I didn't have time to bring the rifle up, so I shot from my hip.

The bullet lodged at the base of his skull and cracked it. He fell forward, then he raised up on his back feet, turned sideways, and rolled over on his side and down the hill. I ran to him and his feet were twitching, but that was just nerves, 'cause he was dead in two seconds.

I never seen a rack this big before. Down home you count every point big enough to hold a man's ring on it, so this was a 21-point rack. I had it mounted, not just a head mount but a whole shoulder mount, on a big shield-shaped board.

Just for fun one night I took it over to Edd Haddock's place. See, Edd was trying to shoot a deer with his single shot .22 rifle on his own place. That way he could turn it in on a farm tag and never have to pay for a license and he'd still be legal—he didn't know he was still illegal 'cause you can't hunt deer with a .22.

Edd kept that rifle in the corner of his living room so he could go out in the early morning and late evening, 'cause that's when deer stir. He saw some, but always too far away. His eyes were bad so he had to get pretty close.

Well, this one evening during deer season I parked my car down the road from Edd's, turned off my lights, took that mounted deer head with the 21-point rack out of the back of my station wagon, and walked up to Edd's house. I could see him watching TV through the picture window.

So I snuck up to the house and held that shield with one hand on each side and I put this deer head up in front of the window about how tall a deer would be—then I tilted the board down like it was feeding, then pulled it back up. I did that three times, then I moved it out of sight and hid in Granny's garden behind the grape vines.

I saw Edd head out of the back door with his .22 rifle. He come walking out real slow. I was scared to make noise near the deer head, and I sure didn't want to take off running with it.

A hunter is supposed to verify he has a deer in his sight before he shoots, but you can't count on someone who ain't a veteran hunter. He might get buck fever. Anyway, Edd sees a rack that big, he just verified it's a buck.

I heard the door slam when Edd went back inside, so I went back to the car and put the deer head in the trunk, then I drove up and walked into Edd's house. I was waiting for him to mention the deer but he never did, so finally I asked about deer hunting and he said there was a big buck in the yard a little bit ago.

"Why didn't you tell me?" I said. "I got my spotlight and gun in the car!"

"It was right out here by the window."

"How big was it?"

"I'm going to tell you, Tom, it was the biggest rack I ever seen!"

"Edd, come on, you're telling me the biggest buck you ever saw was dumb enough to come right up to your house?"

"Ask Granny!"

"Well," I said, "I'm coming back here in the morning. I'm going to get that sucker!"

"Not if I get him first!" Edd said.

"I'll be here in the morning looking for him," I said. "What way did he go? How big did you say he was? How many points?"

"I never had a chance to count them, Tom, but it looked like a bush to me."

I put on a show, going down the road with my spotlight and all.

Edd's boys looked for that buck the rest of deer season. About two days before it was over, I told them what I'd done to old Edd.

Granny said, "I wish you'd of told Edd. He looked for that deer all week. I told him, 'It's probably Tommy,' but he didn't think so."

Edd just said, "I owe you one."

                                                   ∽

This last one isn't really a prank—let's just call it hunter's retribution.

One time I was out coon hunting with my dogs. I heard them barking at a treed coon, so I hopped in my car to drive around to where they was instead of tramping through the woods. On the way I drove past an out-of-county pickup with a dog box in the back.

As I pulled off the road to park, I heard my dogs barking and saw a light shining about where they were. I heard gunshots, then barking like a coon fell out of the tree, then quiet. Then the light moved off through the woods.

This guy stole my coon!

Taking coons other hunters' dogs treed is like leaving a farmer's gate open or shooting a pregnant doe or setting a trap within three feet of a fence—you can catch more, but you get guys' dogs. These are things you just don't do.

So I took the wheels off his pickup and put each hub on its rim, with the wheels flat on the ground. I kept the lug nuts, then wrote a note in the dirt on the pickup door:

You got my coon but I got your nuts.

Seventeen

Tom Henry

Virgie Reed was this old widow, real snoopy, the type that listened in on her party line, and one time me and my buddies Ricky, Tudie, and Norman Dale were hunting right next to her place. Virgie called the law and claimed we was trespassing.

Fred Drummond, the game warden, was waiting when Ricky came out of the woods. Fred arrested him and took his gun. Then he got Norman, and when I came out next, Fred told me he just read the others their rights and he had to take us in. Pretty soon Tudie come out of the woods, so Fred got all four of us.

He took our guns and fined us each $25. The bond was $50 and we had hardly any money on us, so we sat at the police station for about forty-five minutes. Norman's mom got him out, Tudie's dad got him out, Fred Wheeldon loaned me $50, and Rick called his grandpa at the dry cleaners.

We went to court and pled not guilty. The judge asked if we wanted a lawyer.

"We'll represent ourselves and we want a jury trial," I said. You should have seen their faces. A jury trial for trespassing! It got in the paper, four guys for trespassing, and the next week it said four men were taking trespassing charges to a jury.

Everybody said stuff like, "We know you guys. Anyone else going to a jury trial, we'd think they're innocent, but you guys?"

I told them, "Come to court and watch."

Court day comes and the prosecutor asks do we want to proceed and I say we do. Then Tudie pisses him off with some smart remark, so now he really wants to get us.

"You can't all talk," the judge said. "One of you has to be the spokesman." We huddled and decided on me.

So I asked the questions of the jury. "How many of you hunt deer? How many own property in this county? How many have No Trespassing signs?" That kind of question. We started with eighteen jury members. They knocked off three and we knocked off three, which left twelve. Fred Drummond just sat in the corner with a satisfied look on his face. He knew he had us. This was the first time anybody had ever taken one of his trespassing arrests to court.

Virgie Reed testified first. She knew I had a dune buggy. I asked her if she saw a license plate on the dune buggy.

"There wasn't one."

"What color was it?"

She said it was green. I got her to tell what day it was, then asked her if she was sure the dune buggy was there that day. And was she sure the guys that shot at her a few days before had that dune buggy? And what was the four trespassers wearing?

"Three of them had a hat on, and that red that deer hunters wear, and they all wore blue jeans, and they all had rifles."

I thanked her and got Fred Drummond up there—he was in the jury room when she testified. He never actually saw us on Virgie's property. I asked him what we were wearing when we came out of the woods.

"I advise everybody, even though the law isn't yet in effect, to wear fluorescent orange," he said.

"What was I wearing, Fred, when I come out the woods?" I said.

"Camouflage clothing."

"What was Tudie wearing?"

"A cowboy hat with a distinct tail feather on it, and no shirt."

"Norman Dale?"

"Fluorescent orange, and Ricky had a brown hunting jacket on," he said.

"Look at the conflict between what Virgie Reed says we was wearing and what Fred Drummond says," I told the judge. "And another thing, your honor, I have right here a receipt bill of sale from Chuck King for the dune buggy. Look at the date on this and you'll see I sold my dune buggy two and a half months ago. Plus it's a different dune buggy—it's obvious she saw four different guys."

I would of kept talking, but the judge said sit down and be quiet.

The jury went into the room and about two minutes later they came back out. The head juror, a great big guy, got up and said, "Not Guilty."

I went up to Fred Drummond and stuck out my hand.

"Nice try, Fred, but you ain't got me yet." He just turned away.

To rub salt in the wound, we went right over to the *News Gazette*. If we'd been found guilty, there'd of been a big article about it, but they'd only put one in if I paid, and it had to say "advertisement" on the bottom real small. I took a four-inch by three-column ad, big bold print. It said: "Raymond McAnally,

Tom Elliott, Rick Cleaver, and Norman Gideon were found Not Guilty in Magistrate Court Monday afternoon on charges of trespassing on the property of Virgie Reed."

When the paper came out, I bought 25 of them and put one in Virgie Reed's mailbox and one in Fred Drummond's—one in every mailbox of somebody that said we was guilty.

⌒∽

At first, Faith was just one of the Patterson kids that came over to my house.

I was working for Charlie Patterson, who said if I liked the woods so much, why don't I get a trailer and put it back on his place? I bought a 1952 Zimmer and put it on his land, but I didn't have water or power back there.

I first started fooling around with Faith in that trailer.

One day at dinner Charlie said to Deloris, "Hey, Big Girl, looks like we got a deer trail going out to the bachelor's."

I never dated Faith, like taking her to the movies or bowling. I used to take all the Patterson kids but never Faith by herself. When I worked for Charlie I'd eat at the Patterson's, and to pay them back I cashed a $600 income tax refund check and took four of the Patterson kids to the Piggly-Wiggly. We filled up the back of my pickup with groceries, then backed it up to the Patterson's porch. We had a regular assembly line loading it all into their cupboards.[21]

Me and Faith had something special in common that she never knew about. She was born on my tenth birthday, but hers was the only birthday we would celebrate, 'cause November 23rd was Henry Hillenbrand's birthday. Tom Elliott's birthday was January 16th.

I wanted to marry Faith, but it wasn't no easy decision. Why it was tough is I kept thinking about Patty and how I stalked her when she started going with other guys and how I wound up going so nuts I shot her. I wasn't exactly worried about it happening again, 'cause Faith wasn't like that and anyway I'd learned my lesson. But it was on my mind.

Now, I knew I'd never love Faith the way I loved Patty. All I had to do is close my eyes and Patty was there—like I could talk to her anytime I wanted. But Patty was dead because of me.

---

21 I got this after two hours of begging Tom Henry for romantic times with Faith. "There wasn't none," he said. He fled to other stories and I brought him back. "I need romance," I pleaded. "I thought this was non-fiction," he said.

And that thought led to another. Because of what I did, I was a fugitive. At any moment the law could catch up with me and Faith suddenly would lose her husband. Was it fair to put her in that situation? On the other hand, she was cute, she was fun, and we was good together—and I'd been down here two and a half years by that time, so it felt safe. And I did love her.

One thing for sure, I couldn't never tell Faith about my past. It would be dangerous for me and a burden for her. Once she knew my past, she couldn't tell on me 'cause she loved me but she'd have to tell on me 'cause of the law.

෫ఞ

Soon as we was married, I got a job at the chicken plant, so me and Faith had money for a better place to live. That old trailer wasn't no place for a woman, with no water and no power. I spotted this cabin on a 40-acre plot and talked to the owners about renting it. They thought I was joking at first it was so dilapidated, but they were happy to have someone keep an eye on it. I rented it for $20 a month and we moved to Lodebar.[22]

I built an outhouse at Lodebar. Fixed it up real nice, so nice it became kind of a joke, then I dolled it up even more. I wired it and installed lights and a fan, carpeted the floor wall to wall, hooked up a TV, hung venetian blinds and curtains, and screwed a full-length mirror on the inside of the door. The outside was varnished oak.

෫ఞ

Just up the road was a pink house with a great big sign, about four-by-six foot, nailed right up there on the triangular part of the siding leading to the peak of the roof. The sign said in bold letters: BEWARE! JUST A LITTLE WAYS DOWN THE ROAD, YOU'RE GOING TO MEET CHRIST.

The house belonged to Bill Hunt, an old man people told stories about. In his younger days he made enough moonshine to float a ship, carried a pistol and a bowie knife while he ran his still. He romanced his wife by ringing a cowbell in the woods. The neighbor lady would come running out and they'd have sex in the field underneath the tree.

---

22 The name "Lodebar" was given to this house later, after Tom was saved. It comes from the Biblical story of Mephibosheth in I Samuel 9. How that name came to be applied to Tom's house will be explained when it occurs.

On a dare as a kid, while the teacher at Pucket Church was bending over cranking up the bucket on the well to get water for the kids, Bill lifted up her skirt. One time he put a frozen hornets' nest in the church, and a few hours later when they started getting warmed up, they came out buzzing all over.

Everybody was scared of him. Just his looks would scare you. He was the meanest guy for miles around.

But then he got saved, late in life, about sixty-five years old.

You should have seen him—smiling all the time, happy in the Lord. You'd never know it was the same guy except for that bulldog look that was just his.

Bill used to walk along the road and I'd yell out to him, "Beware, Bill Hunt! Just a little ways down the road you're going to meet Tom Elliott." He'd just wave and smile at me. Anyone who nailed a billboard up on the peak of their house seemed a little lulu to me!

When I saw him walking down the road I'd zoom right next to him. He wouldn't budge an inch. I don't know how come that guy's alive today, 'cause he'll play chicken with you. You can't scare him. I can see why he'd of been so feared before he got saved.

Once I saw Bill Hunt up at Dean's store.

"You can keep trying to run me over all you want," he said. "The Lord won't let that pickup hit me."

I bought him a Pepsi and we sat down to talk.

"Bill," I said, "if I didn't jerk that steering wheel over, by golly, I believe that pickup would hit you!"

"The Lord is the one pulling the steering wheel over."

I'd see him on the highway and I'd pick him up sometimes. He'd smile and witness to me, quote scripture and tell me about the hen gathering her chickens under her wings, say that's how the Lord was protecting him. I'd cuss and he'd say, "I'll pray for you."

"Don't waste your time. Pray for someone else."

"The Lord's going to bless you for picking me up."

"I'd much rather you just thank me for the ride, it'd do me more good."

Bill was a prayer warrior at Bunker Hill Church. He'd go up there two or three hours before the service started and just pray. Sometimes I'd pass by his house and the window would show just the top of his head and you could see his hands lifted up in prayer, then I'd come back by forty-five minutes later and there's old Bill with his hands still lifted up in the air, praying.

I just laughed. Back then, all Bill was to me was an old religious nut.

⌒�〜◯

Faith's teenage brother Leroy was having problems at home, so he used to come over to our house. I told Leroy his mom had already been over looking for him and I didn't want to get in no trouble with her, but he could stay in the house till one then he had to be out 'cause Faith got home at one-thirty.

I gave him my sleeping bag and told him to put it on top of the hill by the pond. Lodebar had these giant cedar trees, made a nice cover. Leroy stayed there a few days, inside whenever Faith wasn't home, outside whenever she was.

One day I took him with me to a job interview at Emerson Electric. I had to cross the state line from Missouri into Arkansas and I knew taking a minor across state lines could get you in trouble, so I stopped the car and made him walk across the state line. He got back in the car in Arkansas. We did the same thing on the way back, laughing and thinking it was a big joke.

That night Faith spotted him and told her mom, who came over with Vicki.

"We know you're helping Leroy," Deloris said. "Where is he?"

"He's up there," I said, pointing up the hill.

"Bring him over when he comes down," she said.

"There's no way he's going to come with me," I said, "and he's too big to carry."

"Well he better be over there by tonight, or I'm going to call the law."

"If the law can find him here, more power to them," I told her. "They know where he is and you know where he is. He'll cool off and come home. If I do bring him home, what are you going to do? Tie him up?"

Leroy didn't go home that night, and Faith told me Deloris had signed a warrant on me for contributing to the delinquency of a minor. The next day me and Leroy were building my shed and we heard a car crunching up the gravel road real slow, so we hid in the woods and watched. Here came Bill Estes, the cop, walking up the driveway. I had the chain up across my drive, so he had to walk in.

Soon as he saw no one was home, he walked around, snooping in my cars and pickup. Then he looked in my outhouse, and in my shed, and at the serial number of my chainsaw, and in the windows of my house. He looked in my pressure system and lifted up the lid, then walked back to his car and took off. That made me mad, all that snooping. He tried to catch us two more times. The third time he walked right into the house!

So the next time he come we took our hammers and snuck around through the woods. He was at the house, this time looking in my ditch, checking out my tractor, my toolboxes, my brush hog. He had no right to snoop like that, so I got on the driver's side and Leroy got on the passenger side of his car's back window, and both of us hit it one time with our hammers. It stayed in, but it crazed so bad you couldn't see in or out.

We went up on the hill to watch, and you should of seen him when he got to his car. Usually he drove off real slow, but this time his wheels were spinning in the gravel. We had a good laugh.

I went over to Edd and Ada's that night and I called up Earl Spears from there.

"Heard you got a warrant out for my arrest, Earl."

"Where are you?" he says.

"Never mind that," I said. "You ain't going to get me at the house, 'cause I won't be there. But I'll tell you what, I'll be down there tomorrow morning at ten."

"Okay, see you then."

I talked to a lawyer, then I talked to the bail bond guy. I borrowed a friend's car so they wouldn't recognize me and arrest me before I turned myself in, then I drove to town. I wanted to be sure everything was set with the bond before going in, or they might have to hold me in jail. I had to avoid that, 'cause when they hold you in jail they fingerprint and mug-shot you.

I went to the sheriff's office at ten. They served the warrant, the bail bond guy posted bond, and I went home. While I was there, I saw Bill Estes's car parked in front of the office. It had the whole rear window duct-taped. They never said a word about it.

ᏼᎧ

Three weeks later we're in court. Charlie wore a new flannel shirt and a new pair of Big Smith overalls—to him that was dressing up. When I first got to the courthouse, Charlie looked away from the Jesse James posters on the walls and nodded at me.

"You know it ain't my idea being down here, don't you," he said.

"Yeah, I know, Charlie, and you better not be caught talking to me if you know what's good for you."

"All right, by golly."

I took the stand, then Charlie, Deloris, and Leroy went up after me. Charlie was impossible for them to question. He played the stupid and the hard of hearing role.

When Leroy took the stand he told them he ate but didn't sleep in my house.

"Did Tom take you with him on any job interviews?" the prosecutor asked.

"Yes."

"And where did Tom interview when he took you with him?"

"Emerson Electric."

"And in what state is Emerson Electric, if you know."

"Arkansas."

"Arkansas. And from what state did you begin this car trip?"

"Missouri."

"So you're telling this court Tom drove you in his car across a state line?" Boy, the prosecutor was grinning! He had what he wanted.

"No sir," Leroy said. "He dropped me off and I walked across the state line."

The prosecutor stopped like he'd been shot. He looked at Leroy, then back at me. I was the one grinning now. But he wasn't beat yet.

"Leroy, when did Tom tell you to say that, way back then or just now before trial?"

Before Leroy could answer, I yelled out, "I didn't tell him to say nothing! I beat you fair and square."

The judge told me to shut up, but I said it again, louder this time, so the judge said I was in contempt of court and raised my bail $3,000.

Whoa! This is more serious than I thought!

"Do you have the money, Mr. Elliott?" the judge said.

"No, not on me," I said.

"Bailiff, take Mr. Elliott over to the jail," the judge said.

Now I've done it. If they book me, they'll fingerprint me.

"Your honor," I said, "may I speak to Mr. Patterson a second?"

He granted it, so I walked back to Charlie.

"Charlie, you probably didn't hear." Deloris was sitting right next to him at his side in the second row. I kneeled down. "That judge up there just raised my bond because of my outburst and they're going to put me in jail. I only have twenty-eight dollars, but I got money owed to me from the cordwood plant. I need $300. Will you loan it to me?"

"Sure." He reached into his Big Smith overalls and opened his thick billfold, pulling bills out one at a time. "That'll do you?"

"Yeah, thanks, Charlie. I'll take care of you soon as I get the cordwood money." I walked up to the bench and said, "Your honor, how do I pay this?"

"Give it to the bailiff and he'll take you to pay it. But before you do that, I want to have a word with the state's attorney. Have a seat."

They had their word, the state's attorney went and got some records, then the judge took a ten-minute recess for the state's attorney to talk with Charlie and Deloris in a jury room.

Back in court, the judge asked Deloris if she wanted to drop the charges, and she said she did, on the condition I wouldn't harbor Leroy no more.

When I saw Charlie to give the money back, he told me Deloris was on his case all the way home.

"Big Girl was pretty hot to trot, but she'll get over it, I reckon. I may not get any more lunches for a while, so I guess it's back to eating blackberries in the woods."

ॐ

When Faith told me she was pregnant, the first thing I thought of was Winkie. How is she? What family is she growing up with? With Junior as her grandfather, it was a real concern. I often thought about it, but there wasn't a thing I could do except worry. If I made one contact, they'd have me. I was a fugitive for a double murder, and for that they don't never stop looking.

As Faith grew bigger, I grew more excited. I'd screwed up the first time— now was my chance to get it right.

When we found out it was a boy, I got even more excited. A boy will become a man, a man will carry on my name. Well, not my name strictly speaking, but still mine. Tom Elliott was going to have a son, so right then I decided he was going to be Thomas.

One day I was building a fence on Fred Haddock's place when Bill Baker drove up and told me Faith was at the hospital. I zipped up there in no time.

130

Faith was in the bed and there was this big round clock in front of her. She was already in labor. She had a long labor, over eight hours, and they finally had to induce the delivery.

She grabbed the stainless steel bar with her right hand and Deloris with the other. She looked at me like she wanted to strangle me, so I just went to the waiting room. When he came out, Thomas's feet and hands was all wrinkled up like from being in bath water too long. Patches of his skin was like burned marks.

During the couple days Faith was at the hospital, I got some old blue paint, and since Thomas didn't have his own room I painted just the two walls that made one corner from window to window. That's where his crib was.

Now we were a family, Faith got out this family Bible, so big you'd need a backpack to carry it back and forth to church. She wanted me to fill in my family tree.

I used my parents' real first names and substituted "Elliott" for their last name.

೧๋

Life with Faith wasn't nothing like the way it was with Patty and Winkie up in Joliet. I married Faith because I loved her, but I never loved her like I loved Patty. Patty was my soul mate, that once in a lifetime chance at real happiness.

But Thomas was a different story. As much as I loved Winkie, I probably loved Thomas even more. Maybe that's because he was a boy, or maybe it's because he was my second chance to get it right.

As I came to realize how much I enjoyed being with Thomas, I thought about what my dad said to me after the murders: "I pray someday you'll have a boy. Then you'll know the love I have for you."

Well, his prayer was answered. Now I knew.

And having Thomas just got better and better. First, when he was a baby, it made me happy just to hold him. But then when he started to talk, what a blast! And when he could run around and play, and go places in the pickup with me, he became my buddy.

Even teaching him to pee was fun, 'cause here's how I did it. I used to throw bread out my back door at the bottom of the steps and I'd call the chickens, "Here, chick-chick-chick." And I'd pee on their heads while they ate. They don't care about getting hit in the head, but they got little tiny holes where their ears are, underneath their feathers, and if water gets in them they shake their heads back and forth real fast.

Thomas got a kick out of that, so I told him, "Stick your weenie out there." He'd try and try. "Pee-pee on the chickens." Finally a little trickle come out that fell short, but he practiced till he could stand on the bottom step and some pee would just make it to their heads. He'd start peeing on a chicken and it'd take off, so he squeezed hisself to wait for another one. "Daddy, it hurts!" But he wouldn't let go.

Sometimes I'd be riding in my pickup with Thomas and see a deer. I'd stop next to the highway and tell him to pee. He'd pull his wee-wee out and act like he's peeing, and this worked good 'cause people coming by would just think he couldn't hold it no longer. The trouble with Thomas is he'd look at the deer I'm shooting at. I tell him to look away but about two seconds later his head turns to watch the action. I couldn't really blame him.

And then I'd tell him, "Now, don't tell Mommy about shooting that deer."

And he wouldn't, but over supper he might say, "Daddy, you going to go get that deer?" And his face and his tone gave it away to Faith.

"You taking him out and shooting deer? Don't you be shooting no deer with Thomas in the car."

So next time I said, "Thomas, you got to keep quiet if you want to go with Daddy."

Thomas and me, we was real close.

Eighteen

By now the top bunk of cell 3-49 was filled with manuscripts and transcripts, newspapers and notes, and the wall behind it contained a multi-page graph of the book's action.

One afternoon as the line made its way back to the cell house from the School Building work assignments, I headed to the yard. Up on the gallery, Dave, a Northsider from next door, stepped into our cell with Tom Henry when they locked up the line.

"In three weeks," he told Tom Henry, "I'm taking Hendricks's money. The Northsiders won't let me touch his shit until Brett leaves."

"He's pretty big," Tom Henry said. "And he's willing to throw down."

"I ain't afraid of him," Dave said. "But don't say nothing to him. I got nothing against you, Road Dog. Actually, I ain't got nothing against him neither except I want his money."

Tom Henry told me about it when we locked up for the count after supper. I had to leave again when the evening school line was called, and when I returned to the cell after class he said there'd been some developments.

"Is it bad?"

"It's not good," he said. "Let's wait till the runners lock up."

"I'll start typing now and we'll talk when I lay off about eleven, okay?" I rolled a sheet into my typewriter and rat-ta-tatted on my portable Olympia. When I was done, Tom Henry made coffee then turned up the TV so Dave and Little Johnny in the next cell wouldn't hear what he said.

"They come back tonight, the two of them. They was asking who owns the TV, where you keep your Lifers, stuff like that. They told me not to tell you, so cover me on this."

"Of course."

"They said they was going to come back later. Guess they mean tomorrow."

The next day, no fewer than six Northsiders warned me that Johnny and Dave were going to extort me for "big money."

Johnny came by to talk to me before supper, saying he'd speak to me later that night about "something." That evening as I stood on the gallery, waiting to get into my cell after recreation, he approached me again.

"How long you been on this gallery?"

"Why? Who wants to know?" I was already in confrontation mode, but just then another Northsider came by and Johnny had to leave.

"I'll be back," he said.

When he did come back, the guard was only about ten cells behind, locking guys up.

"Hendricks, I ain't got much time so I'll come right to the point. You're going to pay rent or you'll get stuck."

"Listen, Johnny, I've got natural life —"

"I don't want to hear it. Pay or bleed, mother—"

"Well, I'm not about to pay, not you, not anybody."

"We'll be here when the doors roll, you son of a bitch."

"I'll be waiting." I paused for effect. "And I'll be ready."

"Lock it up," the guard said.

I entered the cell.

"Well, I guess this time it's do or die," I said to Tom Henry, who'd heard the exchange.

"How can you be so calm?" he said.

"Trust me, I'm not."

"Well, you couldn't prove it by me."

"I've got a drop of flight mixed in with a tank of fight. I know it sounds crazy, but I'm tired of worrying. I'm ready for them to bring it on!"

"Yeah, it does sound crazy but I know the feeling."

"This might be the best thing that could happen. If they attack in the morning and I mess them up—and I mean really mess them up—I'll never have to go through this again."

"Be sure they're inside the cell," he said. "Shut the door if you can so they can't get out. And don't stop until they're unconscious."

"Understood." I paced a little. "I'm loaded with adrenalin. How about recording for a while, then I'll make my battle preparations."

"You sure you're up to it?"

"Yeah, it'll take my mind off of what I've got to do in the morning. Plus I might be in Seg tomorrow, so let's get this recorded and I'll leave it up to you to hide the recorder and guard the tapes until I get back."

"You might be in the infirmary tomorrow."

"Either way you'll have to watch the tapes."

∽

We recorded until two in the morning, then I got ready to fight.

Tom Henry got out the Northsider shank he was holding. I sharpened two pencils, a 4H and a 6H, then poured a cup of bleach into a ceramic coffee mug and dug out an old stinger. By the time the doors rolled in the morning, the bleach would be boiling and that stinger would never again heat coffee. I pulled two cans of Campbell's tomato soup from my stash, shoved them deep into the ends of doubled socks, and tied them off.

Tom Henry picked out the largest of his paint brushes, sharpened the end in a small barrel pencil sharpener until it wouldn't feed in any further, then switched to a bigger one to finish it. He cut the brush off, glued an eraser over the end, and slid it onto the paintbrush dowel.

"Why the glue?" I said. "I'm going to be pushing, not pulling."

"I'll be the one doing it," he said. "And after I push, I'll pull it out to push it in again. If it gets bloody, it'll be slippery, and the eraser's got to stay on 'cause that's how I'll pull it out."

"This is my fight," I said. "When the doors roll, you step out right away. I'm going to stay in the back behind this curtain like I'm on the toilet so they have to come in to get me. If you can roll the door shut, that would be good."

Tom gave me a measuring look.

"You sure about all this? You're plenty brave, but do you know how to fight?"

"I read about it in a book once," I said with a tight smile.

"The best advice I got is, surprise wins fights. Don't wait till they get to the toilet. Come out charging when they're one step inside the cell. That's when I'll shut the door."

"Okay."

I slid under the bottom bunk and went to sleep.

༚

The next day there was no school—teacher's conference—so we could have slept in if not for the promised invasion. But Tom Henry had stayed up all znight.

When the guard rapped the metal baton on the bars in the morning, I popped out from under the bunk and made my preparations. Tom Henry got up and stood by the door. When it rolled he stepped out quickly, but no one was around.

"Come on, Big Stuff, you can go to breakfast!"

"No, that's okay. I'm not really hungry. Maybe I'll just have a nice hot cup of bleach."

That was Wednesday. Nothing happened all that day or that evening. Johnny and Dave were on gallery runner duty but they never stopped.

The next night two different Northsiders stopped by and asked Tom Henry for the shank he was holding.

"I don't like the looks of that," I said. "Are they reducing my defensive capability?"

"Maybe, but I don't think so. Curtis went to the Adjustment Committee today for that ticket he got a couple weeks ago when he wouldn't let them search his cell. They sentenced him to Seg. I think Northsiders are moving the shanks in case he talked."

It turned out Tom Henry was right. Nothing happened that next morning. For a few days I stood near the cell door every morning, a soup can sock in one hand and Tom Henry's sharpened paint brush in the other. When the doors rolled and I peeked out and saw no one lurking I'd step back into the cell, put away my weapons, and go to breakfast.

After a week of nothing, I realized my ordeal must be over.

❦

It was Tom Henry who next incurred the wrath of Little Johnny. A Northsider showed up at the cell asking for his piece. He gave it over to the guy, who told Little Johnny, who promptly grabbed it and ran back to our cell.

"Hey, get over here!" he told Tom Henry. He was red in the face and pointing his finger. "I'm the chief on this gallery. I told you keep this piece in your house and don't give it to no one except me! I should freakin' stick you with it, you son of a bitch, just to teach you a lesson."

Tom Henry took the piece back without a word—but as soon as he had it in his hand, he exploded.

"Now what are you going to stick me with, you son of a bitch?" he screamed. "I got the piece! You little sawed off runt, coming to my house telling me you're going to stick me!" He was shaking with rage.

Johnny disappeared.

It was a side of Tom Henry I hadn't seen before. I put my hand on his shoulder.

"Dude, calm down. Are you okay?"

Tom Henry turned and looked up at me, a big grin on his face.

"I'm fine. Sometimes you got to give 'em a show."

"Well, if that was a show, you belong on stage."

∾

A couple of days later an article appeared in newspapers throughout Illinois with a story I already knew. It said Susie's estate, worth over $121,000—which under the law could not go to her murderer—had been divided up among her siblings, all five of whom had returned their share of the money to me.

"That's good news and bad news," I said.

"How can it be bad?" Tom Henry said. "It's great that Susie's whole family believes in you so much they turned down the money!"

"Yes, that's the good part," I said. "And when I think about it, I realize I wouldn't want it not to make the news—it could really help me with public opinion, which lawyers say doesn't affect the law, but I don't believe them."

"So what's the bad news?"

"Every thug in this place thinks I just got a hundred thousand dollars!"

That night Tom Henry sat at his desk cutting paper into small squares. He wrote large numbers on each: 21, 22, 23...

When I got up in the morning, glued to the wall near the cell bars was a sign with a small hook, and on that hook were numbered squares.

The sign said: TAKE A NUMBER.

Nineteen

Tom Henry

M e and Faith wasn't really fighting but we wasn't getting along neither. We never talked to each other but see, we was almost never home at the same time. I worked during the day, she dropped Thomas off at her mom's when she left for the second shift, I picked him up when I got home from work, and that's how our lives went—together but separate.

I was always out hunting, trapping, fishing with my buddies. Most times we'd stay out all night coon hunting. Faith was always on my case, giving me those sourpuss looks that just made me mad and wanting to leave the house again. She never appreciated my practical jokes, and we was always poor.

༄

Leon, who worked for Phil, was always trying to get me to go to their church. He come over, talking to me about religion, pretending to be looking after his cows on Connie's place.

I told him, "Leon, I don't want you around here talking about going to church. I'm not interested!"

Then Phil come over and gave me this pitch like a life insurance salesman.

"Been doing any hunting?" he said. "I got me some good beagles."

But I knew what he was there for. Beating around the bush, trying to get brownie points up at the church: "I brought Tom out by witnessing."

So I hit him direct on it.

"Phil, I know what you want. I ain't going up there!" All he knew about it was from the Revelations, 666,[23] the mark of the Beast.[24] To me, he might as well of been talking German—or Greek, 'cause it was Greek to me.

Leon come back a couple weeks later, same old song.

"Tom, seriously now, I don't want you joking, cause I got to admit it makes me a little mad when you joke about my faith. You know I was an alcoholic, right?"

"Leon, I never knew you was an alcoholic till I saw you sober one time."

---

23 Revelation 13:18
24 Revelation 16:2

138

"And you know how I used to run around with women, how I been married several times, how Bill Oler tried to witness to me, and the doctor told me I'd have to stop drinking, and I did for a while but soon I was back to that blackberry brandy. You remember how I used to buy it by the case?

"Then when I was in the hospital, getting operated on, Dad passed away. I knew it was because of my drinking that I couldn't even go to my own dad's funeral, but I kept at it even after I got out of the hospital.

"Then one day when I was out with the hogs, Bill came over and witnessed to me again. You know why I didn't run him off? Because he was there when I was in the hospital, visiting me and praying with me. He took his time out to help me when he could have been running his dozer, making money. And right there I broke down and prayed and cried to the Lord. Bill held my hands and we prayed together. And the Lord changed my life overnight. You remember?"

I did. When I first met him, Leon was a big, tough, loud-mouthed drunk. No one liked him. We'd talk about him behind his back—what the hell does Connie see in him? He ain't got no money and he ain't got no friends. That's one reason Leon was always over at my place—I was one of the few who would put up with him. And it was tough, because he was always wanting to whip me, and by golly he was ornery.

So, yes, I sure remembered the change in him, couldn't hardly believe the difference when he got saved. He'd come to my house and I'd try to make him mad, just to prove there wasn't nothing to it.

"Leon," I'd say, "let's go to Anderson and I'll buy the blackberry brandy and we'll talk about church." I tried to make him cuss me out like before, but I just couldn't or he just wouldn't. This was a new Leon.

"I'm going to keep praying for you," he said, "so you can have what I have."

"Get this through your skull," I said. "I *don't want* what you got!"

That's how it was with Leon, always witnessing to me from the time he got saved, but I couldn't get too mad at him 'cause now he really was different. He kept coming over to my house, pestering me about coming out to church. He just kept wearing me down.

I liked the guy, I just didn't want what he had to offer. I thought I was just as good as him now, religious or not. I worked seven days a week, I didn't have time to waste in church. Plus I wasn't about to quit chewing tobacco, drinking if I felt like it, or cussing when I wanted. None of that stuff hurt nobody.

So this one time I'm splitting wood with a splitting maul, Leon's talking to me a mile a minute about religion but I'm not listening to him. I'm occupied with my wood splitting. He can tell I'm not listening, so he says, "Let me split a little of that."

Now, I know the only reason he offered is to get my attention.

"Leon, I'll split it later. Just come on in and let's talk. What do you want?"

"I want you to come to church with me."

"Leon, we been through this before. I'm too busy."

"What have you got to do? I'll split the rest of this wood or help you dress out some deer meat or whatever. That'll give you time to come to church."

"I don't want you to do my work. And I don't want to go to your church."

"I know what the problem is—I remember in my own life. You know how I used to be, Tom. I wasn't afraid of nobody. I'd go into the rowdiest beer joint and I might get my ass whipped but I'd be back the next night. But I was always scared to go into church. Most people are."

"I ain't scared, Leon."

"So how come you won't go up to church?"

"I just ain't no Christian and no religious person and I ain't going to be no …" Hypocrite is the word I wanted, but I didn't learn it until I got saved.

"I'll compromise with you," he says. "If you go to church with me, I'll help you with whatever job you pick so you'll have the time. You won't lose anything. You'll take the deal if you're not afraid."

This was on a Tuesday night, and Leon had the sense to shut up while I thought about it.

So finally I said, "Leon, I'll make a deal with you all right, but this is it. I'll come up to church and stay for the service, no tricks, if you promise me you won't say another word to me about it. If I ever go again it'll be of my own free will. I don't like the idea of going even this time, but just to get you off my back, I'll go. How's that sound?"

"We have our Wednesday night service tomorrow—I'll come around about six-thirty and pick you up."

"I said I'd be there, you ain't got to get me. I got a pickup."

"Okay, don't raise your voice."

"Well, when I say I'll be there, I will! What time does it start?"

"Seven."

So a little before seven the next evening I pull up to the Bunker Hill store, which closed at six, park outside it and watch the church. I waited until about one minute after seven, then parked out by the road and walked into the Bunker Hill Church and found a seat in the back. They was singing hymns. Dan's boy was leading the singing and he saw me back there, but no one else did.

When they quit the singing they had prayer requests. After a few different requests I heard, "Let's not forget Tom Elliott."

I'm thinking, these people really care about me. They don't even know I'm in here. Three or four got up there by the altar and prayed, and when they turned around to come back to their seats they seen me. One of them got me a Bible. Then there was a sermon.

To me, it didn't seem like a sermon, just like a guy talking. I liked his little story and his message. I didn't know they listed the books in the front of the Bible and I couldn't find the place, but when they turned to something I flipped the Bible open so it looked like I was reading along with them. I liked just what the preacher was saying anyway.

When it was over, about eight-thirty, everybody talked to me, real friendly. I didn't want to talk to anybody inside the church, 'cause I felt like it was sacred in there and I couldn't talk without telling dirty jokes and cussing. But as soon as we got outside into the open air, I felt at ease and talked for a long time. A lot of them had to get home, but some stayed and talked with me.

Now, I had a deal with Leon, and he was as good as his word. No one come over to my house and bothered me about going to church. So one Sunday morning about two weeks later, I turned on the TV—which I knew better than to do 'cause we only got three stations and on Sunday morning they was all religion—and I watched Pastor Pack. He talks about Revelation all the time. He sits behind a desk and shows these pictures and when he reads, the words go across the TV screen. Anyone can understand that.

I walked back and forth into the kitchen, made coffee and bacon, listened to Pastor Pack, went outside, chewed tobacco, came back in, and here was Kenneth Copeland on the TV. He's kind of funny. I watched him for a while. Now, this guy's all right! He was walking around, strutting like an old rooster getting his feathers ruffled, and I liked how he talked about animals. I could relate to that. I didn't wander around anymore. I stayed there and watched him. His program ended and I thought about going to church.

I didn't know what time the services were. I'd been by there hundreds of times but I never noticed what time they met. So I just decided to go over there. I went into the kitchen, cleaned up, shaved, and got dressed. Of course I never dressed for church before. I put on my old flannel shirt, my blue jeans, my nice belt, my cowboy boots, and off I go to church.

I sat down this time in the fifth row. Ronnie Tosh was preaching. I enjoyed the service, and after it was over I was just jabbering like crazy right there in the church—I wasn't thinking about watching my mouth in this holy place, I was really relaxed and feeling good. You know how a good sermon kind of sticks with you for a few hours, making you feel that glow?

Kenneth Copeland's message from the TV was still inside me and Ronnie Tosh's from the church added to it. I felt like I was brimming over with good things. I don't like getting cleaned up, but this was worth it. They were all so friendly and welcomed me up there that night. So I began going regular.

Ronnie started having altar calls after the services. I didn't like that, he was singling me out. Who else could it be? These people been coming regular to church, so they must be saved. They don't need to find the Lord. He's stepping on my toes. I didn't say nothing but I missed a few times to get even with him.

Phil started coming over to my place. He sold me a Smith and Wesson .38 pistol for $150 'cause he needed the money. We got to be buddies and I started going up to church again with him. At one altar call for people who didn't know the Lord, I wanted to go but I didn't feel like making a fool out of myself. But I finally went up there.

That's why I'll always go up at an altar call if I feel the Spirit leading me to, 'cause I know there may be someone there who wants to go up to the front but they're too shy, and if I go first they might feel more comfortable. I remember how it felt that time.

After I got up there I kneeled down. As soon as I did, here came Noble, Dan, Leon, Herman, all of them around me. I said to myself, hop to it, by golly! If you want to give me ten dollars or if you want to give me a milk cow, Leon, you sure can, so if you've got the Lord like you say, I guess you can give me that, too!

Here I am kneeling down, and this one's touching me and that one's touching me and they're praying for me—it really made me feel good. Wanted.

Well, I *was* wanted. But this was a better kind of wanted.

Naturally, when I get up I'm shaking and happy and feeling good, and they're all shaking my hand and telling me I'm saved now. That was easy! Noble Flowers is crying, wiping his eyes. Ann, this real sweet lovable woman is crying and telling me about how long they prayed for me, not just at church but when they was at home saying grace, too.

I went home and the first thing I thought of was, boy, now I'm saved I got to quit cussing. Every time I cussed I'd catch myself—I was serious about it. When I'd catch myself saying "hell," I'd slap my hand down on my leg, "God damn it, I got to stop that—oh, look what I just said!"

Now, I figured the devil's going to work on me harder. Before I was his and he didn't bother with me, but now I'm serving the Lord, so he'll try to trip me up. Maybe all this is the devil. I just have to keep fighting him.

As time went on I tried to read the Bible, but I didn't understand the King James with its thees and thous so I got me a Living Bible.

When I read about sin and heard in church about confessing your sins, I thought, How can you remember all your sins? Are you supposed to list them all out for God, starting with the worst to the least bad? Like I got to list out ten thousand sins? First I killed Patty and George, next.... See how dense I was? I'm learning all this on my own. I figure if this is God's word, I just have to read it and I'll learn everything I need to know.

Now, you got to remember I was just reading the Bible for a few weeks, plus I couldn't read all that good anyway. Up to that point, after high school I hadn't never read hardly anything except hunting magazines. I never had a Bible as a kid. But now they told me, "That's God's word and that's how He speaks to you."

So I read it. And I learned a lot.

Noble Flowers told me to get off that Living Bible 'cause I was asking too many questions. He said it was fine at first but as soon as I grew a little I needed something more solid. So he took my King James Bible home and marked some verses in it.

He's the one who taught church Bible class on Wednesday and Sunday nights, and he also held a Bible study at his home. I went to that one and I started going over to Phil and Jean's house too. I was looking up to Phil, because he was a good talker and it seemed like he knew quite a bit.

So all these people had been with the Bible class long before me and they was all saved, but I was learning just as much as they was, and look at the way some of them are talking about pussy five minutes after we closed the Bibles!

Why, I don't need to worry about all that to be a Christian!

What happened was after a while I just gradually faded away from that group, and they started praying for me again.

❧

Bonesy was a cur, a collie/shepherd mix, and he mated with a Wagner black and tan and had a litter Thomas got to watch being born. Thomas and me took a rag and helped the mother wipe them off, then I put the runt of the litter into Thomas's hands.

Ringtail, the mother, got up thinking Thomas was going to hurt her pup.

"Thomas, you can't pick him up no more," I said, "or Ringtail will get worried and she won't be able to give her pups any milk."

Thomas fell in love with that little fellow, so I kept it for him. We named it Runt.

When the puppy was about seven months old, I was up in my shed working and Thomas was playing outside when I heard this tearing sound in the outhouse. I had a fifty-pound sack of dog food in there, and when I went in it was tore open. Runt had his nose buried deep in the sack and it was him making that rustling and tearing sound as he nuzzled in for more food. His rear end was sticking out—I pulled his tail so hard his feet come out from under him, then I grabbed him by the back of the head as he tried to get up and banged him on the side of the outhouse, then I picked him up and threw him out in the weeds, madder than heck.

I cleaned up the dog food he'd spilled and put it in this round galvanized can and swept the rest outside onto the ground.

I wasn't even thinking about Thomas till I turned around and saw him.

He never looked at me like that before–when I went to pick him up he was scared of me! I remember when I was a kid, going into my bedroom with Rosie, crying, 'cause Mom and Dad were fighting out there. Every time we heard something bang, we'd think one of them was hurt.

Boy, if I remember that, I know Thomas will remember this.

I promised myself right there, I ain't never going to let myself get mad like that in front of Thomas again. Over a dog eating dog food! How could you blame the dog, really, when you stopped to think about it?

∽

I bought a goat off Ricky Cleaver, one heck of a milk goat—I mean a Dolly Parton bag on it—for sixty bucks. I could of bought goats all day for twenty, but this one was gentle. A real nice goat.

So I'm sitting in the outhouse reading a hunting book and I have the door open, and little Thomas is by the porch swing fastened to a Post oak about 10 yards from the outhouse, pushing his toy truck into the goat's legs. The goat backs up and puts her head down and Thomas follows it with the truck and bumps into its leg again. So the goat puts her head down again, but Thomas don't take the warning. The goat raises both hooves up, rears back and thwacks Thomas in the shoulder. She spins him around and he starts crying.

Now Bonesy starts growling—I'm stuck in the outhouse, 'cause I was just in the middle of my business—and the goat turns and raises up with her legs about eighteen inches off the ground threatening Bonesy!

"Get her, Bonesy," I shout, just like I sic him on coons when we're hunting.

Bonesy jumps and grabs her underneath the throat. The goat raises back up and tries to get away, but Bonesy just squeezed and his teeth punctured the goat's jugular vein and the blood pumped out with each heartbeat.

So here I am, pulling my pants up, running out there to try to help the goat, but it's too late. She's gone. A sixty-dollar goat, and I only had her two weeks! All I could do was butcher her and get ten bucks' worth of meat.

What I liked about the whole thing was how loyal Bonesy was to Thomas. After that, I never worried about Thomas when he was with Bonesy.

∽

One deer season Bonesy came home whimpering, his leg all bloody and bent up. It was plumb busted. Someone had shot him and the bullet had went through his left leg.

I saw how bad it was, so I took him out back to put him out of his misery. The way he looked at me, though, I just couldn't. I didn't have tags on my Jeep and Faith had the car, so my neighbor offered to take me and Bonesy to the vet. I was just going to have him give Bonesy a shot to put him to sleep.

"Can you do anything for him?" I asked the vet.

"I can't fix the leg—the bone's shattered. But I can amputate it."

I got to thinking about how much Bonesy loved hunting, and how would I feel if they were deciding whether to kill me or cut off my leg.

"Go ahead and amputate," I said.

I went back up there two nights later. You should of seen old Bonesy when he saw me! He tried to get up but he wasn't used to three legs yet, so he fell down twice before he made it over to me. The leg was off and the hair was shaved around the area and he had stitches. But he was happy, wagging his tail.

He learned to walk and run okay, but about four weeks later Bonesy got to where he couldn't hardly move. I took him back to the vet and he said it was lead poisoning—he never got all the lead out of there. So he cut a slice and put a solution in it and sewed it up, then gave me some more medicine. So I paid that bill and took Bonesy home again.

Well, he wound up foaming at the mouth. I went up and told the doctor and he says bring him in next week.

"Naw, I need something for him right now."

So he gave me some medicine for pneumonia and I give it to Bonesy for about two nights. A few mornings later I go to push the screen door open, but Bonesy is laying there. So I nudge him with my foot and say, "Move, Bonesy," but he don't stir. So I go out the back door and come around and bend down. I don't have to nudge him to see he ain't going to move.

Bonesy was dead.

I didn't want Thomas to see him so I carried him into the trees till I got home from work, then I buried him in a private area in the woods.

∽

That night I said, "Thomas, can you come out here with Daddy? I got something to show you."

Thomas followed me out there to where the fresh mound of dirt was. I kneeled down and put my arm around him.

"That's Bonesy there," I said.

"*Where's* Bonesy, Daddy?"

"Right there, where the dirt is," I said. "He died this morning."

Now Thomas is crying and I'm holding him. After a while we picked some wildflowers together and we made a wooden cross.

"He'll be happy in heaven," I said, "'cause there's lots of coons there, and you know how old Bonesy likes hunting squirrels and coons." Real soft, I said, "We'll see Bonesy again."

Then I said a little prayer about Bonesy.

Now, that came back at me later on, during the divorce when Thomas was at my place. I was saying my prayers—"Remember Grandma and Grandpa, help them to know about God, and help Mommy and Daddy get back together, and that I get to see Thomas more—"

And Thomas cut right into my prayer. "Don't forget to tell God about Bonesy, Dad."

Tears came to my eyes so I couldn't hardly talk, but I said, "Yeah, God, don't forget old Bonesy."

Twenty

Tom Henry

friend of mine who worked at the trailer plant where Faith worked told me Faith and this guy named Otto Hanson was going out together. I acted like I knew all about it, but when Faith got home I sprung it on her.

"Who's Otto Hanson?"

She jumped like she was shot! "Otto who? What are you talking about?" So it was true. She didn't say no more about it and I didn't either.

When I come home from work a few days later, all my furniture and all of her clothes were gone from our house.

So was Thomas.

◌

Faith never told me she planned to move out. She left me before for a couple days then come back. I thought she wanted me to go after her but I didn't. I just let her go. This time she didn't come back.

She got a lawyer from Neosho, so I talked to one from Anderson. He wanted $300 and Faith's wanted $800. I got papers served on me—Faith wanted me to pay all her lawyer fees plus this great big sum per month, 'cause I was making good money logging for Hines.

After Faith left I stopped associating with my regular friends as much. Mostly what they'd tell me is just to forget about Faith and go out drinking and partying. I started getting away from friends that knew me and Faith because it was so hard not to be asking them about her. What's she been saying to you? What's she been up to? Who's she been with?

I asked the people at church what I should do and they said they'd pray for me. They said God will bring me and Faith back together again, but other friends said forget her and move on.

◌

I looked for Otto Hanson. I had no idea where he lived—nobody I asked knew nothing about the guy. I had the woman in the personnel department get his address from his job application. Turned out it wasn't the right address, but they gave me a relative's name in Sulfur Springs who would know where he lived. The place was a big upstairs apartment where several guys lived together over a garage with one girl. When I went out there, a couple of them was working on their motorcycles in the garage.

I went to the door and said, "I'm looking for a guy called Otto Hanson."

One of them said, "I'm Otto Hanson. What do you want?"

"I'm Tom Elliott. My wife is Faith Elliott. You need to leave her alone."

"Get out of my face, man," he said. His buddies were smirking. "She's separating from you and she wants to lead her own life."

I got in my car, which was parked right by the open door. I pull out my blue Bible and start showing him scripture, the one that ends, "let no man put asunder."[25]

He thinks a Jehovah's Witness is talking to him. Then a couple more of his buddies come out and they start mocking me.

"Wait a second," I say, "I got one more scripture for you."

He starts laughing harder, and I reach under my seat where I kept my .357 revolver. I always keep the next chamber that's coming up empty in a revolver, but looking at it from the front all he could see is five bullets in five chambers.

As I brought the revolver up I cocked it. He heard it, so he knew it wouldn't take much to pull the trigger. You can shoot a revolver without cocking it, but it takes a lot of pressure. Once you pull the hammer back a slight touch will do the job.

I gritted my teeth and shook like I was real nervous. Now I had his attention! No more funnies. His buddies didn't know what to do.

"You can laugh at my Bible," I said, "but you better hope I keep studying it, 'cause if I ever stop, you're dead men."

෨

I was trying to catch Otto and Faith out together on a date. I hit all these dancing places in Neosho, Joplin, over in Arkansas, and sometimes I even had to pay a door charge to get in and look around.

"When you was riding around the Neosho square, a couple on a motorcycle with helmets waved to you and you waved back," a friend told me. "That was Faith and Otto. Otto thinks it's funnier than heck, 'cause you waved at them while you was looking for them."

---

25 Matthew 19:6

That made me so mad I drove to Otto's apartment the next Friday night. I found Faith's clothes and sliced them up and I wrote "Helter Skelter" on the mirror with lipstick. I had to write real small at the bottom 'cause I ran out of room.

I knew Otto and his buddies might be coming out to get me at Lodebar, so I made my bed up to look like someone was in it and had just enough light in the room so they could see it. I put a piece of plywood over the two holes in the outhouse and slept there. But they didn't come, so after two nights I moved back to Lodebar.

One night I heard my dogs barking, so I got my shotgun and crept out the back door and through the sage grass. Otto and his buddies had parked on the main road, and I shot right at the car. When they left, it was on foot. The next day the car was gone when I got home. Who came and got it I don't know.

Instead of going to church and Bible studies, I was spending Saturday nights running around like a detective, looking for Faith and Otto. I couldn't even get up Sunday mornings. And I started drinking again. I'd sit out there and watch them on a date—I might be over by the railroad tracks or behind a tree, and I chewed tobacco 'cause they could see a cigarette.

Stakeouts, drinking, setting traps ... this took up all my time and made me not want to go to church even if I had the time. I was thinking, everything is just like with Patty again. I'm drinking again, spying on them—it's all the same. I'm going to lose Thomas just like I lost Winkie, only worse, 'cause there'll be a new man living with Faith.

Anything I could think of to make me madder, I thought it. Then I drank some more.

What happened in 1970—which I'd never dreamed *could* happen—*how can I keep it from happening again?*

I figure the best thing all the way around is to kill myself. That way I don't have to worry about doing nothing to Faith. Can you imagine what they'd say to Thomas? Probably exactly what they was saying to Winkie now.

Those guys coming to Lodebar, I shot right into their car. Heck, I could of killed them!

I couldn't let that happen again.

I went to this guy and bought eight speed pills. They call them bird eggs 'cause they're blue with little black specks on them. I'd been taking them to stay awake following Faith and Otto around.

I drove out to this field and parked the car. I was drunker than heck but I still needed more nerve, so I popped all eight bird eggs at once. Then I sat in my car listening to the radio real loud and getting one heck of a pain in the middle of my chest.

I opened my shirt and turned my dome light on. My chest was quivering, felt like I had a real bad heartburn. I thought to myself, I'm going to end up dying by an overdose! I'd rather go any other way than to have a doctor do an autopsy on me and say I was a drug addict.

So now I *was* ready to shoot myself.

I had this .38 pistol I bought off of Phil. I put it to my head and held it there, but I couldn't do it.

I tried again. Each time I put the gun up to my head, I got the picture in my mind of all this squishy stuff, spaghetti, all over my car. Why that should matter I didn't know, but I couldn't do it. I couldn't even pull the hammer back. Drunk and out of it as I was, I still knew if I pulled that hammer back, just the sweat on my finger could let that trigger slip and I'd be gone.

I don't know how people ever kill themselves. I wanted to do it, I got all psyched up to do it, I even got myself drunk and stoned to do it, but I just couldn't shoot myself.

I still wanted to die, though, so I thought of another way. Where I used to watch deer through my scope, over by Penitentiary Bend—boy, that would be the place to do it. I drove down Dabney Rock Farm Road—high-tailing it 'cause I was thinking when I get there I'll just veer off the road, shoot off the precipice, and plunge to my death.

I'm flying like a maniac, the wheels in my head spinning just as fast as the wheels on my car. But then I think what if I go over that sucker and hit a tree? Not die but just get crippled. Everybody would laugh about that!

So I pull up to the side of the road and plug my spotlight into the cigarette lighter, then I use it to try and find the right place so I won't get hung up on my way down. After a minute I find a perfect clear path, so I tie my hanky to a bush by the side of the road to mark the spot. Soon as my headlights hit it, that's where I'll go off.

I backed my car down the road around a couple small bends—tough to do when you're drunk. I sat there with my door open and my motor running, drinking. I opened that Bible Noble Flowers had marked in and looked at a picture I had of Faith and Thomas and thought about my past and everything that was going on, then put the Bible down—I didn't read nothing out of it, just looked at the picture. I finished my bottle, threw it out the window, looked again at the picture, and took off.

I floor-boarded it so I could get up enough speed. I didn't just want to ride down the side of the incline, I wanted to fly like they do in "The Dukes of Hazzard," 'cause the creek's way down below. I got up quite a bit of speed, probably about forty miles an hour, and I come around the bend in the middle of the road where everybody drives unless you meet someone, then you pull over.

Now, it was a one-lane gravel road. There's a little hump of gravel on each side, then a ditch the grader makes for the water to run in. I saw the hanky up ahead, just at the point the road curves right. The hanky was on the left, and I started to veer off the road a little ahead of it.

Well, my left wheels caught the loose gravel on the side of the road and my car skidded, ending up on the right side of the road with the back wheels in the ditch and the front of the car sticking out onto the road. The rear chrome bumper was resting on the dirt just past the ditch towards the woods.

After I figured out why all the noise had stopped, I climbed out of the car and kicked the door with all my might—you know, the way a drunk does when something goes wrong. I put a big dent in the sheet metal. This was a '76 Dodge wagon, real nice, all deluxe, air, power steering, the works. I got back in the car and tried to gently ease it out, but no go, so I got mad and floored it and dug myself in deeper.

Now I can't think of what to do. I figure I'm going to have to walk home, only a three-mile walk if I go through the woods. So I look underneath the seat, 'cause I've put plenty of whiskey there, but there wasn't none, just empty bottles. I threw those bottles down the slope where I'd planned to plunge to my death.

I get back into my car and turn my tape player on and I start listening to a religious tape. I'm thinking and kind of snickering more than listening. I still got the Bible there on the seat and I turn the tape player off and the dash light on but I don't open the Bible.

I'm talking out loud to Faith, calling her a bitch, looking at her picture with Thomas, thinking how I could cut her picture out and leave Thomas's. "You're lucky I don't take you and your boyfriend out, then myself." But now I'm leafing through the Bible and I see some of the marks Noble made. So I start reading these verses—nothing else to do out there in the middle of the night.

I read the story in Acts we had in the Bible study about Saul on the road to Damascus.[26] And different verses, John 3:16, a lot in Romans and some in Galatians, and I'm thinking about how Noble and different ones would come over to my place and try to help me. And I'm thinking, they really care about me. Look at old Bill Hunt, look at how he took me underneath his wing. Look at Leon, and all the rest of them.

So I'm reading them verses, thinking about the Christian people that's been kind to me. The verses are making sense. I get to wondering is there really a God? I don't know. I'm so mixed up.

Then my thoughts swing back to wanting to kill Otto and Faith, but no more wanting to kill myself. Then I swing back to the idea that I should just kill myself for everyone's benefit.

Finally I get back to rational and stay there. Heck with killing myself. I got my life to lead, I got Thomas to look after. I look up again at his picture. It might of been the worst picture we ever took of Thomas, but to me it's beautiful.

I thought about Mom and Dad and wonder how many days of service calls late at night he did just to let me stay in school up in Chicago, and I not only didn't never repay him but put him through all kinds of hell.

I stopped thinking. I decided to go home.

❧

I got out my bumper jack. I had to dig away the dirt to set the base of the jack in so it would catch the bumper. I jacked the car up on an angle. Each time I got the tires up high enough I put rocks under them, first one side, then the other. On the right side, my jack started to bend over, digging deeper and deeper scratches in the tailgate.

When I thought the car had enough rocks under the wheels, I hopped in and gave it the gas. It just spun, kicking out the littler rocks and gouging the tires on the bigger ones. I undid all the work I'd done in just a few seconds.

---

26 Acts 9

I was stuck, but at least cars could get around me. I had all my chainsaws in my car, 'cause I was taking it to work. If I left the car someone might come along and steal them, so I decided to hide my guns and chainsaws and all in the woods. So I'm putting them in the leaves, and as soon as I put my hand on the first chainsaw it come to me: You fool, that's how to get out of here. Just cut down a sapling, put wood blocks under the wheels, and drive out.

Well, I started my chainsaw up out there in the middle of the night. No one's going to hear me way out here. I cut a small tree into about sixteen chunks of wood. I jacked up the car and put the wood in first from side to side, then lengthwise.

I got the car up finally to about four inches higher than the road then gently drove it out of the ditch. I got my chainsaw and jack, put them on the floor-board—too tired and drunk to put them in the trunk—and put everything else into the car and drove home about ten miles an hour, I was so deep in thought.

&

This was three or four Sunday morning. I pulled into my trailer, walked up onto my porch, thinking about God—and death.

I had this one good tape of Pansy—Bill's late wife. She got hit by a train down by Noel, and Bill's never been the same since. Now I'm listening to this tape of Pansy playing the piano and singing a gospel song and I'm thinking about how she's dead now. Next I'm thinking about death, about Patty dying. I can't say I ever thought too much about George dying. Not that I'm not sorry. Of course I am. But what has always, always been on my mind is Patty dying.

I started to think about how crazy I been acting these last few weeks. So I went out and got the galvanized pipe with the ends screwed on and the gunpowder in it, the plastic explosives, my guns, everything but the chain-saws, and brought it all in the house.

This tape of Pansy's is still playing. Once when Bill Baker came over and I was out there feeding Bonesy chicken bones from the truck stop, I got that tape playing to make Bill feel good. He heard me playing it and was real tickled. But now I'm playing it and thinking about how Bill lost Pansy and how I lost Patty.

I don't even like piano playing, but now I'm listening and thinking about this one picture Bill had of Pansy playing at some kind of shindig in a long pink dress. A few weeks after she died, Bill sent the roll in to be developed. When he got it back, that one picture really broke him up.

It had a clear image of Pansy in her long pink gown, and at the top there's a faint image of the same picture of Pansy but just her shoulders and head and she's way up in the clouds. It had a special meaning for Bill, like God's telling him don't worry about Pansy, she's with me. She was real religious, but Bill wasn't. He never had no time for it. But he had that picture right in his living room where he could show people and look at it.

Here I was listening to this tape and I could see that picture in my mind, and it started a whole new line of thought going. I went into the living room to get my coffee and there was my Bible. I started looking through it, really reading it this time. I came back to that part about Saul on the road to Damascus, about him killing and persecuting those Christians.

This was interesting, just like a regular book. I was reading it right through, really enjoying it. Why would God pick someone who went around killing Christians to be blinded, then to be a goody-goody guy to witness to Ananias, to go to the street called Strait?[27]

I started thinking about myself. Has something blinded me? How come all these happy people tell me they know there's a God? How come God don't talk to me like he talks to other people? I mean ones I know have something: Leon, Dan Mullin, Edd and Ada. These people have got to be hearing God or seeing God. No matter what happens, they say, "Praise the Lord," and they mean it.

Now I'm thinking, how come God picked a guy like Saul to do His work? How come he didn't pick out a nice Christian, why this type of guy? I'm just like old Saul—only I didn't intend on killing them. I didn't even know what I was doing. If God could forgive Saul, he can forgive me too. He might not want me to be one of these apostles or anything like that, but he has to give me a chance if he gave Saul one.

So I read all kinds of verses. I read I don't know how many that didn't mean anything to me, but then I came to the one about knock and ye shall receive,[28] and the little simple ones a Sunday School teacher would use.

I read the ones Noble had marked, and read before and after them to get their meaning, and I started to get some meaning for me out of them. I tried to

---

27　Acts 9:1-19
28　Matthew 7:7,8

get myself in the mood to talk to God. How can I talk to God when I just got done cussing Him and laughing at Him? I want to feel it with my whole heart.

I want to be serious with God. Earnest. I talk to people all the time and tell them to have a nice day and I don't really give two licks whether their day is nice. But I don't want to talk to God like that. I just tried to kill myself, but God stopped me. And now them verses, that music, these thoughts, all made me want to really talk to God.

I paced back and forth with my coffee, then I went outside and on the steps right there on the porch looked up at the dark sky, then into the wide-open door of my trailer. I was thinking, Look at this place. I've had it so long, just renting. I ain't getting nowhere in life. It's a good thing my dad can't see me now. He wanted me to be in business, and here I am cutting trees! I lost my wife and my son will grow up away from me. What do I have to lose? I'll try it, and if it don't work I'll tell anybody right to their face!

I really think if it wouldn't of worked for me that night, no one could've ever told me about God again. I believe that. 'Cause I brought myself down to a point where I really wanted forgiveness for what I did, not only to Patty and George but I thought about Winkie, I thought about Faith's life, how I might of gone and done the same thing to her and Otto.

I hadn't never been this serious in my whole life. I knew now I could never go back to Bunker Hill Church unless something really happened to me, 'cause I'd be mocking them. I may be a lot of bad things but I ain't no hypocrite.

And, hey—all of a sudden I'm talking to God out there on my front porch. I said, "All I want is a little peace in my life." And I kept on talking to Him out loud like He's standing right there. It was just a nice flow, like water in a brook, something took over me and the more I talked, the more water flowed over the dam, and then it seemed like I tumbled over and my sins were left in the swirling waters and I shot out clear.

It was a light feeling. I left the turmoil behind. The sun started to rise. I was feeling free and light. It's kind of like when you put Alka Seltzer in a glass of still water, all of a sudden you get a bubbling you can't stop. Even if you put your hand on it, you can't hold it in.

I'll never forget my experience with God. I'll never be able to not believe in God. Oh, I could go out there and lead the worst life there is, just live for the devil. But still, no matter how drunk or what state of mind I was in, if someone come up to me and asked, "Is there a God?" I could never deny it. I might say,

"Yes, and for your sake you'd better believe it. For mine, there's such a thing as backsliding. When you find God, pray for me."

If I broke my leg early in my life, I could go the rest of my life denying I ever broke a leg, but if you took an x-ray you could see the bone built up around that area. You hear people say, "I know I'm going to heaven if I die today." That used to irritate me, 'cause I thought to myself, how can they be sure about something like that? Now I know it's a "Blessed Assurance."[29] He seals you with His Spirit.[30]

⌒⌒

That morning I had the TV on and was watching religion while I was getting cleaned up and dressed for church. I pulled in at Charlie and Deloris's on the way to visit with Thomas for a little, and Chuckie, Faith's brother, come out and asked me where I was going.

"To church."

"You still going to church?" They never knew I dropped out.

"Yeah."

"Hey, can I go with you?" He'd never been up there before!

"Sure, come along, if you hurry."

"Be right with you." He went in to get dressed and came shooting out in a jiffy, still threading his belt through his pant loops.

I took Chuckie up to church and we sat by each other. I sent him to the rack for a couple hymn books and we're singing up a storm. I was singing louder than heck, 'cause I was really feeling good. After singing, we got down on our knees for prayer requests: Bill Hunt's son, Mullin's little baby (that later died and they buried it in the yard), and a few others.

I prayed where I really felt like I was talking to God instead of just trying to fit words into the pattern everyone uses. Here in church the words just came tumbling out and I felt like I really was talking to someone up there past the ceiling.

I kept thinking about what I did. It's like having a tattoo on you and you can't get rid of it. My mind went back to 1970, the way Patty was, so sweet and never hurt a flea, and the way she got treated by Junior and she just took it.

---

29 A well-known Christian hymn, "Blessed Assurance, Jesus is mine! O what a foretaste of glory divine!"
30 Ephesians 1:13

But she wasn't saved. She didn't know a thing more about God than I did. And here I was, knowing I'm saved and there's a Supreme Being and an afterlife, and I took her life! It's like I was throwing the devil's pitchfork at her while I was shooting those bullets, sending her straight to hell. Why should I be allowed to go to heaven? It wasn't fair.

I was better off not being saved than being saved, 'cause now I was miserable with a conscience. I only knew if you're saved you go to heaven and if you're not you don't—I didn't understand about God being merciful and the age of accountability.[31] I couldn't cope with the thought that I'd sent Patty straight to hell.

So right while everybody was kneeling down, praying, and with Chuckie right next to me, I ran out the church door. I got in my car to take off, then remembered I had to take Chuckie home, so I went around the west side of the church and crouched down with my knees bent, my head bowed, and my arms crossed over my forehead.

I was miserable. I thought about what I done a million times and never felt this bad. Why now, when I've come to God, who is supposed to be so gracious, do I feel the worst I ever felt in my life? So I'm crouching down there and out of the corner of my eye I see some shoes and pant legs move into the picture. Four guys came out there from church—Ronnie, Noble, Dan, and Leon. I didn't want to look up, 'cause I was crying.

"Tom, no matter what you say to me, I'm your friend," Noble said, once they saw my needs were spiritual, not physical. "Tell me your problem, I'll be there to help. Don't try to stop me from helping you, 'cause it's obvious you need help. I'm your friend, Tom."

All this before I've said a word. They could tell something was wrong. No one had ever seen me pray by myself before. I never walked out of church before. And the windows in the church are on the same side as the outhouse, so they could tell I hadn't gone there.

It was quiet for a while, them all standing there with me still squatting on the ground.

Finally Noble said, "Are you going to be out to church tonight?"

---

31 This is the Christian doctrine that, while each is responsible to accept Christ for themselves, children and those who never had a chance to know about Him are not accountable and therefore God takes them to heaven instead of judging them for rejecting Christ.

"Don't ask me, 'cause you guys will just make me come to church, and I don't want to come here no more!"

"I'll tell you what, Tom, me and Ann, instead of coming to church tonight we'll come to your house. If you want to leave now, go ahead. We'll take Chuckie home."

"Noble, I'm saying no to both of them ideas. I'd of been long gone and nobody would of bothered with me except for Chuckie. I'll take him home, 'cause I brought him up here. I feel bad about running out of church 'cause of Chuckie—the first time he come to church. But you ain't coming over to my house tonight."

"We sure are. You need us, Tom. Don't you consider us friends? We want to help."

"If you knew how nasty my house is, you wouldn't never think of bringing Ann there. I'll be in church tonight, you got my word on it, 'cause I don't want you coming to my place."

"Tom, I know you will. That's one thing about you—you say something, you'll do it."

After a bit my eyes cleared and I got tired of squatting and I stood up. Noble is a big guy, and old Leon is tough, but their eyes was glassy, not really crying, but close.

When the service ended, I said, "Ronnie, that was one sermon of yours I can't say I remember much from. Your voice don't carry too well in the yard." Just a little joke to tell him I was all right. I hate sympathy.

Chuckie came out there and asked, "Where'd you go?" I told him I just went out to talk with some guys privately. Chuckie wasn't used to churches and he didn't question me no further. I dropped him off.

"You ever want to go up there again, just let me know."

◠◡

I buzzed back up to church that night. Now, I'd never been up in front of the church before, but during the second song I got out of my chair and without asking nobody went in front before we were even done singing. I stood there right at the pulpit and told them everything I was going through—about the divorce, about Otto Hanson, some real private stuff. I told them everything except about Patty and George, and I had to stop myself from saying that.

"A lot of the divorce is my fault," I said. "I married Faith when she was fifteen and she never got a chance to date no one else. I ain't never had no kind of lifestyle for her, a lot of you know I work seven days a week, ten hours a day—but I still got nothing to show for it."

I started telling them about last night in my trailer. All these people thought I was saved a couple months back and I couldn't bear to tell them I wasn't saved when they were praying with me up in front of the church.

How I know something different happened that Saturday night was no one heard a cuss word out of my mouth after. And I didn't even realize it until three or four days later, when someone came to me and told me my talk was different. I had to be told! And look how hard I'd tried to do it before.

When I left the church that night I felt open with these people. I didn't care about their stares. I was free. If they didn't want me in their church, all they'd of had to do is have one person come up and say so and I'd be gone for good, I'd go to another church or worship the Lord at home. But you won't believe how people came up to me and told me how what I said affected them, 'cause I was open about it. They knew they'd heard the truth. A lot of what I said wasn't according to scripture—or even according to reason—but I told them what I felt.

I took up the whole service.

Twenty One

"You know what's missing in here?" Tom Henry said one night as he looked up from a Christmas card he was making for his youngest son. Jeremy had been just eight months old when Tom Henry was re-captured.

"Um … good food, sex, freedom? Maybe you should tell me what you have in mind. My list is a little long."

"Christmas! There's no Christmas spirit in here. No tree, no presents, no …" He sighed. "Remember putting up the Christmas tree? Decorating it? Putting on the lights?"

"There might have been something I left out when I told you about my religion."

"No Christmas tree?"

"No Christmas! We were too Christian to celebrate Christmas," I said with a grin.

"You serious?"

"The origin of the Christmas tree is pagan and Christ wasn't born in December. Plus they object to the drinking and partying associated with a sacred holiday."

"You guys didn't know how to have fun."

"Well, since it has meaning for you and I've resigned from the Brethren, I guess you and I could celebrate Christmas."

"So how are we going to celebrate?"

"Well obviously we start by ordering a tree from commissary," I said.

"Oh, you're real helpful."

ᇰ〜ᴑ

It was early December, 1985. As the days progressed in what passes for normality in prison, I heard no more about celebrating Christmas. I assumed the idea was just a Tom Henry whim. I should have known better.

In mid-December, Friday the thirteenth at about midnight, Tom Henry began pasting my white typing paper onto the cell wall near the front bars. He kept pasting until a three-foot-wide strip of wall was covered in paper from the floor to a couple feet from the ceiling. He used toothpaste, a common adhesive in prison, five dots to a page—one in each corner and one in the middle, not too much or the paper will wrinkle, not too little or it won't stick.

Tom Henry then began drawing with an art pencil. He drew a Christmas tree stand at the bottom, then a tree six feet tall and thirty inches wide at its base. He painted the branches green and the trunk brown and the stand gray— all with black highlights.

"This will be the first time in my life I had a Christmas tree," I said.

"Well, let's hope it won't be the best tree you ever put up."

"Amen to that, brother. How can I help?"

"Here's some Kraft paper—make some ornament balls."

So I stayed up with Tom Henry that night and used a needle to cut forty-five circles of Kraft paper in six different colors. I cut strips of four colors of tissue paper and pasted them into loops and joined them into a chain. We wrote names of family and friends on the Kraft paper circles and pasted them to the tree.

We got out the Christmas cards we'd received and filled some of the empty areas, then hung the tissue-paper chain in large curves over the tree. Tom Henry added the final touch by coloring the light bulb of his high intensity lamp with a red magic marker, then wiring the lamp to the overhead shelf above the front bars so it cast a red Christmas glow onto the tree.

"Man, you're amazing," I said. I backed up as far as I could in the cell's tight confines and admired the Christmas tree. "It's so festive—totally out of place in this setting."

"That's what makes it so necessary," he said.

"I can't argue with that."

Neither could the inmates who shuffled by on their way back from chow the next morning. We saw smiles on faces that had never worn anything but glares.

"Check it out, homey!"

"Merry Christmas!"

"Look at that!"

"You guys are crazy!"

All of it positive, all in good spirit, from black, white, Latino, gang banger, independent, we saw grins or—for those too hard to allow such a breakdown in character—a softening of the features. Lunch brought a similar response, only this time everyone looked as they passed. The word was out. Guards on break from their duties stopped by West 3-49 to see the Christmas tree.

But the tree looked its best during the post-supper return from the Chow Hall. By then daylight was starting to wane and the red light pouring onto the tree from above made it burst off the wall.

"That was something," I said after we were locked up. "Did you see their faces? I'm guessing some of those guys never had a Christmas tree in their house."

"I'm guessing some of those guys never had a house."

"You did it, Tom Henry! You brought Christmas cheer to a maximum security prison. These guys are muggers and rapists and murderers! And did you see their expressions?"

"I'm a murderer, Big Stuff."

"Yeah, but you know what I mean. You aren't anything like what I'm talking about."

"I did enjoy seeing their faces."

"A preacher told me once that when the Bridal March plays and everyone looks backward to watch the bride proceed down the aisle, he likes to look forward to watch the groom watching her."

Tom Henry's face lit up. "We did something good here," he said.

෴

On Christmas Eve, a normal Tuesday in prison, something happened that caused me to start copying all my *Tom Henry* transcripts, chapters, notes, along with my daily journal, and mailing the copies to my family for safekeeping.

Tom Henry was heating water for coffee with his stinger hooked on the side of the cup. You have to keep an eye on it so when the water starts to boil, the level doesn't get below the coil. Tom Henry had just plugged it in when the call came for commissary. He and I left with the line.

When we returned our toilet was black with soot, the smell of burned plastic was in the air, and tiny black ashes had landed all over the cell. The stinger's coil had plastic melted to it.

"You left your stinger on," Officer Joe Saunders said. "Someone yelled 'fire' and I rushed in here and put it out."

"Thanks, Joe," I said. "The fire could've jumped to the blankets and then to my papers."

"Just what I was thinking," he said. "I thought, man, these guys are the only ones doing something worthwhile in here and I'm not letting it burn up."

෴

Thursday, January second, I was back at my desk in the Voc School when Tom Henry stepped in from the hall.

"Check this out!" He, handed me a small newspaper called the *Jewish Week*. "How close can you copy this label?"

"What are you up to?"

"I want to give this to the mail guard to deliver to old Strickler."

I smiled. I always enjoyed Tom Henry's pranks, even when they were at my expense, so I figured I'd enjoy this one even more, having contributed to it.

"I think I can make it look good enough he'll think it's real."

That afternoon our Nazi neighbor got a personally addressed copy of the *Jewish Week*. At chow it was all he could talk about.

"I don't know how those bastards got my name," he said, "but I'm on their list." It was nearly too much for us to maintain our composure as Strickler rattled on about how he could now keep tabs on his enemies.

ᕯ

Later that night Officer Alms came by.

"South House is locked down," he said. "Bikers and blacks got into it."

"Are we going to be locked down?" Tom Henry said.

"I wouldn't bet against it."

Sergeant Sampson was talkative that night.

"They found hacksaw blades," he said.

"Hacksaw blades concern you guys," Tom Henry said, "We're more worried about shanks."

"They found them, too," Sergeant Sampson said.

"So this is going to be a long one."

ᕯ

The next evening Officer Alms stopped by to talk. "They're doing a real thorough shake-down in the South House. Two galleries a day!"

"They finding anything?" Tom Henry said.

"Damn straight! Twenty shanks in one cell, bullets in another, hacksaw blades under a sink of another. This is the most thorough shakedown we've ever done. Ever!" He straightened up and looked both ways on the gallery. "Sinks, toilets, and cabinets have come down."

Our tape recorder!

We prepared for this shakedown like never before.

About noon on Friday a group of guards entered the West House and started on Nine Gallery. They did nine and part of seven, then quit for the day. Saturday they finished Seven and Five, so I typed as far into the night as I could to get everything on paper before the shakedown crews arrived.

I said, "I'll hide the tape recorder deep in this box."

"That could look suspicious, a tape player stuffed down deep."

I thought for a minute. Tom Henry had a point.

"Well, isn't there an expression about hiding in plain sight?"

And so, when they got to our cell about noon, we were ready. Everything had come off the walls, even the Christmas tree. All shelves had been removed along with all wall hangings, including my multi-page timeline of *Tom Henry*. A clipboard held our IDs and permits. The tape recorder was on a box, in plain sight. Both TVs had the Bears game on.

The guards messed the cell up a little, just to prove to their superiors they were on the job, but otherwise all they did was kick back and watch football.

Whew!

꒰꒱

For about six weeks things were prison normal—or abnormal, things were so quiet. You can tell by the single incident that caused a ripple in our lives during this period, a yell from the cell next to us at about one in the morning while I was transcribing.

"Stop that damn typing! Go to sleep, God damn it!" This was Rodeo, one of the Northsider big shots but a pretty good guy. The next afternoon I stopped at his cell after work.

"Sorry about that typing, man," I said.

"I know you need to type and all, but that constant rat-tat-tat gets on a guy's nerves. No more after ten o'clock, okay?"

"How about eleven, Rodeo? No way I can get done stopping at ten. And I'll put a folded blanket under the typewriter to soften the sound."

I stuck to my promise, but it turned out the blanket made so much difference it didn't matter anyway.

꒰꒱

One morning Tom Henry stopped by my office in the school building.

"Big Stuff, I got to move out today." He sat down and pulled his chair close. "The Northsiders told me at lunch they need me to hold a cell for a guy who's on investigation."

"Okay, when can we get back together?"

"They're going to hold our cell and the one I'm going to—I think it's 3-34—for thirty days. They say no one will be moved into either cell."

"Understood," I said. "Do you need my help moving?"

"No, I'm good."

"Hey!" I said as Tom Henry turned to leave. "Take my TV. Maybe I'll get some work done."

I'd been given a rare gift: a cell of my own. I knew it might not last, despite the gang's promise to Tom Henry of thirty days unmolested. I was sure they'd put a hold on 3-34, the cell they were having him hold for them, but I had no confidence they were doing the same for us in 3-49.

Up until now I'd typed what Tom Henry had dictated, which was more or less chronological, but I'd noticed many things were out of order. So I divided his post-Illinois history into ten sections based on major events such as marriage, divorce, Penitentiary Bend, and Thomas's birth. Then I grouped the events whose time I knew into each section and the rest into an eleventh and sent them down to Tom Henry's cell for help.

As he sent the sections back, I laid them on the bottom bunk in stacks, then arranged the stacks. That's how I put the luxuriously large space of a single-man cell to good use.

I finished about nine o'clock in the evening, satisfied I now had a better grasp on the time line of the story, then went to bed totally worn out.

I woke up to a carton of milk in my food slot. The lockdown lasted five days.

On the fifth day, Tom Henry got a letter from Winkie he sent to me to read.

It was one of those letters that can drive a man crazy. Bill, her current boyfriend, had talked her out of having anything to do with her father—she was writing to tell him that she was cutting off all contact.

The letter was a devastating blow for Tom Henry. When he was recaptured by the FBI, Winkie had visited him in the jail in Illinois and started writing him letters. She was fourteen at the time. During the last four years, depending on her mood, her letters might be tender, thanking him for a card he'd sent, or harsh, asking him, "How did it feel when you pulled the trigger?"

He desperately wanted a relationship with her and he'd done everything he could think of to stay in her good graces. But he'd murdered her mother. What could he possibly do to repair such damage?

"It feels like trying to empty the ocean with a bucket," he'd once told me. After I read the letter, I sent him a note.

"I'm so sorry, man," I wrote. "Always bear in mind, this too shall pass." It felt lame, given what I knew he was going through.

When I returned to my cell at two-forty in the afternoon a few days later, I discovered a mattress and property box. They belonged to Pollack, who'd just come out of Segregation (sent there when they found a shank strapped to his arm).

As soon as he knew I had a Northsider cellmate, Tom Henry told them to switch Pollack and him—Pollack could hold the cell for his Northsider brother, whose investigation would soon be completed. It took a week, but Tom Henry and I were cellmates once more. Time to resume recording.

"So where were we?" Tom Henry said that evening, as soon as he was settled in. "I just got saved, right?"

Twenty Two

Tom Henry

I wanted to know more about the Lord, I wanted to know all about the Bible. There were children in our church who knew more than me, and I was ready to grow as a Christian. I wanted to learn the basics, Adam and Eve, the Fall, all that stuff. Then I could go on to more advanced things.

I started to watch all the religious stations on TV and marked down the programs I liked. I bought the Bible on cassettes and got a tape player and listened to tapes in my car when I drove to work. I bought sermons on tape through the mail and listened to them.

I was sleeping again at nights, not even thinking about Otto Hanson. I wasn't drinking or cussing. No more running around like a detective. I started going to Bible studies with Judy, Phil, Noble, having a good time.

The more I kept trying to serve the Lord, the more I felt the blessings. Good things started to happen. I remember hollering up at the sky, "Lord, wait till about Tuesday before you give me any more of your blessings. I can't take care of the ones you given me now!"

I started going to every service at Bunker Hill, not 'cause I felt like I should or 'cause I didn't want to hurt Noble's feelings—now I wanted to be there, 'cause church was the high point of my week. And Bunker Hill didn't have enough services to suit me, so I started going to different churches and Bible studies to fill in. No one will ever enjoy my singing, but at least the Lord could tell which one was me.

I didn't know anything about testifying but I did that too, without even trying. I'd be up in the Bunker Hill store and people would say, kind of round about, "You been going up to Bunker Hill pretty regular. I need to do something like that myself. Old Ronnie Tosh still preaching?"

"Yeah. I really like him."

Then after they beat around the bush, they might say, "Pretty good services up there?"

"I like it there," I told them. "I didn't at first, but now I like it."

But what they wanted to find out was more about my story. They'd of heard rumors about what I said that night and they wanted to hear more.

When they asked me something religious I couldn't answer good 'cause I didn't know enough from the Bible. All I could say is just what Leon and Bill Hunt said to people they witnessed to. "You knew me before and you know me now. Look at the difference."

Then I might say, "Now, I don't know if I'll ever go back to my old ways. I hope I don't. But this I know—I've found the fullness I need in life and I'd rather go to church than do anything else. It's like a family reunion. I feel wanted and loved. Now, maybe your needs are different and you can do fine without the Lord, but for me, this is what I been looking for all my life and I'm happy I found it." What could they say to that?

 ∽

We had a meeting at the church to decide on ideas for the new sign. Noble's design was two two-by-fours with a board and lettering on both sides. Thomas could have thought of that! I felt like we could do better.

So I went home and really worked up a fancy design. I went in there with a drawing measured with a ruler, with the rocks drawn in, colored with Thomas's crayons.

When they saw that, they couldn't say no to me. Look at all the work I put into it. I had a slot with changeable signs for a revival and a photo cell to turn a light on it automatically at night.

"I not only want to do it, I want to pay for it too," I said.

"Tom, it's fine if you want to help, but this is a church project," Dan Mullins said. "Noble will get his feelings hurt. He's been our maintenance man for years."

"Fine, okay," I said, but the Saturday we started on it, Noble didn't show up. His feelings got hurt anyway.

To make my sign, I got some Arkansas rock that a guy who built a big house had left over, and some pieces of marble, and I bought an old bell from a school. I made a framework on the side of the steeple and put the bell there and I had a rope with a piece of chain coming through the ceiling where you walk in the front of the church, so you could ring the bell. For inside the church I bought some rough cedar boards and had a guy plane them down. I used those to make a cedar-paneled section behind the pulpit. I got a little cedar tree about four inches round and I cut it right down the middle with my chainsaw and made a cross. I set the cross in there with the bark showing and nailed it up with horseshoe nails. And I put the American flag on one side and the Christian flag[32] on the other.

❧

It took us two Saturdays to build the planter box for the sign. The second Saturday, I was there working with Frank when a fancy Cadillac pulled up and out steps this well-dressed city guy with a Cadillac belt buckle. He comes sauntering over and sticks out his hand.

"Hi, I'm Bob Melton, pastor of the Mt. Zion Baptist Church."

"I don't think I can shake your hand," I said. "I ain't rich enough." But I shook his hand.

"I hear you're on fire for the Lord. Why don't you come down to my church sometime?"

"Well, I already got one church to fix. I don't have time to repair another."

"We do our own repairs. We'd be happy if you just came to a service."

"How do you like that?" I told Frank soon as he left. "Here we are, working on this sign planter, so he knows we belong here and he's trying to steal us away to his church. Rich guy! He probably don't get enough contributions to make his Cadillac payment."

So that's how I met Bob Melton.

❧

I'd been working on the cedar church door for a while and I'd promised them at church I'd get it done because we had a revival coming up. I was in my trailer working on it and feeling pretty good from a revival I was at in another church that night, 'cause I got into praying in the Spirit there.

So here I am that rainy night working on this cedar door and I go by the window to grab my coffee. The cedar door is on sawhorses in the middle of the room with sawdust all over the place, and I'm just about to take a coffee break when all of a sudden—

CRACK!

The top of the window shattered into the room. A couple pieces hit me, but most of them flew over my head by the door. All I heard was the CRACK, 'cause my air compressor was running. It sounded like a shot.

---

32   To picture the Christian flag, think of the US flag. Where the stars are is a blue background with a red cross. Where the stripes are is solid white.

So I dropped to the floor and crawled into the hallway, then I ran into the bedroom and grabbed EF Hutton. I wasn't thinking about Otto no more, but that didn't mean he wasn't thinking about me. I figured whoever's out there might be waiting for me to run out of the trailer.

There's two doors in my kitchen so I ran in there, unlocked one of the doors, grabbed a metal tray on wheels and threw the rolling tray out. It clattered to the ground, making a big noise.

While it's still tumbling out I run out the other door and slip into the woods. I come crawling through the sage grass, thinking they'll expect me to go through the woods with the trees for a cover. No one would expect me to come across the field, so that's just what I did, putting the strap for the gun behind my neck and crawling army style through the sage grass, which was near two feet tall.

I came out by the apple trees past my garden by my driveway. I checked around me. Nothing. Then I dashed across my driveway and rolled down into the ditch. Nothing. I walked through the woods and back up the driveway by my pond bank, listening for any sound I might hear over the steady beat of the rain, like a car starting up or a gunshot.

Nothing.

I was soaking wet. I figured I'd venture up the lane to my house. That's when I saw the tree fallen right against my house, with one little branch stuck through the window where the glass had been. I stared at it dumbfounded for a second, then I burst out laughing.

I was thinking of getting my chainsaw out and cutting up the tree, but I was wet and cold, it was pouring rain, and I was wore out. So I just went in soon as I rescued my metal wheeled tray, closed the kitchen doors, and tacked a piece of plastic over the broken window.

The next morning I went out there with the camera and took pictures of the tree. It never got uprooted but it split about two feet above the ground, an unusual place for a tree to split. Usually they'll either come out of the ground or split a little higher up the trunk, where they're not quite so thick. I took a whole roll of film.

The tree just missed my pickup by inches, landing between my truck and the trailer. That tree did mighty little damage for where it fell—except to my nerves!

❧

I went up to the front in church Sunday morning and showed the pictures and talked about the tree crashing into my house and how I snuck out around the back, through the sage grass—and they were wondering, what does this story have to do with anything? Ain't he never going to shut up?

I said, "Now this may not mean nothing to you yet, but just follow me. Here I had all them boards all set to nail together, five across this way, two the other, and then I was going to turn it over to put on the slanting one. But because of the tree crashing I never finished the door till the next night. Well, even though I don't like having to cut up the tree and fix the window, I'm real glad that happened.

"Why, you ask? Well, look here. The next night I switched one board around, and look what you see. (I showed them the picture.) See the cross? If I'd put it together the night before, I'd of put the boards in this order" (another picture), "and the cross wouldn't never have showed up. Ain't that remarkable?"

You know, not only was there a cross there, but by me giving that little talk on the door, people come up with more things besides the cross I saw. One saw the shroud, another the blood, and some saw what reminded them of the only door into heaven. What come out of that tree falling was much greater than just a cross being on the church's door.

Now every time these people that heard me talk that day come to church, they'll see something that will put them into a spiritual frame of mind. See the blessing that came of it? And I didn't plan none of it.

∽

I didn't get baptized right away after I got saved. Noble and Ronnie kept trying to talk me into it, but I told them, "I ain't going to get baptized till I understand it." So they tried to explain it to me and showed me from the Bible.

"Yeah, I see it," I said, "but I don't feel it."

We went to Straight Up Rock for Frank and Sharon's baptisms, and they asked me if I wanted to.

"I'm not getting baptized," I said. "Don't keep asking me, 'cause I ain't going to do it."

I was there, though, and I saw Frank and Sharon getting baptized, and I saw Frank go under the water—it was pretty cold—and then I saw him come out.

The look on Frank's face as he came out of the water, the feeling I felt when he hugged me after, the huge smile all peaceful and contented—all of that was what done it. I just knew how happy he was, inside out. And I knew now was the time.

So right there I said, "Hey, I want to get baptized too."

Dan Mullin dunked me under the water as he said, "In the name of the Father, the Son and the Holy Spirit ..." and I come out soaking wet and everybody hugged me and I felt real light.

Afterwards, Dan Mullin and Noble Flowers kissed me on the side of the cheek. On the way home I thought about it—if any man had ever come up to me and kissed me under any other circumstances I think I'd of socked him, but this was different.

∽

That night an evangelist from Edna, Kansas, had a revival at our church. He preached about Mephibosheth. He talked about a place that was desolate, where the water had to be hauled, no bathroom facilities. He said it was a place so bad cockroaches wouldn't live there. He called it Lodebar.[33]

I said, loud enough for people to hear, "Sounds like he's talking about my place!"

From that time on everyone called it Lodebar.

∽

I drove home from that revival with a glow inside, so I thought I'd share it. I pulled into Charlie and Deloris's place and walked into the house.

"I just got baptized!" I said.

Faith was in the corner, giving me one of them smirky looks that usually make me mad, but I was all happy and smiling.

"Faith, I found something you need."

"I need you to get out of here. Mom, tell him to leave!"

"Deloris, you want me to leave?" She didn't say nothing so I picked up Thomas, who was sleeping on the sofa.

"Now you woke Thomas up," Faith said. "Yeah! And I got something *you* need! I got papers that says I ain't got to give you no more visitation rights."

That hit me like a cannonball. I had Thomas in my arms.

---

33 II Samuel 9:4

"I'll take him right now!" I started toward the door. "I'll show *you* who's got visitation rights!"

Then they all jumped on my case. Thomas started crying from all the yelling, so I put him down on the sofa and I left. As I'm driving home I got to thinking how much I still had to learn about being a Christian. What I didn't know was all Faith had is some motion from her lawyer to ask the judge not be let me have visitation rights 'cause we was fighting about everything at the time. But I believed she had a judge's order, so Faith kept me from seeing Thomas for a while. But I snuck around to see him when I could.

What I done that night would come back to bite me during our divorce, 'cause Faith's lawyer told the judge I tried to kidnap Thomas and then he really did order that I couldn't have visitation rights. I don't think that order ever got cancelled, but after Faith cooled down enough I got to see Thomas again. But it sure took a while!

გოo

The German was this old hermit that lived about a mile from me. He had a one-room cabin in the woods. When I was hunting back that way I used to pop out of the woods to talk to him and sometimes he invited me in for coffee.

He kept a few cattle and he fixed farm machinery. He wasn't unfriendly but he didn't talk to people a lot. He didn't have electricity or plumbing or a telephone, and his only heat was a fireplace, but since he lived in the woods he stayed warm.

When I asked once where he was from, he told me he was Hungarian but he escaped when the Communists took over after the war. We all just called him the German.

Clifford Gideon was the German's closest neighbor, and one winter day in early January Clifford went over there 'cause he hadn't seen no smoke from the old man's chimney, and he found the German sprawled on the ground next to an old hay baler he'd been working on, shot through the heart.

The police found a calendar the German checked off every day, and the last day checked off was December 31, 1980, so since Clifford found him on January 3rd they figured he'd been dead three days, which turned out to be right.

There wasn't no wallet in his pants, so at first they thought the motive was robbery, but the next day they found his wallet inside his house with $140 in it and they found a suitcase packed for travel with $4,000 in new $20 bills and then they found another $4,000 in cash hidden in the barn.

Most of his papers was in Hungarian, so they hired a lady from Joplin to translate them. They could tell he was shot with a high-powered rifle and it didn't look like a hunting accident—a single shot through the heart. They could tell the bullet went clear through his body but they never found it.

The German's name was Istvan Kondra. They had trouble digging up any records on him until they figured out he was using a false name. His birth name was Janis or something like that. Istvan Kondra was the name he used when he escaped Hungary. I remember a quote of his they put in the paper, "A Hungarian foot won't fit into a German boot."

Most of what I know about the murder I read in the newspapers. This guy became an officer in the Hungarian army, refused to serve in Hitler's Nazi army, spent three years in a concentration camp, left his country under a false name with fake papers to escape from the Communists, got to the U.S., worked hard, and lived like a miser to save up his money.

He planned to donate his land and money to set up a Hungarian youth camp in the U.S. for the children of Hungarian refugees, a place for them to learn their heritage so they could someday go back to a free Hungary. When he was sixty-nine and had saved over a hundred thousand dollars—most of it in the value of his land—and wasn't bothering nobody, somebody comes along and BAM! One shot to the heart.

⚭

I was drinking a coffee at the store when I read in the paper that Sheriff Lou Keeling had requested help from the FBI because of the mystery surrounding the German's background.

The FBI! I was the last one to talk to the German—the day before he was killed, I was chatting with him at old lady Cheese-eyes' store for forty-five minutes trying to get him to come to church. Everybody coming in and out of the store saw me, and nobody ever talked that long to the German.

Plus I lived less than a mile from him, I was a noted woodsman, and whoever killed the German went in on foot. And I was the only one in the area who loaded and shot steel jacket bullets, which the paper said was likely what killed him.

Should I pack up and run right now, before the FBI shows up? Then they'd think for sure I was guilty. I'd have to start all over with a new identity. I did it once when I was young. That was over ten years ago. Could I do it again? What if I'm just worrying about nothing? I didn't shoot the German, so someone else did. The FBI will find evidence and solve the crime and I'll of run for nothing. Maybe they won't even call me.

Not long after, the FBI called me in for questioning.

Twice while I was in Missouri I was really scared. Once was in the feud with the Hanson brothers, but now I wasn't dealing with some bikers fighting over a woman. This was the law. And not the McDonald County law—the FBI!

I believe I was being watched from the time they told me to come to the sheriff's office. They gave me two days' notice, enough leeway to see how I'd react to being a suspect. I didn't see anyone following me or any strange cars, but I wasn't never where they thought I'd be. Going home to Lodebar I went through the woods south of it or through Fred Haddock's place.

∽

"What were you talking to him about for so long?" the FBI agents asked me when I showed up at the sheriff's office.

"I was trying to get him to come to church," I said.

"Are you going through a lot of depression and stress because of the divorce?"

"No."

"Do you load steel jacket bullets?"

"Yes."

"You know you're the only one around here does that. Why?"

"I do it to save money," I said. "Loading my own ammunition is a hobby."

They said their theory was the killer might've used a steel jacket bullet, 'cause the exit hole wasn't much bigger than the entry hole. They asked me about hunting near the German's place.

I think the stupidest question they asked me is, "Have you ever gotten one of your guns and repeatedly fired it into the air to release your stress?"

They had me take a lie detector test, but they didn't fingerprint me.

Wednesday's newspaper said, "two suspects were questioned," one on Monday, the other on Tuesday (that was me). "After submitting to lie detector tests, they were released. There are now no solid leads in the case."

They buried the German at Tracy Cemetery with a stone that said, IST-VAN KONDRA BORN IN THE COUNTRY OF HUNGARY MAY 3, 1911 DIED IN MCDONALD COUNTY MO JAN 3, 1981.

His murder went unsolved for two years.

Twenty Three

Tom Henry

I went over to Bill Clapper to get help filing my income tax. He's in a wheel-chair, been crippled since he was twenty-one, and he's a Christian. Now, if you're a logger who wants to cheat on his tickets, you don't go to Bill Clapper. I remember when I showed him a bunch of gas receipts I'd made up he said, "Tom, if you used this much gas in your chainsaw, this state would look like Kansas!"

He told me he'd heard through the grapevine about me getting saved and talking at the church.

"I have to come and listen to you one of these times," he said.

"It's nothing, Bill," I said. "I just get up in front of a few friends and talk. You know how it is up at Bunker Hill Church."

"Well, I'm going to have to buzz up there." Then he invited me up to his church, Mt. Zion. He started bringing out religious material, said he knew I was going through a divorce, that Faith and me should get back together and it's all in the Lord's hands. I was getting twitchy, wanting to go, when he said something that made me not care if he kept me there all night.

"Faith was here four nights ago."

"What for?"

"She brought her income tax to get filed. I told her because you were still married last year it might be better if you filed jointly. But she said no, she'd file on her own and you'd want that too."

"Yeah, that's probably best."

"I gave her some books by Oliver Green."

"I doubt if she'll read them," I said.

"I believe she will, Tom, because I asked her to—and she has to come back for another appointment." He said they had a good talk and he told her she needed to give her life to God and He'd work things out for her. Then he brought out a marriage counseling tape. "I played this for her," he said.

I listened to it real close, thinking about Faith hearing this same tape.

Now, Bob Melton had already invited me up to Mt. Zion Church, but when Bill Clapper asked me too I thought I'd check it out. So the next Thursday night I went. After the service, Bob invited me over for dinner sometime, and I went.

"You may as well talk to this wall here as talk to Faith about needing the Lord," I said. "She won't pay no attention."

"I heard you were the same way," he said.

"You're wasting your time, Bob. I know Faith."

"Let me go and witness to her."

"She'll get madder than heck if she thinks I sent you."

"She knows you go to Bunker Hill Church, not Mt. Zion," he said. "She doesn't know any connection between you and me. My job is to go and talk to her. Your job is to pray."

He went once, twice, and kept on going. She started talking to him, about smoking cigarettes, about all kinds of things.

"What did she hit you with?" I asked him the next time I was over there. He laughed, but then I asked, "What did she tell you?"

"She told me some confidential things."

"Like what?"

"It was confidential."

"What do you mean confidential?" I said. "You're supposed to be my friend."

"I'm supposed to be someone you can count on to keep a secret, and I am." He told me she wasn't nothing like I told him. "She's polite and courteous and she's reading the things Bill Clapper gave her. Just keep praying for her."

So I went over to Bill Clapper's and asked him if Faith had been back yet. "I know she's reading your books, 'cause Bob Melton told me. Don't tell her I sent Bob to talk to her."

"If she asks me I'm not going to lie."

"Don't lie, just fib a little bit."

We was all praying for Faith at Bunker Hill Church, me keeping them posted on all the latest. I wanted to make sure they were praying for her 'cause I heard more reports from old Cheese-eyes about Faith running around and I wanted as many to pray as possible. I especially wanted Dan Mullin to pray for her. If anybody's prayers would work, his would.

I got up in front of the church but I didn't say nothing direct about Faith.

"I don't ask for much," I said. "But this one time, I'd like you all to pray for me, 'cause I'm going through a lot." And for about twenty-five minutes they all prayed for me. Not a soul got up till I did.

Two days later, my brother-in-law comes over and says, "Faith got her finger hurt real bad at work. Somebody drove an eight-penny nail into the wood railing of the steps at one of the houses she was working on, and when she jumped down her ring caught on it and it tore her finger up bad. They took her to Gravette Hospital and the doctor wants to amputate."

I knew Faith wouldn't want to see me in the hospital so I just went back home. I felt bad, thinking I'd just asked for all this prayer for her and look what happened. But I got to the verse about it being better to lose your eye and get into the kingdom of heaven,[34] and that made me feel some better.

If God was going to work in her life by this means, I wanted it. But I didn't want her to suffer.

Faith started praying to God about her finger. All her friends who was saved were telling her they were praying about her finger. I mentioned its progress at our church. They all prayed too, and on Friday I heard she wasn't going to lose her finger. So Sunday I told them at church, kind of like a progress report. Then Faith went over to Bill Clapper's to get more religious materials. Recuperating had given her time to read all those books and she wanted more.

Faith started talking to me. Before long she was staying for a few minutes each time she picked up Thomas.

༄

I took Thomas to church after I got saved. I'd take him right up to the altar with me and he'd start asking questions. I prayed out loud with Thomas every time we was about to eat and at bedtime, and I explained to Thomas what we were doing so he could pray too about Grandma, Grandpa, and about his mom and dad getting back together. And about Bonesy having plenty of squirrels and coons up in heaven.

I was raising Thomas to be a Christian. Plus I figured if just one time he'd stop before a meal and say, "Mommy, I have to bless the food like Daddy does," it would have a heck of an impact.

Faith had been sending Thomas to me with just one set of play clothes. Now she started sending him with nice clothes for church. I don't know where she got them, probably at a rummage sale or a yard sale, but he had a little suit, dress shoes and all.

---

34 Matthew 5: 29, 30

Pretty soon he was bringing back things he'd made at church and Faith would say, "What did you learn in church today?" He'd try to explain what the Sunday school teacher had taught him through the things they made.

I had also been using Thomas to find out about Faith. I'd ask him something, then I'd think about it, then a half-hour later I'd ask again, trying to get at it from a different angle.

"Dad, you asked me that before," he'd say. "Don't ask me that no more." When I saw how it was bothering him, I stopped.

✑

I was coming home from Edd and Ada's one night and as I pulled up I saw Faith's car parked right in front of my trailer. What right does she have to be here?

When I walked in, ready to chew her out, she was there sitting in the chair, not with the old sourpuss look but with a big smile spread all over her face.

I said, "What are you doing here?"

"You know," she said.

"No I don't, but tell me."

"Tom, it happened tonight." She stood up and her face was lit up. "I accepted Christ just an hour ago in my bedroom!"

"You did?" I hugged her. "Tell me how it happened. Sit down." But she couldn't sit down. She was too happy. She paced the floor while she told me she'd been reading those books and thinking about what Bob Melton and Bill Clapper had been telling her and noticing the change in my life and she'd decided to take Christ as her savior.

✑

The next night Faith watched for me to come home, then she drove across the road into my drive.

"Oh, you just got home? Why don't you come over and eat with us? It'll be good for Thomas to have you around."

"Okay." I went to Thomas in the car. "Give Dad a kiss, Thomas." He did. "Ask Mom if it's all right for you to come over there with me." It was, so I pulled him out of the car through the window and played with him while I cleaned up, then we went over together.

I had *The Open Bible* edition of the Bible now and Faith had that great big white one we bought years before at a garage sale because it had the family tree in it. She was using it, but she wasn't understanding it at all.

We ate supper, and she knows how much I like to drink coffee so she made me coffee afterward. It was like getting waited on at a restaurant. Napkins, forks, knives, all clean and in order, the meat nice and tender, a couple vegetables, a fancy coffee cup—one of those you can hardly get your finger in the loop—everything nice, clean, and cheerful.

Then I went out to my pickup and got my Bible and we started having a discussion about it. I marked a bunch of things in my Bible and left it with her. She liked it so much I had to buy her one to get mine back. That was the only gift I ever bought Faith that she really appreciated.

The next step was me taking one or two showers over at the Patterson's place. I was thinking of getting back together with Faith but I wasn't sure. I felt like the reason I wanted to get back with her wasn't that I really loved her, it was 'cause I was afraid of losing Thomas and I wanted to make sure no one took my place as his father.

It felt like I was back like when I first got down there—all alone. I had a lot of friends, but all my friends were married and I just didn't fit in with them anymore. I came home from work at night and my dogs barked and that was enough company for me. I was used to being alone, and even though I liked a woman's companionship, I didn't need it now like I did at first.

I told Faith, "You know how I am, and you know how my friends are. I always joke around, I ain't never had nothing for you, and I can't handle money even though I make more than most of these guys around here."

"I know you're not like everybody else, Tom, but if you were, I couldn't just love you, I'd have to love them all."

That got to me, that she had feelings for me.

She comes up and hugs me, then we start kissing. I do believe it was the first time she showed genuine love for me. Then we got more intimate and I wanted her to come into my trailer to make love, but she wanted me to come back to her house. I'm thinking if we go in the trailer I know we're going to make love, but if I follow her over to her house she might get out of the notion.

But we went over to her house and went to bed. The next night I come back for more, but now she's under conviction. She feels bad because we ain't legally married and we had sex.

"Faith, God's the one that joined us," I said. "Man divorced us. In God's eyes we're still married."

"You're just telling me these things to get me into bed, 'cause you know the Bible better than me," she said. "But that don't make it right."

We didn't have sex again until we got remarried, so I know when Jeremy was conceived.

We started going to Mt. Zion Church together. Bob Melton kept asking Faith when she was going to get baptized. She said she didn't understand about baptism and Bob showed her scripture passages. While she was reading the Bible, she ran across this verse about we're all going to get white robes in heaven,[35] so she didn't want to get baptized till she found a white robe.

We looked all over, but the stores we went in said they didn't have no white robes. We went to quite a few stores in Neosho and we finally found this white terrycloth robe. I don't remember what it cost, but we'd been looking so long I didn't care. We bought it.

Faith got baptized at Straight Up Rock in the creek. Bob Melton did it, and I still have some pictures of him holding his Bible there by the water. Afterwards we made that robe the official baptism robe for anyone needing to get baptized. And to make it even more official, Faith pinned one of these Jesus Saves pins on it. That got baptized too.

We kept on going to church for some time.

"You kids really need to get married," Bob Melton said.

"Yeah," I said, "my sex life depends on it."

So we made our wedding plans. I was kind of low on funds, so we went all around looking for rings. I don't have much patience with shopping. I can go to Wal-Mart on a Saturday morning and have two carts full and be on my way home before most women are halfway down the first aisle. We looked at one store in Anderson, then we went to Neosho and we found us a ring she liked. I couldn't afford it, so Faith drew the money out of her account.

We got a marriage license. I knew the clerk of the court in McDonald County and he was kidding me about trying it all over again.

"Well, it's just like my driver's license," I said. "I got to renew it every four years."

---

35 Revelation 6:11

"Oh, I thought you wanted a new marriage license," he said. "To renew an existing one you just go two doors down the hall."

❧

Our second wedding was real simple, but since we never really had a first wedding I guess it was fancy in comparison. For our second time we got married on a Thursday night in church. Our marriage was the service and Bob Melton preached from the book of Ruth—I still got it on tape. Boy, it was good! He told a story about this new preacher in this church who had a girlfriend and asked her to marry him. He told her, "There'll be one restriction on our marriage. I can't ask you to be first in my life. God has that place already. But will you be second?"

It was on point for us 'cause we already tried marriage once and it didn't work out. He was telling us if we just put God first in our lives, all the rest would work out for us.

And I really believe it would have.

❧

It was after that that Eunice Canter come from Texas and joined the Mt. Zion Church. The first few weeks she was there she was real nice, got in real good with the ladies there.

Then she started causing trouble. Every time Bob Melton spoke in church, she'd start an argument with him right after, real loud. She wanted us to get a new preacher.

She come over to my house one night at Christmas time with a present for Thomas, a truck that cost $40. Faith was thrilled. Eunice starts telling me all these highfalutin' things from the Bible, going through it faster than I can turn the pages.

All of a sudden she says, "Bob Melton made an advance toward my sixteen-year-old daughter."

Boy, that took me by surprise. "What did he do?" I said.

"He made an advance."

"What was it? Did he touch her or say what he wanted?"

"He just did something. I can't tell you what it is."

"Well, you got to tell me more than that before I'm going to help you get Bob kicked out of the church."

"Just believe me, he did something."

Eunice come over again a few days later, this time with details. By then she had the ladies in the church all worked up good. She'd told them when Bob hugged her daughter, which is the custom at Mt. Zion, he patted her on the butt.

"I'm going to do the right thing and confront Bob Melton," I said. "I'll go over there right now and see what he says."

"No, no, no, don't do that!"

"It's no more than right, Eunice," I said. "I don't know the Bible like you do, but I know if we got a problem in the church, someone should go to him instead of talking behind his back, then if he won't listen, two or three go to him, then if he still won't come to reason, the whole church has to do something."[36]

"At least give us a chance to talk about what we should do," she said. "Different ones at the church are concerned." She wanted for us to take a vote on it without him, then tell him he was out.

I knew that wasn't fair, so I went right over to his house.

 ﹏

"Bob, I got to talk to you about something private."

"There's nothing you can say to me you can't say to Sarah."

Sarah was just coming downstairs, so I told Bob, "I got something out in the pickup I want you to see," and we went out together.

"I figure you can tell Sarah if you want," I said, "but I wanted to leave it up to you. There's a problem you should know about."

Now he could see I was serious. "What problem?"

"Eunice says you patted her daughter on the butt when you hugged her. You always been a straight shooter, so I need to ask. Is it true?"

"It is most certainly *not* true," Bob said.

I told him what Eunice was saying, and while I was still talking, he ran into the house.

"Sarah! Come here!" And he told her. Boy, you talk about hot! He couldn't sit down talking about it. He wanted to go right over to Eunice's house and get her daughter to tell the truth.

---

36 He's paraphrasing Matthew 18:15-17

The next Sunday he preached one heck of a sermon. He said, "If Satan can't tear a church up from the outside, he tries it from the inside." He talked about people squabbling, just like the Children of Israel getting tired of the same old manna all the time. Boy, I'm going to tell you, he was riled up! And then he resigned, right there from the pulpit. Everyone was in shock.

∽

Eunice started running the services at Mt. Zion Church, and she come to my house and asked me to preach there. I turned her down.

"Are you sure the Lord hasn't called you to preach, and you're the one hindering the Spirit?" she says.

"Eunice, I feel real sorry about what happened to you as a child"—her father had raped her, we'd found out—"and I can't imagine how horrible that must of been. But you can't take it out on innocent men. I know how you broke up that church in Texas and how you got kicked out of another church and how you accused leading men in both those churches of moral sins." I didn't add that I knew she'd been to see a psychiatrist.

She didn't try to deny none of it.

"You're following a man," she kept saying. "You ought to be following Christ."

"I'm not following a man, but I do look up to him, and rightly so."

Now, when we found out them things about Eunice's past, I went to Bob.

"Why don't you tell people what you know about her? It's true. She's spreading rumors about you that ain't."

"You can't fight the Lord's battles with the devil's tactics," he said. I'll never forget that. It's good advice.

Eunice got some young guy to preach in the church. But he'd gone to seminary and he was educated, and he wasn't going to work for one third of the offering! Pretty soon the church didn't have nobody. Now, it's not even operating.

Bob started preaching at the Baptist church in Stella, a bigger church. He's still there, and Eunice has split up a Nazarene church. It's funny, 'cause she's a nice woman most of the time, just as sweet as can be. Flirty, too. When she talks to you she puts her hand on yours and laughs so sweet, but she's a snake, just waiting for you to make some kind of a move, then BAM, she's got you.

∽

Faith felt guilty about what she'd done with Otto and she got the idea God might punish her by making Jeremy be born with something wrong. While she was pregnant, she used to kneel down for an hour at a time and beg God to make Jeremy come out all right, not punish the baby for what she done. I prayed with her.

But once Jeremy was born Faith stopped needing me. Even before he was born she quit sleeping with me, so me and Thomas slept together—me and him got real close on account of that. After Jeremy was born, when I'd be playing with him or changing him, Thomas would get real jealous.

Not too long after Jeremy come, a friend says, "I hear your wife rented the old Carter house."

I didn't know what he was talking about but I acted like I knew about it. I didn't say nothing to Faith, just come home about three-thirty in the afternoon the next day knowing she didn't expect me till after dark. She had all her clothes in the back seat of her car and Deloris was there with Scotty and Becky's pickup.

I never said a word. I even helped them carry things out. I knew Faith wanted me to say something so she could get mouthy with me, but I just treated her nice. The whole second marriage I treated her real nice.

One wisecrack I did make, as she was about to drive off I called out, "You got supper made?"

Our second marriage was short but not sweet. I ain't sure what happened. I think Faith married me partly 'cause she got saved and now we had something in common, and partly 'cause Jeremy was on the way. But I think later she realized she liked her freedom better. I don't really know. We never talked about it.

Me being a suspect in the Kondra investigation probably didn't help.

Twenty Four

"Bob and Betty are coming for a visit," Tom Henry said one evening. They were headed to a craft show where they were going to sell Tom Henry's cards. The proceeds would go to his boys.

"Great!" I said. "Ask if I can interview them for the book."

I spent the rest of the evening writing a letter to Bob and Betty, introducing myself and naming the subjects I wanted to ask about. A week later I headed up to the visiting room for my first book interview, which lasted a couple of hours. By the time the basketball game aired that evening, I'd typed thirteen pages of notes.

"They're the most important Missouri witnesses because they knew you so well," I said after the game. "Especially since you lived with them after Canada. But not even you can line everybody up to come visit me one at a time. I've *got* to get out if I'm ever going to finish this book."

"When's your appeal going to be decided?"

"Any time now," I said. "They've had it six months."

∽

The very next day I received a letter from my mother, who wrote that Steve Vogel, the Bloomington radio journalist who was writing a book on my case, had been in touch with the court, and a decision was about to be issued. That was the good news. The bad news was that Vogel was trying to prepare her for a negative decision.

He turned out to be right. The appellate court affirmed the convictions, I learned from my Bloomington visitors a few days later. The decision had been unanimous.

"I just can't believe it." I said, pacing the cell. "Did they read the transcripts? Did they even look at the evidence? I can't believe it, I just can't."

"I'm sorry, Big Stuff."

He could have talked about the Illinois Supreme Court, or the U.S. Supreme Court, or the federal habeas corpus appeals—everyone in prison was familiar with these. But right then he had the wisdom just to say "I'm sorry" and let me sort through the crushing disappointment on my own.

The appellate court had been my best chance. Sure, I could appeal to the Illinois Supreme Court, but that court wasn't even obligated to hear the appeal. They could refuse, just as the U.S. Supreme Court could and often did.

At my sentencing hearing, the judge had ruled that the crime I'd been convicted of met all the requirements for the death penalty. He'd then proceeded to astonish the courtroom:

"I am not personally convinced that the defendant has been proven guilty beyond a reasonable doubt. I cannot in good conscience apply the sanction of death unless I have been convinced of his guilt beyond a reasonable doubt. I have not."

At the time, my lawyers were exultant about this bizarre ruling and its unusual rationale. They told me that besides keeping me off death row, the judge had given me a get-out-of-jail-free-eventually card. But now it occurred to me that had I been sentenced to death, my appeal would have gone directly to the Illinois Supreme Court, where I believed I'd have gotten a fairer shake than in the appellate court.

So if the Illinois Supreme Court accepted the appellate court's decision and refused to rehear the case, I'd be doomed because of a judge who had said I hadn't been proved guilty. If it weren't so tragic, it would be comical.

Just as these thoughts were circulating, Officer Alms stopped by to talk.

"East House is locked down," he said. "Someone threw a heated mixture of bleach and baby oil into a guard's face. His skin peeled right off his face and he may lose an eye."

When he was gone, I turned toward our cell bars.

"Thanks, Alms, for reminding me what kind of hellhole I'm stuck in for the rest of—" I stopped and turned to Tom Henry. "Sorry. I'm being selfish. This hellhole is home to both of us."

"No, Big Stuff, there's a huge difference," Tom Henry said. "I killed two people—I belong here. But you? Man, you don't belong! You got to get out of here. And I ain't just saying that 'cause of the book."

❧

"I got a call pass this morning for a phone call from my lawyer," I said the next evening. "He's going to appeal directly to the Illinois Supreme Court."

Just then the mail came, bringing each of us a letter. I looked up from mine with a wry smile.

"This is the wife of a friend of mine. He's a Christian, she's not. She writes, 'I think of you—I can't say pray for you—every day.' I like that—if I could get my Christian friends to stop praying, I might have a chance at justice."

But a Christian is a tough audience for a comedian who wants to mock Christianity.

"Sorry," I said. "That was a joke. I get frustrated sometimes."

Tom Henry held up his hands. "Did I say anything?"

"Let's just say your face was eloquent in condemning me."

"You keep mocking God, it's not my face that's going to be condemning you."

"Touché," I said.

♋

"Do you think dreams mean anything?" I asked Tom Henry out of the blue one morning.

"I don't know," he said. "In the Bible God talked to people through dreams. Like the king Daniel interpreted a dream for."

"Nebuchadnezzar?"

"Nebuchadnezzar, right. He first told the king the dream, then he interpreted it. If someone tells you what you dreamed, you got to believe him about the meaning."

"I think dreams are just random brain waves," I said. "But last night I had a dream I've had before—when I was in jail. I'm with my family and all five of us are walking down a street together, right down the middle, no cars, talking among ourselves and happy, and people on each side of the street are looking at us and saying, 'Look how he loves them. There's no way he killed them.'"

I paused to collect myself. Tom Henry remained silent.

"I mean, it's not logical, but that's my dream. And I had it again last night. I've been thinking about it all day."

We were quiet for a while.

"That brings me to something I've been thinking about, something I want to talk to you about," Tom Henry said. "I mean, *with* you about."

"Shoot."

"You sure this is a good time?"

"I'm as introspective today as I'll ever be, so yes, it's a good time."

"There you go again, college boy, hitting me with one of them four-sylla-ble words, making fun of my ed-u-ma-ca-tion—hey, that's five syllables! How do you like *that*?"

"I'm very impressed," I said, smiling for the first time that day, "but what was on your mind before your five-syllable thought?"

"Look, I seen you read book after book. You ace your college classes. You can do math in your head like me on a calculator. You got a good mind. Why don't you use it to help yourself?"

"You mean to study the law?"

"You don't need to study no law! Your lawyers know the law. What you need to do is what no one else can do like you can—shine your mind on your own case. I'm talking about the details—footprints, blood, wounds, fingerprints, stomach contents, the stuff they talked about at your trial."

"I don't know what I could do. I was there in court. I saw the evidence, I've read the transcripts, the reports—"

"The autopsy reports?"

"Well, no. I never—"

"Have you looked at the pictures?"

I flinched. I stared out of the bars and shook my head.

"Why not?" Tom Henry said.

"That's my wife. Those are my kids. Do you know how they died?" I shook my head again. "No!"

"That's what I'm saying. You ain't studied the actual crime you're in here for. Look, if I'm sure about anything after living with you for two years, I'm sure you didn't kill your family. That means somebody else did. There's got to be some detail, something no one caught. There's *got* to be! And you need to figure out what it is."

"I appreciate what you're saying, but how can I do that?"

"Let me put it this way, Big Stuff." He pointed at me. "How can you *not*?" He let that sink in for a minute.

"Look," he said, "if a bear's charging at me in the woods and I got a stick and a high-powered rifle, I'd use the rifle! You got the State of Illinois against you, with all their attorneys, prosecutors, police, investigators. They even pay the judge! You got one lawyer and he's got other clients. You think he stays awake at night thinking about your case?

"You can avoid the hurt and rot in prison or you can study up on your case. Choose your pain. The answer—something that proves your innocence—will be in the evidence. The blood, the wounds, the stomach contents, the time of arrival or departure, details, facts you can analyze."

"What you're saying makes sense. But how—"

"Why don't you let me start it? I'll read your transcripts, look at the pictures, study the reports. Maybe I can point you in a direction. But then you're going to have to apply your brain. God gave you a good one. Use it."

∽

That conversation was an epiphany for me. In the days to come I decided on a two-pronged attack. I'd apply my own mind to my own case, but that wasn't all I'd do.

Ever since my first visit to my business lawyer, before my arrest, I'd been advised to keep my mouth shut and not talk to the press—"If you talk to them they'll only hurt you." When I'd spoken into to a camera—in a fog, just hours after being told my family had been murdered—I'd repeated what my church friends had been whispering in my ear: my family was better off in heaven now with Jesus. Viewers thought I must be guilty—or at least crazy.

It was true the media had done me no good. But as I thought about it, I realized they could only repeat what they were told, and for the most part only the prosecutor and police had talked to them. And what did I have to lose? I was already locked in prison for the rest of my life.

So I decided that not only would I agree to be interviewed by the media, I'd invite them to talk to me. And research the evidence in my case with Tom Henry's help.

He was as good as his word. He read some of my voluminous transcripts, paying particular attention to the scientific evidence: fingerprints, footprints, blood, stomach contents—autopsy stuff. I didn't wait for him to finish his research. I started my own. We compared notes and collaborated. I didn't really have any illusions we'd discover anything new, but I was grateful just for the hope the process gave me.

∽

"I got something, Big Stuff!"

I was on my way back from the yard, not even inside the cell yet. The guard locked us up and left.

"Okay," Tom Henry said, starting right in. "So the state's expert says the children died about nine that night, but Susie come home about ten-forty, and you left the house before midnight to drive all night to start sales calls in the morning, right?"

"Right."

"Now, I got to ask—didn't the fact you left at midnight to drive through the night make the police suspicious? How'd you explain that?"

"I'm sure it made them suspicious, but I never had to explain it because they asked around and everyone told them that was my pattern. Sometimes when I couldn't sleep I'd stay awake all night, so I'd go to the office and work to make the time useful. Susie used to laugh at me."

"I notice you have weird sleep patterns," Tom Henry said.

"This from a guy who stays up almost every night?"

"But then I sleep in the day."

"Yeah, we're a couple of nuts. But let's keep that secret to ourselves."

"Meanwhile, back at the ranch," Tom Henry said, "we know the kids were alive when Susie came home, 'cause there's no way she would of gone to bed without checking on them."

"*We* know that, but other people don't know that."

"A mother of three children comes home and don't tuck them in?"

"It's obvious but it's not proof."

"Okay, but let's at least agree *we* know, so we'll start with it's a fact the children were alive when Susie got home."

"Oh yes, it's a fact."

"Which means she was killed first."

"Well, I'm not sure that follows, logically. You're trying to *prove* something here. That the children were alive when she arrived home doesn't prove she was killed first."

"Okay, then let's start with this—it does prove the state's expert witness, Dr. Baden, was wrong. If the kids was alive at eleven, they can't of been dead by nine."

"Right. Susie arriving home with the children still alive would prove Baden wrong."

"Okay," Tom Henry said. "So it's up to us to prove Susie was killed first. That's what I done! My proof is in the hair."

"The hair?"

"The hair. If your children got killed before Susie come home, then why weren't there no hairs from the children on Susie?"

"Well, let me play devil's advocate," I said. "The murderer could have killed the children, then cleaned the axe before killing Susie."

"But there's hairs from your children on the axe. If the children was killed first, some of the hairs on the murder weapon would of come off when it crashed down on Susie's head …" He saw the look on my face. "Sorry to talk like this, but—"

"No, I signed up for it."

"The point is, there ain't no children's hairs on Susie."

"Again, the murderer could have cleaned the axe," I said.

"No, he couldn't. Because the children's hairs *are* on the axe—just not on Susie."

"Well, he could have gathered them up and put them there."

"Aha! That's what I been waiting for you to say!"

Tom Henry looked like he'd just won the lottery, and his excitement was contagious. He set his coffee down.

"Now we come to what I got," he said. "Remember, I ain't only a hunter, I'm a trapper. I know animal hair. And human hair is like animal hair, it's hollow inside. Now, I seen hairs on my hatchet, and an axe don't cut hair— it smashes it. So the end is smashed flat and stuck to the hatchet with that smashed end right by the edge. There's no way you could place the hair like that. Any expert could see the difference between a hair cut off and placed on an axe and a hair that got on the axe from a blow to the head. They wouldn't even need to magnify it.

"And remember, there ain't just hair on the axe, there's blood. That's how the hairs stick to it. I seen hairs and blood on my hatchet many times. No way you could place hairs there with your hand and make it look the same as if it got there from the hatchet's blow."

I shook my head as I took in the implications of what he was saying.

"Do you know I paid those useless lawyers over half a million dollars, and they never noticed this?"

"Right. Susie was killed first," Tom Henry said. "The rest is easy. Baden was way wrong about the children being killed by nine. Susie eats raw vegetables around nine-thirty, and raw vegetables takes a long time to digest according to all the experts, and she didn't have nothing in her stomach at the time of her death.

"Now, if you killed her she had to die before midnight—well, earlier than that 'cause you'd have to clean up and everything, so let's say eleven-thirty. That's two hours after she ate raw vegetables, so what I'm saying is I didn't just find proof you didn't kill them, I found proof you *couldn't* of killed them. So, that'll be half a million for me!"

"Let me tell you, what you've found is worth more than that—the bums who were paid that much got me convicted." My grin was as big as Tom Henry's.

"And, remember, that's not even mentioning the unidentified footprint in your house or that it was probably two murderers or that Grace never ate mushrooms and mushrooms showed up in her stomach contents, showing someone tampered with them. So you got a great chance if you win a retrial."

I couldn't sleep a wink that night.

༄

Now that I had a story to tell, I reached out to the media. Several journalists soon contacted the prison asking for an interview, and one was set up.

The night before, I stayed in from supper to type out my notes. At supper Tom Henry told Cat Man, a sharp old con who'd been in and out of the joint his whole life, about my interview. After supper he stopped by the cell where I was typing.

"Dude! Did the press help you when you got arrested?" Cat Man said. "They're no good. They only want to hang you. When they get here tomorrow, tell them, 'Hell with you! Go home!' You give that interview, I guarantee you not two nice words will be printed."

I thanked him for his concerns and kept typing.

The next morning I was summoned to the Guard Hall. The journalists arrived about nine fifteen. Two girls with 35 millimeter cameras, one man with a TV camera, two newspaper writers, one TV reporter, and the radio journalist Steve Vogel who was writing a book about me—so far I'd refused to speak with him.

They started by taking pictures of me in the library (Cat Man worked there—he held a newspaper over his head), then the school building, then my cell. Tom Henry was there, so one of the reporters latched onto him. Tom Henry was answering questions about me at high speed and the reporter's pen was flying.

"What kind of batteries does that pen use?" Tom Henry asked. Before the surprised reporter could respond, he resumed his torrent of words.

After that we returned to the assistant warden's office, where the cameras and recorders were ready. I began my spiel.

I explained why the prosecution expert's "proof" was so unlikely. I walked them through Tom Henry's observations about the hair and stomach contents. I spoke about our suspect in the murders, ticking off the evidence against him.

I talked for well over an hour.

❦

I was back in the cell before Tom Henry returned from lunch.

"You were the topic of discussion," he said. "Rick in electronics said you'll be just like another guy here who was innocent. When all his appeals run out, after six and a half years, he killed himself. Rick said all real intelligent people are like that—they can't handle it. They snap."

"Did he have anything useful to say?"

"He advised me not to be your cellmate when that happens."

A couple of days later when the newspapers arrived in the library with stories of my interview, Cat Man showed up again at our cell.

"I don't mind saying it, Hendricks. I was wrong. Don't know how you pulled it off, but you got some damn fine coverage out of those reporters—and one of those reporters was damn fine herself."

❦

Tom Henry was approved as a printer, and soon after that I became a reporter for the prison newspaper, the *Menard Time*, the office of which was housed in the basement of the school building along with the print shop. This allowed Tom Henry and me to both cell together and work together, thus further facilitating our book project.

A few days later I was detained for an attorney phone call. My lawyer was disturbed that I was talking to the media.

"It's just not a good idea, David. You have no control over what they'll write. Say they want to write something you never said. What are you going to do? You're a convicted murderer. You've got no credibility. Let us handle your legal case through the legal system."

Yeah, and look at how well the legal system has done so far!

"Thanks for your advice," I said. "I'm not forgetting how important your work is. I just want to add my two cents."

"Well, I can't stop you, but I hope you'll consider how foolish it would be to antagonize the state's attorney," he said.

A few months later I got another call from my attorney's office, but this time it was from his assistant. I picked up the phone in the Print Shop and she came on.

"Are you sitting down?"

I slumped into the chair. The Illinois Supreme Court must have decided not to—

"They're going to hear your case!"

I was too excited to concentrate after the call so I took a shower and returned to my cell.

"Great news!" Tom Henry said. "Guess that means we better finish my story. We're getting close. This chapter will be called 'Canada.'"

Twenty Five

Tom Henry

I met Steve Slater when I was driving home from work one evening. He was hitchhiking, looking to go to Arkansas, about ten miles up the road.

"I'm not going that far," I said, "but you look hungry. You had anything to eat?"

"No, but a cup of coffee'd be just fine."

I turned around at the bottom of the hill and we went back to the truck stop.

"Order whatever you want," I said.

After we ate, we shot pool in the back room. I noticed he carried his Army duffel bag with him from one room to the other. When he was bending over for one of those hard-to-reach shots, his pants leg come up and I saw a knife sheath on the side of his boot.

We stayed up there until about seven-thirty.

"Well, by golly, it's already dark," I said. "You might as well sleep at my house, 'cause nighttime you don't want to be on the highway. I'll take you to Arkansas in the morning." At the time, I was logging near Arkansas.

So he came home with me and I was showing him my mounted deer heads and my shell reloading stuff.

"I always wanted to know how to reload them shells," he said.

"Well here's how," I said, and I showed him how it was done.

I never did take him to Arkansas. He started spotlighting with me, coon hunting, loading shells. I noticed Steve was pretty good in the woods. He said he'd traveled all over the country with the carnival.

I told him about my dream of hunting big game.

"I've shot me hundreds of deer," I said, "but can you imagine the feeling of shooting a bear, or a moose?" He told me about going to Colorado, staying in a cabin and catching trout in the mountain streams, and about the snow up there.

"I know a place neither of us has been," I said. "Canada! I know hunting and trapping, you know cold and snow, you got no wife and mine's divorcing me. And Canada's got bears!"

౷

There was another reason I wanted to leave: the law was trying to serve a subpoena for my divorce. I couldn't let that happen—now I was saved, no way was I going to place my hand on the Bible and swear to tell the truth "so help me God," then say my name is Thomas Charles Elliott!

So we started getting ready for Canada. We cleaned out my house and fields, got rid of all the junk I collected over the years. We took seven pickup loads to the sale and spent that money on supplies and camping gear.

Old John Carter, the process server, couldn't get to me at work, 'cause I was working across the state line. He tried to get me at the house, but I avoided him there and I didn't never go to town. Instead I sent Steve to pay my bills and cash my checks. To pay my bills, I signed blank checks and Steve filled them out.

My friends didn't like Steve. They asked me why I was hanging around with him.

"Don't go with him," Phil said. "He's got evil eyes."

I did notice Steve was wary of the law, just like me. I knew why I was, but why was he?

❦

Steve was in a big hurry to get going, so we started our trip early in September. Our first stop was the Longview Bank. My account still had about $1,400, so I wrote a check out for that, cashed it, and we took off.

At the Canadian Port of Entry at Emerson, the guy told us to pull over to the right and unload the pickup so they could search it. They finally said, "Okay" and gave me this little piece of paper to carry in my billfold.

We drove about eight miles before we saw a restaurant on the left with a little sign, "Cafe." I wasn't really hungry, just relieved about making it across safe, but I couldn't tell Steve that.

What a place! They had a mounted mallard duck, a goose, a bear head, and even more in this other room you had to unhook a velvet rope to get into. You had to go through that room to use the restroom. I went twice, just to look at the elk and moose paintings.

Boy, I've come to the right place!

❦

A couple miles down the road we picked up two girls hitchhiking.

"Can we sit together by the door?" one of them asked.

"Heck yeah," I said, "I won't ride next to no strangers!"

Me and Steve was laughing.

"You don't want to ride in the camper," I said, "'cause I only fastened it with c-clamps." So Steve slid over and they got in.

"We were at a party and the guys were trying to get fresh," they said, "so we took off."

"I'm just a bojacker[37] coming up to hunt and fish and trap," I said. "Lucky we stopped at that restaurant or we wouldn't never of met you."

"I got an apartment in Winnipeg," the girl called Lucy said. "That's the next town."

"We ain't going to Winnipeg."

"You have to go through it," she said.

When we got to her apartment, Lucy cooked us something to eat.

"I have friends who can tell you all about the bush country," she said.

The next afternoon me and Lucy and Steve went to this fancy sports bar with big-screen TVs. A lady named Lorraine who knew Lucy came over to our table and ended up coming back to Lucy's apartment with us.

Steve and Lucy seemed to be hitting it off—he even kind of took to her baby—so about eight that evening I took Lorraine out for supper to a restaurant six blocks away. Lorraine had long coal-black hair, a thin face and slender figure, thirty-nine and divorced. She was a lobbyist for poor people at parliament. Her job was talking and she was good at it!

When me and Steve took off, we didn't tell either of the ladies we was leaving. We didn't find out till later the feelings we left behind us.

༺

We stopped at a store in Vermilion Bay run by a helpful old lady and we stocked up on the supplies she recommended.

The last town on our way north was Red Lake, where we first met Eskimos. They look like barrels with arms, legs, and a head, plus huge smiles that show a mouth full of stained teeth, friendly as heck.[38] They told us about Stormer Wilderness, a log-cabin store an old bachelor Indian tended.

When we got there, he said the road only went a hundred miles farther north.

---

37 A southern term for a hillbilly.

38 The Indians Tom Henry calls Eskimos are actually Pikangikums, a tribe of the Ojibwe Indians. Eskimos live 300 miles further north.

"Is that all?" I said.

He looked at me kind of funny. "How much farther you want to go?"

"I want to get me a bear."

"There are bear, moose, fish, beaver, foxes right here. Why you want to go further?"

"I want to go where no people are."

He laughed. "You don't want to go there!" He shrugged like, you're crazy but it's none of my business. "You can drive a hundred miles to a bridge, but the bridge is destroyed. Leave your pickup there, no one will bother it."

We drove the truck to the bridge and watched an Eskimo paddle by.

"I thought we were going where no people are," Steve said.

"We ain't there yet."

We loaded the canoe for the first of four trips, about three hours each way. We took the first load that night, hid the stuff, came back. By then it was dark, so we slept in the tent. We made three trips the next day and the last trip was one way. It was an awful lot of work, moving everything in a canoe.

Now we had to decide where to build a cabin. The closer we settled to a trading post the easier it would be to trade but we'd also be closer to people, and the best hunting and trapping was where there weren't no people.

We found an area on the map that would take about four more moves, maybe ten miles each move. Each move would take two days. We started out with our first load, but after about four miles as we came around the bend we spotted the perfect cabin site. We landed our canoe and walked around, had to climb up the rocks on the face side to get to it.

We built the cabin there about sixty feet above the water. It took us three weeks.

෧෯

The canoe is the best way to travel in that part of Canada. You can see a lot more animals than walking, 'cause a canoe makes very little noise and there's no foliage on the water. And you can paddle right up to things. You can look into the roots of trees, where the water has eroded the soil, and see the dens of mink, otter, muskrat, beavers.

We ate mostly meat and we didn't fry too much, 'cause most of the food we brought up with us like rice and potatoes and beans was all dried so we had to boil water anyway. We boiled the meat right on the bones, then when it was tender we scraped it off and mixed it in with the rice.

I started to think how I was going to get my bear. We hadn't seen none yet 'cause we hunted during the day and bears come out at night. One day we made a set with buried ducks, and two days later the whole place was tore up. No hair in the trap, but tracks and claw marks all around. A bear had to of done that.

I told Steve, "That's how we're going to get us a bear!" We didn't set a trap, we just buried the bait, then about two hours before daybreak the next day we paddled the canoe across from where we buried the meat. We turned the canoe over on the bank and leaned against our backpacks, eating peanuts and waiting for our bear.

We heard a noise, not any big cracking noise like a bear might make but a rustling like a deer coming through the woods or the brushing noise you make when you're walking through a cornfield or—

But it was a bear, and when I saw it I didn't know what to do. Should I shoot now or watch?

I decided to watch. I had this fellow in my rifle scope, sniffing, putting his paws on the feathers in the meat and pulling it up with his mouth, kind of tearing it. I watched for a while, then shot him once in the base of the shoulders. He goes down and twitches his feet a couple times and that was all there was to it!

Steve paddled and I kept the gun pointed. We get out and walk up to the bear, and—oh, boy, what a feeling! I carefully poked with the end of my gun barrel and there wasn't no movement.

There was no way we could carry him, 'cause he must of weighed 250 pounds. I'd say he was about five foot tall. We skinned him—without his hide he looked just like a short, heavy-set man—cut him up and quartered him right on the bank.

"I ought to clean out the skull and put it on my head like the Indians do on TV," I said. "I wish the people from Missouri could see me now!"

∽

It was getting cold. The only good thing about the cold was that after the first frost there wasn't no more dang mosquitoes, no more grease on our faces, no more constant buzzing by our ears. With the cold coming we decided to make a last trip to the trading post. We had plenty of furs to trade and we needed supplies for the winter.

We got out our map and headed for the trading post, and on the third day of canoeing we found it, but it was shut down for the winter.

Talk about disappointed! And what about our supplies?

We'd figured on sleeping in our tent by the trading post until the plane brought our stuff, so we'd been eating up our best food, our chocolate bars, granola bars—we thought we were going to get more. Now everything was changed. We wouldn't starve to death, but you get tired of eating meat and meat and meat. You need variety. And look how fast this winter's coming in on us! How long will it last?

⚃❧

One evening we're sitting outside the cabin door, close to the fire. We finish eating and are heating up some water for coffee by hanging it over the fire with an s-hook.

"For the first time in my life I'd rather have food than money," I say. "I'd of taken any price for them hides 'cause we can always get more."

"Damn it! Damn it!" Steve says.

"Just think about someone finding our skeletons. That'll help you survive!" Steve doesn't smile.

"Nothing's ever been right my whole life," he says. "I was treated like shit as a kid, my dad left when I was young, I fought with my stepdad and my mom sided with him, then in Vietnam and even after—it's all been shit."

He has his gun in his hands, cleaning it while he talks.

"I killed in 'Nam, and I found out it don't bother me to kill." He reloads the gun and he's rubbing the outside of it with his oil-soaked chamois rag. "It don't bother me to kill. I didn't just kill in the service, I killed in civilian life too. I'm not just a soldier, I'm a murderer. In fact, I'm wanted by the law. That's why I came up here with you."

He lifts his head to look at me.

"And now you know too."

Is he really thinking about shooting me? I remember Phil telling me I shouldn't go with him, he has evil eyes.

"Look, Steve," I said, "I ain't had a good life myself. I'm going through a divorce, I'm up here away from my kids, I think about them all the time. Bet you think about Lucy back in Winnipeg and that little baby."

He don't say nothing but his face softens a little bit.

"Heck, it's rough up here," I said, "but we're going to make it. We'll get out of here and go logging or work on the oil rigs somewhere. We'll make it! Right now it's rough, but just think, if we keep trapping, in the spring when we go back into town, look at the money we'll have.

"Think of the fun we can have with that money. We can go back to Winnipeg and look up Lucy and her baby. But you know full well the only way we'll ever get out of here alive is if both of us work together. Neither of us could make it out of here by hisself. We need each other."

I've got my gun in the holster, but there's a piece of leather holding it in. No way I can slide my hand down to unlatch the holster. He'd notice.

Now, I'm drinking coffee and smoking my pipe. I'm thinking I'll drink this cup real quick and when I grab the next cup I can throw the boiling water in his face.

But I know deep down that if he wants to shoot me, I'm dead. I was right about us needing each other to survive, though. And whatever Steve is, he ain't stupid.

෨

The snow was getting deep and it was hard to walk around and so we needed snow shoes to get through the winter. That's when we thought about the Indians—we saw them once, planting fir trees. They had children with them so they must live near there.

We packed some jeans, a little money, and a few things to trade, then we canoed to where they lived. We expected to see wigwams but what we saw was six houses. There were thirty people in the village, and Buckeye was the one we talked to. He was a little taller than me and a little heavier, a real likable guy with black hair cut straight all the way around about earlobe level.

"The trading post was closed," I told him, "but we need some stuff before winter sets in. Can you help us?"

We got two sets of Bear Paw snow shoes, a bunch of pressed fruit and wild rice, some beef jerky, and flour. We gave him all our pelts, six pairs of blue jeans, two pairs of sunglasses, a Swiss army knife, and some money.

෨

The Indian girls are cute as buttons when they're young but uglier than sin by the time most of them reach thirty. When they talk to you, their breath stinks. That's from tanning their hides—they bite on them to soften them. They're real friendly, though, and if I ever decided to stay I don't think it would be any trouble to persuade one of them to become my wife.

It's real lonesome up there. Two men together who ain't homosexual just don't cut it. You might not think about it until you go to an Indian village and see women, but when you see them in their buckskin outfits with their smiles, that sparkle in their eyes, it does something to you. They got wide hips, big butts, small breasts—hard to tell 'cause they don't wear bras—and they wear long-sleeve men's flannel shirts and light red cotton underwear you can see 'cause it hangs out longer than their skirts.

◦◦

We made it back to the cabin, but it was getting so cold we had to pile on all the clothes we could—our thickest gloves, our warmest coats, face masks to keep our cheeks from freezing, and we had to carry Sterno with us. It got to where it was near impossible to tend our trap lines. In the snow we had to be real careful walking up and down hills, especially when we was alone, so we didn't slip and break an arm. We teamed up when we went very far from the cabin and we always went together in the canoe.

We're drinking coffee and talking one night about how we'd like to get the heck out of here and how there are a lot better places to be and how much snow is outside and how cold it is and how we can't even trap or hunt and how we never realized it could get this cold and heck, it was just November!

I'm thinking about Thomas and Jeremy.

"Sure would be nice to see the girls in Winnipeg," I said. "We could sell our traps, I could sell my canoe, maybe a gun or two."

"I'm ready to get the hell out of here," Steve said.

The next day we paddled down to where we left the pickup. We cut blocks of wood and put the Sterno can on them and heated up the engine oil. We squirted lighter fluid in the carburetor, pumped the gas a few times, cranked it, and the truck started. We're happier than heck to go, even with the snow and ruts on the road.

We drove back real careful.

◦◦

When Lucy opened the door and saw Steve, boy, her eyes lit up! We took hot showers, shaved, cleaned with soap. I went downstairs to wash our clothes.

After putting the first load in the washer, I came back upstairs and there's Lorraine.

She laughed at me for going up there this time of year.

"We built that cabin like I said we would," I said. "We did some trapping—and I got me a bear ..."

Steve and Lucy became lovers. I slept alone on a big throw rug.

Lucy and Lorraine tried to talk us into staying and getting jobs there, but I missed my boys too much. Steve talked Lucy into coming back to the states with him.

We sold our furs and my guns, except EF Hutton, then we decided to take off—me and Steve and Lucy and her baby.

ᢙ

We drove to the border at the Emerson port of entry.

"Do you have anything you want to declare?"

"No."

They looked at my driver's license, ran it on their machine, looked through the back of my pickup, told us to get out, pulled my defroster hose down, and looked behind the seat—that's where they found the bear hide. Since I hadn't declared it and didn't have a hunting license, they told us to follow this guy back to Winnipeg.

He led us to the jail. The bear hide is what got me caught, but what they charged me with was selling guns without a license. The guy I sold them to said he got them from two Americans in an old pickup with a topper. They took me downstairs where they had this machine with glass and a blue light. I put my hands on it and it made a kind of ding, and that was that—they had my prints.

It happened so fast. All these years I made sure never to get fingerprinted, never to even have my picture taken. People down home said I was camera-shy. Now a blue light shines and a little bell dings and they got me. If this was the U.S. the fingerprints would tell them my real identity, and that's all she wrote. Lucky for me this is Canada.

So I decided the best thing to do was sneak back to the U.S. and never go to Canada again. I could only hope Canada and the U.S. don't have no kind of fingerprint exchange. I'm too old to start a third life somewhere else and I'm not about to leave Thomas and Jeremy the way I left Winkie.

All I could do was hope and pray—and think about the fact that the duty on that bear hide would of been about twenty bucks.

෧෨

They come in and questioned me like I was some kind of terrorist. I told them how we hunted and trapped and built a cabin, and how cold it got up there, and how we decided to leave, and here we were. At first they were skeptical, but pretty soon they realized I was telling the truth and they seemed to relax and enjoy the story.

They held me on the weapons charge and I signed a release to allow Steve to take the pickup away. My bond was $150. I had the money, but it was too late that day so I bonded out the next morning.

I asked around, talked to different guys. "How can you get across the U.S. border without going through the port of entry?" They told me about a port of entry above Bismarck that's closed from one o'clock to five in the morning.

We took off the next night and drove through there with no problem.

Twenty Six

"Mail!" The guard pushed a few letters through the food slot. Tom Henry stepped up to take them.

"Thanks, officer." He looked down at the top one and froze. "It's from Winkie."

His hand shook as he opened the envelope, then he started reading and in a minute he was smiling big. It was a newsy letter with details about her and the love of her life, along with a picture of them. She attributed her long delay in writing to her residence in Canada, and while she didn't end the letter by calling him Dad or saying she loved him, she did end with a casual, affectionate, "Take care."

That was all Tom Henry needed.

෴

For the last few months I'd been trying to orchestrate the help of my family and Susie's family in my publicity campaign. At last, their efforts had borne fruit. Susie's brother told me that New York journalist Jimmy Breslin, who had recently launched the TV show *Jimmy Breslin's People*, wanted to do my story.

"That show's national," Tom Henry said. "It goes good, even bigger ones might be interested."

The morning Breslin was due a guard unlocked the door at eight forty-five.

"Hendricks! They want you in the Guard Hall by nine."

The interview didn't get under way until ten. I watched Jimmy Breslin come in through the double doors, look up and around, observe the technique by which one door was secured before the other was opened. The TV camera was set up and Breslin got going with me.

"I don't have a good feeling about it," I told Tom Henry as soon as I was returned to our cell.

"What went wrong?"

"Nothing went wrong—he just didn't seem interested. He's a renowned investigative journalist. You'd think he'd be all over the details. But he was tired and kind of out of it, to tell you the truth. I'm an American citizen who committed no crime and I'm locked up in a maximum security prison for the rest of my life after losing my family to a vicious murderer who's still out there. That's the story, and I don't think he gets it."

On a Thursday three weeks after the interview *Jimmy Breslin's People* aired my story. It wasn't negative, but it was short and superficial. It started at 1:05 a.m. and ran for 10 minutes. It offered no opinion. Here's what the prosecutor says, here's what Hendricks says. We'll never know the truth.

∽

I hurried to the Guard Hall one morning to see Jerry, Liz, and family. Liz and Susie were sisters, close in age and closer in relationship. My two little nieces monopolized my lap. We discussed the Illinois Supreme Court.

"The oral arguments went well," Jerry said. "Our lawyer seemed very earnest and the justices grilled the state's lawyers rather than ours."

Of course I told Tom Henry what he'd said.

"Maybe something good's going to happen to you for a change,"

"I hope so."

"Which reminds me of something I been thinking about," Tom Henry said. "This might seem a little gross, but check it out. If you get a new trial, I think you need to put on a hair and blood demonstration, maybe with a real fresh-killed animal."

"You mean strike an animal with an axe to show the jury the way the hair and blood smear onto it?" I said. "That seems, well, more than a *little* gross!"

"Obviously *you* can't do it, and your lawyer can't neither. But an 'expert' could do it. And that expert would be cheap—any trapper will do. He can't kill the animal in front of the jury, but if he brings one in that's fresh killed …"

"I'll just put in a request to have that famous hunter and trapper Tom Elliott furloughed from prison to conduct the demonstration."

"Mock me if you want, but it ain't a bad idea."

It was a bad idea, but the principle was good because it was graphic. You aren't just giving the jury a story and leaving them to form their own mental image—you're giving them your image to go with your story. I wondered if we could show photos or maybe even a chart. Thanks again, Tom Henry!

∽

A few weeks later I opened a letter from my lawyer.

"He assures me I'll be retried if the Illinois Supreme Court grants a remand," I said.

"Isn't a remand an order for a retrial?"

"Well, that's usually what happens, but remand just means to send back. They're sending my case back to the state's attorney. It's his decision whether to retry me or not, just like it was his decision to try me originally."

About a month later, I received a letter from my mom.

"Steve Vogel told her the Illinois Supreme Court's decision will issue within the next two weeks," I said. "He saw my name on their advisory. She writes, quote, 'Vogel told me an early decision usually bodes ill for the petitioner, but it may not be so in your case.'"

What turned out not to be so was a decision's being issued in two weeks.

∽

A shadow darkened the bars and we looked out to see Sergeant Sampson with a plate of fresh fruit covered in cellophane.

"You guys want some fruit?"

"Is the Pope Catholic?" Tom Henry scooted to the front to take it. "Thanks." Fresh fruit was very hard to come by because inmates stole it to make hooch.

Sergeant Sampson wanted to gossip. "You hear about Mark and Fang in 23?"

"No. What's up?"

"Last night I caught them rubbing each other with baby oil."

We chuckled about it.

When Sampson was about to leave, Tom Henry said, "Sergeant, why don't you stop back by in half an hour or so?"

"Why? What you got up your sleeve?"

Tom Henry drew himself up to his full height, put on his most serious face, and said, "If I tell you, I'll have to kill you."

Sergeant Sampson left laughing, but he was back half an hour later. Tom Henry handed him a sign and some masking tape. The sign said:

Powder and Oil Massage.
Above the waist, one pack.
Below the waist, three packs.

In early December, Tom Henry looked up from a letter he was reading.

"It's from Rosie," he said. "I'm a grandfather!" Winkie had called Rosie and told her to tell him. He returned to his letter and after a minute looked up again with watery eyes.

"It's a girl," he said. "I have a granddaughter."

∽

In mid-December another letter arrived from my mother. She wrote that my case was scheduled for an opinion to issue on December 21. That day I got up at seven-thirty, wrote out the phone numbers to Vogel and Holliday—two journalists I'd promised to call when the decision issued—and went to the yard on my running card just before nine. I paid a gang-banger for a phone call.

"They confirmed it," were the first words I heard.

The Illinois Supreme Court had confirmed the denial of my appeal by the Fourth District appellate court. More simply, I'd rot in prison.

Christmas in prison is never easy. That Christmas was the worst of my life.

∽

In January I was summoned to the Guard Hall for an attorney phone call.

"What steps can I take from here?" I asked my lawyer.

"First," he said, "I plan to file a petition for a rehearing with the Illinois Supreme Court. When they deny that, it'll go to the U.S. Supreme Court and then, assuming they decline to hear it, to a federal court on a habeas corpus petition."

"What are my chances?"

"David, I'm not going to lie to you," he said. "They're not good."

∽

If the courts weren't going to help me, then I'd redouble my efforts in the media.

Inside Edition expressed an interest in my case. I gave them the information they asked for in a phone call, and they were encouraging. A few nights later, I called my mom.

"*Inside Edition* decided not to do your story," she said.

"Why not?"

"They asked the investigator for the names of the models you slept with, and he told them you didn't sleep with any models. They lost interest."

❧

Later that month, two pieces of news arrived in the mail. The first was a typed note from the warden's secretary.

"The petition for rehearing was granted," I told Tom Henry. "The state is ordered to file a brief in twenty-one days."

"That's great news. Didn't you say there was no hope for that?"

"I didn't expect it," I said. "That same court just ruled against me."

"Something must of caught their attention."

The other interesting piece of mail that night was the Bloomington *Pantagraph* newspaper, with a review of Steve Vogel's book, *Reasonable Doubt.*

"It says Vogel thinks I'm probably innocent," I said. "Hey, check this out! Vogel thinks Susie was killed before the children. I wonder if he figured that out by the hair and blood, like you did."

"I doubt it," Tom Henry said. "He's not a hunter or trapper, is he?"

"Probably just realized how unlikely it would be for Susie to come home and go to bed without checking on her kids."

❧

December brought a letter from my mother.

"Mom says *Inside Edition* is interested again," I said.

"That's good news," Tom Henry said. "They're not just national, they're big."

"Yeah, but all they care about is the sleaze, remember?"

"What've you got to lose? Anyway, you said yourself, 'in for a penny, in for a pound.'"

The *Inside Edition* interview was the last Thursday in January. Jeff Cole asked me to talk about my family, but when I started describing Becky's long pigtails I broke down and couldn't stop crying. It took me a while to compose myself.

I felt bad for Cole because I thought I was wasting his time, but he was pleased. My emotion gave him the drama he needed.

The *Inside Edition* broadcast wasn't just a success—it turned the tide of public opinion. Over the next days I heard nothing but positive reactions from loved ones and friends, convicts and keepers.

"*Inside Edition* convinced lots of people by using emotions, not facts," I said. "I'll take it, but it doesn't seem fair."

"Well, people decided you were guilty based on emotions without facts! So why not bring them to the truth the same way?"

"You've got a point," I said.

"I just hope the Illinois Supreme Court justices saw the show," Tom Henry said.

∽

However happy I was with the reactions to my *Inside Edition* interview, Tom Henry was even happier a month later—grinning, nearly bouncing, when he showed me his letter from Winkie. She'd enclosed a picture of her and her baby girl.

I read the letter and studied the picture as I tried to imagine what it would feel like, all those years being estranged from his daughter, then having her reject him—for understandable reasons—when he was recaptured. He wasn't sure if she'd ever come back around. Now she sends him a photo of her daughter, his granddaughter.

Tom Henry was bursting with pride. He sent Winkie a three-page letter that took him five hours to write, so careful was he not to offend her.

Within a week he got her reply. She was furious at him for writing about his boys.

"Maybe she needs to have you all to herself." I said. "She hurts from all the years without you and it's painful for her to think of you with other children."

"I just wrote about Thomas and Jeremy so she could relate to me as a father," he said.

"Well, the good thing about it is, if she didn't care so much she wouldn't get so angry."

∽

One day in July, I told my civilian boss I needed a favor. "If you don't feel you can do it, I'll understand."

"What do you need, David?"

"The Illinois Supreme Court's decision in my case will issue this morning. I've asked my mom to call you and tell you what the decision is as soon as she learns it, because I have news media I've promised to talk to and I want to be prepared, one way or the other. I need to know before I face them."

"For you I'll do it. But make sure you don't throw me under the bus."

About nine-fifteen, I was at the urinal when my boss stepped up to the next stall and held out a note so I could see the words: "You get new trial."

I stayed at the urinal a moment longer. I'd read it right, no mistake about that. But it had been so long and the news had always been so negative up to now, this was hard to believe. The realization spread through me, drop by drop. A new trial! Fireworks went off in my head.

My boss reminded me not to let the media know that I knew.

"I heard it on the radio," I said. He nodded but didn't look convinced. "How about I ask them to tell me what the decision is before the interview?"

"That's more like it," he said. "Remember, they want you in the Guard Hall by ten."

Four reporters representing six news organizations participated in my mildly celebratory interview.

∽

"We'd better hop to it, my friend," I said in the cell that night. "I'm probably headed out of here in a few days and you have a lot more story to tell."

"I don't have that much more," he said, "and I think you'll be here more than a few days. But let's get a move on!"

Once again, Tom Henry was right. Four more months would pass before we'd say goodbye.

Twenty Seven

Tom Henry

Me and Steve pulled in two days later about three in the morning. I drove three miles past Bob and Betty's driveway and parked in the woods. Steve, Lucy, and the baby fell asleep and I piddled around in the back until daybreak before I woke Steve up.

"I'm going to walk down to my friends' place," I said. "Stay here by the pickup."

By the time I reached the house, Bob had already gone to work and Betty was feeding the rabbits. She invited me in and cooked me breakfast.

"I hope you aren't mad," she said, "but we didn't know where you were, so we've been getting your mail and there are a whole bunch of hot checks." My mailbox was right next to theirs.

"Hot checks? I don't write hot checks! What are you talking about?"

She went into the other room and got them. Steve had cashed the checks I'd sent him into town with, all right—then he'd wrote his own checks for that amount and cashed them just before we left, so no one found out till we was gone—no wonder he was in such a hurry to leave!

It didn't take much figuring to realize Steve knew I was finding this out right about now. Since I'd walked three miles to Bob and Betty's it was probably too late to catch him, but I had to try.

"Betty, let me borrow your car!"

"Bob took it to work, Tom."

I walked back there and to no surprise found my pickup gone and my belongings by the side of the road, so I headed back to Betty's and told her what happened. She wanted to call the police right away, but I said no.

"Lucy and her baby come into the country illegally and I don't want to cause her no trouble."

That evening, Bob drove me to get my stuff and we put it in his garage: my chainsaw, backpack, sleeping bag, mess kit, cast iron skillet, and six duffel bags full of clothes. We talked about the bounced checks. What was I going to do?

Bob and Betty said I should stay with them while I figured things out, which was fine with me. We talked about how I might pay off the debt. I had EF Hutton and my chainsaw. I needed EF Hutton to get meat, and I needed the chainsaw to make money, so really, I didn't have nothing to sell.

We decided not to let anyone know I was around for a while.

Bob and Betty went to my friends and told them about the checks—didn't say I was in the area, just that I needed help to pay off some debts that weren't my fault. Several pitched in and we paid the checks all off. All this time I'm staying at Bob and Betty's but no one knows.

Bob was welding outside of his garage one evening and a spark must of got some of the leaves smoldering, 'cause about three-thirty that morning Betty sees flames.

"Wake up, Bob!" she hollers. "The garage is on fire!" We get out there fast as we can, but there's no way to put it out in time. All my belongings were in there, Bob's welding torch and all his other equipment, and a few hundred feet of cedar lumber for the church.

The fire department come out, but they had to get there all the way from town. They was too late—might as well have pissed on the fire. They did keep it from spreading through the woods, at least.

The only thing I had left was some clothes and EF Hutton, 'cause I kept it in the corner of the bedroom where I was sleeping.

Everything else I owned was gone.

⁓

Phil pulled up at Bob and Betty's one day to visit. I could hear him from my room.

"Edd Haddock passed away," Phil said. "The funeral's set for one-thirty tomorrow afternoon."

Edd was like a father to me. There's no way I'm going to miss his funeral. I know there's bound to be a lawman there but I got to pay my last respects to Edd.

The checks are paid off, so I ain't worried about the law for that. The divorce is still coming up and once they know I'm back in town they'll try to serve me with papers, but I figure I can avoid that. As long as Canada don't send my fingerprints to the U.S.!

So I came out of my room.

Phil drove me to the funeral. I scrunched down in the seat and waited till everybody went in there before I did. All the seats was full and there's six people standing in the back, so I stood in the back too.

When it was time to pass by the casket they started from the back, and I was the second one. Here I am, walking past my neighbors and friends that all think I'm still gone—you should of seen them looking at me. Now, Faith with Thomas and Jeremy plus all the Patterson family are sitting on the right side toward the front. I looked toward them when I first started to walk forward but then I just looked straight ahead and went to the casket in front.

The guy in front of me paused a couple of seconds and walked by. I stood there looking down at Edd Haddock for about a half minute. Edd had a brand new pair of overalls on. I put my hand on top of his and said a few words to him. I had tears in my eyes when I walked away. Faith and all the Pattersons was looking right at me.

I walked out and everyone went to their cars. The hearse pulled to the front and me and Phil took off. We knew they were going to bury him at Union Cemetery, so we parked in the woods across the way and watched everyone going in and out.

That night I got a thermos of coffee and some chewing tobacco and walked to Edd's grave and sat there with him a long time, then walked home.

For a few weeks after I came back from Canada, I didn't have no vehicle. After Steve stole my pickup I couldn't afford another one, so I either got a ride to church from somebody or most of the time I just walked.

I had to figure out what I was going to do for a living. I started going with Bob to work and helping him out, running a scraper machine at Cooper's Construction. One night me and Bob and Betty went for dinner to the Mustang Drive-in over by Powell, Missouri, and on the way home, here was this cop car following us. I was sitting in the back seat.

"Bob, turn on this next country road to the right up here."

"Why?"

"Cause there's this cop car following us."

"So?"

"Well, just turn."

We got a quarter of a mile down that road and pretty soon those headlights turn to follow us. Coming down a country road?

"Grab a left." We did, they did too.

"Pull up in this yard and see if they go by." We didn't even know the people. We just pulled up in their yard, shut the lights off, and killed the motor.

I was in the back seat behind Bob, looking out the window to see if this cop car went by. As soon as I saw the trees behind them light up red from their brake lights, I knew they were going to pull in. I'd be trapped.

I opened the door, jumped out, shut it behind me, and took off running. The car turned in and pulled right up behind Bob and Betty's car, shined the lights on it, then they backed out and drove away.

∽

An hour and a half later I showed up at Bob and Betty's. Bob sat me down in the kitchen.

"You ain't going to bed," he said. "If we have to stay up all night we're going to find out what the problem is."

"Now, Tom," Betty said. "You tell us the truth. You don't want to file charges against Steve for all those checks. Why not? You know he's the one who signed them. And he stole your pickup. Why don't you file charges? Is it your pickup? You got a title?"

"You know I bought it off Bill Baker."

"Okay, now, we've talked this over and we can't figure it. Your last divorce, you drove to Pineville and picked up the papers and went to court fighting it, and this time you don't want to fight nothing and you don't want them to serve you the papers. What's going on?"

I just kept lying and they knew I was lying.

"Tom. We can tell you're in trouble but we don't know what kind," Bob said. "Help us help you. There ain't nothing we won't do for you. We'll hide you from the law if we have to, but you got to be truthful with us."

"Don't worry," I said. "You'll never get in trouble with the law on my account, 'cause if anyone comes, I'll be gone."

"Are you expecting the law?" Betty said. "Because if you committed some crime before you got saved, the statute of limitations ran out long ago."

"Some things take longer to run out than others," I said.

There was a window in the room at Bob and Betty's that looked down at the driveway, and I moved the dresser so the mirror on it would let me look out from where I was sitting in bed. And if lights came in while I was sleeping, their reflection would shine on me.

A month after Edd's funeral I told Bob and Betty I wanted to live by myself. They couldn't understand it, since I had such a nice setup with them. But I told them I wanted a place of my own. I used the divorce as an excuse.

"We've both been through a divorce," they said, "but we never acted like you."

Now, at the time Bob was going to doze this old hog shed, so I got the idea of living in it. There was a perfect spot on Ricky Cleaver's property where Thomas got on the bus in the morning, straight across from Charlie and Deloris's driveway.

I wanted to see Thomas. Now, Faith still had this order that I couldn't see him, so I was borrowing Bob's pickup and following the school bus around and waving at Thomas. How could they stop me from seeing him from my "home" when he got on the bus?

Me and Bob and Ricky brought the hog shed over on a low-boy trailer. We set it up on Ricky's place across from the Patterson's drive, right where I wanted it. We built a floor by making a frame of two-by-tens and nailing tongue and groove boards to it. The bottom of the hog shed walls were rotted and uneven, so we snapped a line and cut them straight with a chainsaw, then we nailed the shed to the floor.

I put an old wood stove in it for heat and built a front porch to stack my wood on. The hog shed was real small, about the size of this cell. I just had a bed, a dresser, a shelf, and a wood stove. The sheet metal roof made a racket when it rained. The wind whistled through it 'cause of the knotholes in the wood, so I mixed flour and water with newspaper to seal the inside walls. It looked kind of neat inside. Cozy!

I cut a hole in the back end with the chainsaw and put in a window where I could look out and see the bus when it stopped to pick up Thomas. I liked the idea of waking up early in the morning to see him at the bus, maybe going out to talk with him. I'd ask him about school, how he was doing, then I'd see him in the bus, running to the back, pressing his nose against the window and smiling and waving to me. That by itself made living in a hog shed worth it.

I started going over to the Patterson's in the evening, talking to old Charlie and seeing Thomas. I didn't talk to Faith, but I was on good speaking terms with the rest of the family. After a while I started hauling logs for Charlie.

They never served the divorce papers. After they couldn't find me for so long, they put a notice of the court date for the divorce in the paper. Someone told me they saw it. So I wasn't worried about them finding me, 'cause they'd quit looking.

∽

Christmas was coming, so I went to Western Auto in Anderson and bought Thomas a mini pool table, one of those $45 jobs with the small balls and miniature cue sticks. I bought a smaller present for Jeremy, who was still a baby.

I was invited to eight different places for Christmas dinner. One was Charlie and Deloris's. "Big Girl's going to put on a big spread," Charlie told me. "Why don't you come over and sink your teeth into some of that cherry and pumpkin pie?"

∽

After two years of investigation, the murder of the German was still unsolved, and far as I knew I was still the primary suspect because of the steel jacket bullets and because I was the last person seen talking to him. But I had two things in my favor—I'd passed the polygraph and I didn't have no motive.

How they solved the murder was by doing nothing.[39] An informant come to them. He was a friend of the guys that did the murder and they'd told him about it.

It turned out the German was shot by my own brother-in-law, Leroy Patterson! Two friends of Leroy's were at his house, drinking and talking about how boring life was and how they were going to get away, have some adventure. They'd talked about it before and the three of them planned to leave but they didn't have no money.

---

39 McDonald County Sheriff Lou Keeling said, "We were looking literally all over the world for answers, and the killer was right next door."

"Why don't we rob the old German?" Leroy said. They all agreed and one friend went to his car and got his rifle and the three of them walked through the woods to the Kondra farm. When they got near the house, Leroy said, "Give me your rifle and let me go up there and check it out," so his friend handed Leroy his rifle and Leroy left his dog with his friends in a gulch and he sneaked—walking and crawling—to the farm and saw the old man outside working on a hay baler.

He crouched down a while watching, then he shot the German once and saw him fall to the ground. The others went inside to look for money while Leroy stayed outside as a lookout. Just after they started searching the cabin, Leroy yelled, "Somebody's coming!" So they ran out of the cabin with nothing to show for their trouble.

That was the last day of December of 1980, and they all went to a New Year's Eve party that night.

In January of 1983 all three got arrested and charged with capital murder. Leroy admitted shooting the German. He pled guilty to avoid the death penalty and he was sentenced to life, which meant he had a chance at parole. The other two went to trial and got off.

∽

I wanted to start logging on my own again, so I told Herman Tanner what equipment I needed. His son Jess was just graduating from high school. Herman figured it'd be a good investment, me being a good logger and a hard worker, plus his boy would learn a trade. Phil was also out of a job at the time. Herman said he'd help me out, and when he sold his cows for $23,000 he loaned me $11,500.

I found a truck and tractor to fix up. The truck I had to put a bed on and it wasn't long enough, so I extended it. The tractor had a bucket, but I needed forks, so I welded them out of old truck axles. The chainsaws I bought brand new, three of them.

The first patch we cut was Granny Harrell's. No other logger would move in 'cause it wasn't a big enough patch and all the good trees were way down in the hollow, but Granny Harrell was having a hard time after Homer passed away and I told her I'd try to take logs off the place. We worked there for two months and we made her about four thousand dollars off it.

Then we went just a little down from Bob and Betty's, where we logged until May 2nd.

That's the day I seen this Jeep Cherokee come up the lane. In it was State's Attorney Roger Carlin, Sheriff Lou Keeling, and a guy in a suit.

Seeing the three of them coming toward me, I could pretty well put two and two together. No use going to my pickup and trying to run. I got off the tractor and they opened the doors of the car, no guns drawn. They didn't need none.

"You Tom Elliott?"

"I sure am!"

"I'm from the FBI." The guy in the suit showed me his badge. "It's been a long time, hasn't it, Henry Hillenbrand?"

Twenty Eight

Tom Henry

"You might as well have the money from my billfold," I said to Phil. "I won't need money for a while."

"What's going on, Tom?" Phil's voice was trembling.

"I'm on the run for murder," I said.[40]

I already had handcuffs on me. I turned to the FBI agent.

"Can I take my Bible?"

"Where is it?"

"In my truck."

"Tom," Sheriff Keeling said, "when you get this straightened out, you're always welcome in this county."

They loaded me into the back seat and joined up with another FBI agent who was waiting on the road and they drove me to Springfield that afternoon.

About eleven the next morning, they brought me before a judge in Greene County and charged me with flight to avoid prosecution. Some deputies there took me over to the Greene County jail, right across the street.

McDonald County Prosecutor Roger Carlin later told me how they got me.

"The FBI lab in DC compared the prints Canada sent after your arrest there," he said. "The FBI found out Tom Elliott was Henry Hillenbrand, so two agents came to see us. We checked your driver's license at the sheriff's department. Your name was on that copper plaque of people who helped remodel the old jail! I took them to your house but you weren't home, so we drove out to where you were logging."

༄

The first phone call I made—they gave me ten minutes—was to Applegate's. My dad asked me a whole string of questions. I asked him how Rosie, Gloria, and Mom were.

"I'm going to get you a real lawyer," Dad said.

"Dad, I already pled guilty. I don't think a lawyer would do me any good. Don't go spending your money on me, 'cause I believe it'd be just a waste."

---

40   Phil Collier told me, "When they took Tom away, I sat on a log and cried for an hour."

That was it. My 10 minutes was gone.

We got phone calls twice a week. I took turns, calling Missouri one time and Illinois the next. I called Bob Melton and Buck McDonald. I talked to Rosie, Mom, and Dad.

∽

"Hillenbrand! You have a visit."

"Who is it?"

"Uh, a Faith Elliott and Deloris Patterson." All this time Faith and I ain't talking. I figure all she wants now that she has me where she wants me is to give me those smirky looks, knowing I'll spend the rest of my life in the penitentiary. I got enough pressure on me without having her across the glass acting snotty.

"I don't want to see no one," I said. But what if she brought Thomas and Jeremy? I needed to see them, have my eyes record them like the lens of a camera.

So I yelled out down the corridor just before the guard shut the big steel door, "Wait! I'll go down there."

The visit was nothing like I was worried about. Faith sat there looking at me and crying. She couldn't believe it.

"How come you never told me?"

"Faith, I couldn't tell you—I loved you. If I told you, you could of gone to jail someday just for knowing. No, if I had it to do over, I'd keep it a secret again. 'Cause I loved you."

"No matter what happens, stay close to the Lord," she said. "The boys will always know you're their father, and I'll write you and tell you about them and send pictures." She asked me to give her the address and phone of my family so she could get in touch.

Jeremy was too little to understand what was going on, so he was crawling on the floor by Deloris, but Thomas sat there staring at me.

"Tell Daddy you love him," Faith said. "Tell him we'll be back up to see him again. Tell him we'll go up to Illinois to see his mom and dad."

"I love you, Daddy." Thomas said.

"I love you too, Thomas. Be a good boy for Mommy." I looked at Faith. "How'd you tell him?"

"I just said you had to go away for a long trip."

It was all I could do not to cry in front of Thomas.

"I got some pictures in my billfold I want you to have," I told Faith. "Give my Swiss army knife to Thomas when he's old enough."

"I will," she said.

Faith[41] kept bringing the boys every Thursday to see me. She rode with Deloris, or Buck McDonald, or Bob and Sarah Melton.

Bill Hunt, the old man, was eighty-six by then. He took the bus from Kansas City on a non-visiting day. They wouldn't let him see me, so he walked back and forth on the sidewalk in front of the jail, singing hymns. They told him to go but he wouldn't. Finally they let him in. I talked to him through a wire mesh door.

He thanked me for helping him in Missouri and he said I'd been a spiritual uplift for him. He told me it was all in the Lord's hands.

"Remember all those years before you got saved how you used to pick me up on the highway?" he said. "The Lord answered my prayers then and he'll answer them now."

Let me tell you, it's a heck of a feeling to know someone that old would come that far just to visit you. After ten minutes they told him to leave. Bill Hunt put his palms up to the screen wire and prayed out loud. He prayed for about fifteen minutes.

The guards didn't interrupt him.

∽

My second day in the Greene County Jail a deputy said I had some visitors from McDonald County. It was Sheriff Lou Keeling and State's Attorney Roger Carlin. They talked to me real nice for about ten minutes.

"Is there anything we can do for you?" Lou Keeling said.

"I've known you for a long time, Tom," Roger said. "This is a shock to me. I guess it's one of those things that happened when you were younger. You sure aren't like that now."

And then they got to the point. They asked me if it was a relief now that I was caught. They complimented me on my faith and said it'd be good for me now, as one of God's followers, to help them with the information they wanted.

---

41 Faith told me, "When Tom was captured, I thought it was a mistake. When I found out it *was* him, at first it frightened me that I lived with someone like that, then I realized he must have been a different person then.

They said I was welcome back in McDonald County when I got out. They wanted to know everything I knew about whatever illegal was going on. Who was poaching, who was running marijuana, who was making moonshine, anything I could think of. It'd help me make it right with God for what I did, they said, plus they'd put in a good word for me in Illinois.

I didn't have nothing to tell them.

෴

One morning the guard hollers out, "Hillenbrand! Lawyer phone call."

I went down there and waited in a room with two guards. The phone rang, I picked it up, and this guy said, "Henry?"

"Yes."

"This is Max Gulo. I live around the corner from your dad, and he's retained me as your counsel. Here's my advice—I want you to fight extradition. Don't sign any papers. That will give me time to see what we're going to do."

"I'm not coming back?" After all these years of running, I was finally going to be able to see my family. That was the only good thing out of all this!

"Don't worry. They'll get you back here, I just want you to stall them."

෴

A couple weeks later, they took me to court. The judge had the papers from LaSalle County.

"Is your name Henry Hillenbrand?"

"Yes."

"You have a right to fight extradition. Do you wish to waive that right?"

"No."

It took them three weeks to come and get me. Governor Thompson of Illinois had to sign the papers.

෴

One evening I got word the guards who were going to take me back would be there in the morning to pick me up. So I stayed up and wrote four letters. I drew a picture for Thomas and included it in my letter to Faith.

After breakfast the next day they were there: LaSalle County Sheriff Wahl, Investigator Klein, and Officer Nole. They gave me a LaSalle County jumpsuit. They handcuffed me inside the building, fastened my cuffs to a six-inch-wide leather belt they buckled around my waist, put leg irons on me, and walked me out to the car. Herb Klein sat with me in the back seat. Kenny did the driving.

We came into Streator through the south side of town right up Park Street. It was good to see the new bridge and houses I recognized, but when we went by St. Mary's Hospital a flood of bad memories rushed through me. I thought about them doing the autopsy on Patty with her head already smashed open from me hitting her with the rifle, and the holes in her body from me shooting her.

We drove into Ottawa toward the county jail where I escaped, but it wasn't there.

Officer Nole saw me looking. "They tore the old jail down," he said.

When we were just a couple blocks away from the new jail, Sheriff Wahl said, "We've got a surprise for you, Henry."

"What's that?"

"We arranged for a special visit tomorrow with your parents." Boy, that made me think! I was excited but nervous. When they said, "Why didn't you contact us, at least let us know you were okay, all those years you never even wrote us a card ..." what was I going to say?

"Do you think you're going to want to be put in a cellblock or do you want to start out in isolation for a little?" Sheriff Wahl asked.

"I'd like to be alone," I said. "I got a lot to get straight in my mind."

"Anytime you want out of isolation, just tell one of the guards and we'll put you with the others." So into isolation I went. A guard asked if I needed anything from the commissary. I said no, then I thought about how nervous I was about tomorrow's visit, so I asked for some Bugler.

I paced back and forth rehearsing my speech to Dad and Mom, saying it out loud in my isolation cell. The jailers looked in on me every fifteen minutes. I wonder what they thought when they saw me all alone, talking. I tried to picture what Mom and Dad and Rosie would look like—I hadn't seen them for thirteen years.

స్తు

In the visitor area three stools were on my side behind a piece of safety glass. It had holes with wire mesh to talk through. They put the inmate in first. I smoked when I first got there, but I didn't want them to see me smoking so I put the cigarette out before they showed up.

They walked into view, Dad holding Mom's hand, and Rosie with them. They stopped and we just stared at each other for a few seconds. I was leaning over the stool pressing my face up to the glass, looking each of them over. My dad looked at me starting with my face, then down to my feet, then slowly made his way up my body like he was trying to take it all in, then looked into my face again.

Finally Dad said, "Sit down, Martha. There's Henry, you've been waiting to see him—don't stop talking now!"

She didn't. She talked so fast I couldn't hardly follow everything. She pulled out her handkerchief and cried. She told me she'd been praying for me all these years and she knew God would bring her little boy back to her.

She asked about the boys and Faith. She told me about people from Missouri that had called and told her how long they'd known me and what I'd been doing there. I thought I was going to tell them what I'd been doing, but they was already pretty well caught up.

Mom kept putting her finger on the glass, reaching out to me. Watery eyes, yak yak yak, happy as could be. She asked how long I was married, what I was doing for a living, then she asked about the boys. Dad got in a word once in a while.

When Mom got up for Rosie to sit down, Dad leaned in and said, "I want you to know I've forgiven you for what you've done."

"What I want to know is did you forgive yourself?" I said. Dad looked puzzled. I meant to say don't blame yourself, but it didn't come out right.

Rosie had a glow about her.

"What's your name Anderson for?" I asked. I knew our twenty minutes was about gone.

"We've got plenty of time to talk about me," she said. "Let's talk about you."

A guard said, "Time's up!" Rosie got up and kissed the glass and they all told me how much they loved me, then I walked back to my cell like a person sleepwalking.

❧

I paced back and forth and thought about my family and Patty. Things I hadn't thought about in years came flooding back. Then I thought about Thomas and Jeremy, out there with no father. How can I be a father to them here? The only way I could deal with it was to open the Bible and ask God to take me out of those thoughts. But even the verses I read would remind me of something and jolt me back.

During lunch the second day I found a clump of something in my soup. I picked it out with my spoon. It looked like paper inside cellophane. I set it in my sink and got toilet paper and sponged off the broth. It was a note.

"You don't know me. My name is Tom Bailez. You escaped with my dad, Tom Garrett. I'm dating your daughter, Winkie. She's okay and real pretty. She'd like to see you. She got adopted by Norman and Sally Pence. Don't pass a note back in the soup or on the tray. Just give it to me when I come up here or I'll lose my trusty job. And don't get caught talking to me."

Before I even finished my soup I wrote a reply: What does Winkie think of me? Do you have a picture?

He came around later that night mopping the hallways and I heard a *psssst*. I jumped up and gave him the note. I tried to look through the food slot in our steel door but all I could see was this little skinny sawed-off runt from the back going down the hallway.

I couldn't talk with Tom Bailez 'cause my solitary cell was right by the dispatcher, so I sent a note to Sheriff Wahl saying I wanted to move to the cellblock. Within a couple hours, the steel door opens and he comes in.

"You ready to be with other guys?"

"Yeah, Sheriff."

About two hours later, they took me to D block. There was only four in there. This tall thin fellow looked at me.

"Henry! Just how the hell are you?"

It was Billy, a guy I knew when he was a kid, he used to come down to our restaurant, real mischievous, always wanting to play pool, and I'd let him sweep and give him oddball jobs so he could earn money.

We sat down at the table and talked.

"Tell these guys I used to work for you," he said. "They don't believe me. Tell 'em, Henry!"

Billy had something to be proud of—he knew the famous Henry Hillenbrand.

༄

I wanted to keep in contact with Thomas and Jeremy. Thomas was almost six, Jeremy was almost one. A couple of the guys in my cellblock got newspapers.

My boys couldn't read, so the only way I could think of to show them I cared was to copy the newspaper cartoons, change them a little and make them bigger and mail them to Thomas and Jeremy.

One cartoon I copied was a flock of ducks flying out toward water. The leader you have to make good, but the other ones you just draw as vees behind him. They're flying right next to this passenger jet. The leader duck has his head turned in the air. The change I made was that by each window I drew a human head silhouette, but in one window I drew a duck silhouette with his tongue sticking out. Smart duck.

I kept sending them cartoons and pictures in jail and later in the penitentiary.

ↄ∾

One day I got a letter from Thomas. He drew and colored a picture of Lodebar, with a crooked chimney and a sidewalk. There's no sidewalk there but he put one in.

I only had a pencil but I decided to draw him a picture of where I lived.

So I drew the cellblock—the long table where we ate and played cards, where the TV was when we rolled it in, where the sink and toilet was, and the outside area where we played basketball. I drew where we took a shower and where my bunk was. I put "Dad" by my bunk. I drew the windows, camera, doors, and I shaded it in, dark and light, and spent quite a while on it. Then I mailed it to Thomas.

I come back from that Sunday's visit and they called me out a few minutes later. I thought I had another visit, but they put me in an interrogation room. Herb Klein showed me the drawing.

"What's this all about? You planning an escape?"

"No!" I said, "my son sent me a picture of his house down home and I decided to send him one of mine."

"In such detail?"

"I got a lot of time."

"I'm going to have to put you in isolation."

"For drawing a picture?"

"Yes, 'cause you're an escape risk—be a lot of heads rolling around here if you escaped. There'd be a lot of questions to answer and a lot of forms to fill out."

"I got no plan to escape!"

"That's right," Herb said. "You're not getting away from us again!"

"Herb, I'm a different person now than I was then. I did the drawing 'cause I love my son."

"Sorry, Henry, but I got to put you in isolation."[42]

They put me in isolation and there I sat on that bare steel bed. Nothing in the cell. No one to talk to. After a few hours they brought my stuff, so at least I had something to do.

I was in there for two days. Then they came and put me in B block. So I got to meet a different group of guys.

I read my Bible a lot. I watched Kenneth Copeland on Sunday mornings and I always went on Sunday afternoons and got literature for witnessing from the visiting preachers.

♾

Sheryl, one of the jail guards, told me, "I'll never forgive you for what you did. Patty was one of the sweetest persons I ever met. Whatever they give you, you deserve it."

I hated to hear her say I deserved whatever I got but I couldn't argue with her. Patty was the sweetest person I've ever known too, and I'll never forgive myself for what I did either.

♾

Tom Bailez would sweep right near the cellblock bars, and if he kept his head down we could talk. He'd call Winkie at night then he'd talk to me. Winkie wants to know this, Winkie wants to know that.

Rosie brought Mom every Thursday because Dad had to work, then on Sundays they'd come over after church. They never missed a visit.

It was a regular Sunday visit when Rosie brought Winkie.

I didn't know she was coming but of course I knew it was her right away. Rosie held her by the hand and Winkie sat with the other hand in front of her mouth.

"Don't be scared, honey." Rosie leaned in to the wire mesh. "Look who I brought to see you."

Winkie sat on the stool and stared at me.

---

42 They never sent Thomas the drawing.

"You look beautiful, just like your mom," I said. "I recognized you 'cause your teeth are just like hers." It was one of Patty's best features—her two middle upper teeth had a gap at the top but touched at the bottom, making a tiny dark triangle when she smiled.

Rosie put her hand on Winkie's shoulder.

"You know what we talked about last night," she said. "Don't be scared. Just tell him."

I sat there waiting and looking at my little girl. She was dressed perfect, not a hair out of place. She must of spent two hours getting ready.

"Where was you when I needed you?" she said.

I just started to cry.

Twenty Nine

In December of 1996 I flew to a northern state for an interview with Tom Henry's daughter, in the townhouse Winkie shared with her husband and daughter.

She began by showing me the charm bracelet Henry had given Patty when they were teenagers. It's heavy with charms.

"During the summer before I went into third grade," Winkie said, "I was looking through my kindergarten yearbook and I came across a picture of me. The caption said, 'Hillenbrand.' I asked my mom why it said that, but she just told me the yearbook must have made a mistake, and that satisfied me.

"Then in third grade I was with some kids in the bathroom, and they were saying there was no Santa and I said, 'No, my parents said there is,' and they said, 'You don't have no parents. You were found on railroad tracks.' I told my parents about it, but nothing was said, and it didn't really hit home with me even then.

"When I was in seventh grade I started working in the counselor's office and I remember once when the counselor left the room I looked in the file cabinet, 'cause it had all our files, and under 'Pence' it had my birth certificate but the name on it was Hillenbrand, and I went home crying. My parents were furious and called the school, 'cause that certificate should have been destroyed.

"Before, when I was eight, my parents had told me the school made a mistake when they printed my kindergarten yearbook, but this was a birth certificate, and now I was twelve, and I wasn't about to accept that kind of lie. But I still couldn't get any answers out of my parents. They just said, 'You're our daughter and we love you.'

"That was the end of it for them. I was just supposed to shut up."

෩

"I was fourteen when Henry got captured. I came in one evening and my parents sat me down and said, 'Listen to this.' It was the local station, *WIZZ*, and it said, '… and from the relationship there was one daughter, Winkie Jean Hillenbrand.' I went upstairs and sat in my room the entire night. I was sorting out everything.

"And you know what? The biggest thing about it was, I was eager to see him. I was eager to know everything, but I didn't think it was something I could ask my parents about. My mom says now in her letters she wishes I would have talked to her, but I don't think that was something I was able to do. They shut me up a lot of times, and all of a sudden I'm going to say to them, 'You lied to me?'

"At school, kids I'd been going to school with since kindergarten said, 'I knew about it all the time, but my mom would never let me tell you.' And teachers—'Hey Winkie!'—pulling me in the teachers' lounge, 'I just want to let you know …' These were people I'd never had any relationship with. Now all of a sudden, they're saying, 'If there's anything you want to discuss, my door's always open.'

"It's like a burning building—people stand around and watch. I was a spectator sport.

"So I was in ninth grade, and me and this girl I hung out with, after our Saturday afternoon chores we'd walk down to the library and I'd look at everything.

"So I was reading all I could about Henry and about the murders and my parents were worried. One day they said, 'How would you like to visit Henry at the jail? You're so full of questions, maybe seeing him will do you good.'

"At the visit, I was sitting there before Henry came out, 'cause I remember just looking at that bare manila concrete wall, and the door opened and he came out on the other side of the glass.

"Henry started talking to me. He was in that orange jump suit, and he looked a lot different than I thought he would. He said right off the bat he loved me, and I didn't think too much about it at the time. But in some of the early letters we wrote, when I'd get a little spiteful I'd say, 'How can you love me? You don't even know me.'

"He wrote back, 'You're my daughter. I always known you.' It felt kind of comforting, 'cause I thought at the time, with how tough my life was, it would've been nice for him to come and get me. Isn't that distorted—like I wanted to be kidnapped? And in my letters I used to ask him, 'Why didn't you come and get me?'

"Anyway, when I came back home and started asking even more questions, my parents said I was confused.

"'Maybe you should go to church camp and think things over, because of your not knowing who your real father is,' they said. I think they were insulted."

Winkie paused then and closed her eyes a long minute.

"There's one question I wrote Henry he's never answered that I still want the answer to," she said. "'How did you feel when you pulled the trigger?'"

Thirty

On a Tuesday in February, Henry's sentencing hearing—technically the Hearing in Aggravation and Mitigation—began in the circuit court of La Salle County, Judge Alexander T. Bower presiding. It was Valentine's Day.

In Tom Henry's case, since he'd pled guilty fourteen years ago the prosecution wanted a full evidentiary sentencing to detail the brutality of the murders and his offenses as a fugitive after the murders: escape, kidnapping, and burglary, as well as life on the lam, where his every breath was a crime against the state.

∽

On the morning of June 29, 1970, Keith Hilliard was delivering newspapers near St. Mary's Hospital.

"I seen a man with a rifle," he said.

"Do you remember where you first saw the man?" the state's attorney asked.

"I seen him by a car in front of the main entrance to St. Mary's."

"What did you see him do?"

"He was getting something out of the back seat. He put a covering over it that come out of the car and he started walking toward … it would've been west."

"Did you get a chance to see what he had in his hands?"

"It was a .22 rifle."

"Was the stock on the gun?"

"Yes."

∽

Police Officer Kenneth Jackson testified that he received a call at 7:25 a.m: "Get a police officer here as fast as possible! There's a woman being beat on the head with a club."

"Do you need an ambulance?"

"Yes, and hurry!"

While he was on the radio calling for the ambulance, another call came in telling him there was a gun involved.

"Upon arriving at the scene, what did you see?" the state's attorney asked Officer Jackson.

"I observed a female body laying on a back porch. The face was turned partly up and kind of twisted like at the legs."

"Now, while at the scene, did you talk with anyone?"

"Mr. Tony Gibbons. He told me he saw the incident take place and Henry Hillenbrand had done this. So I radioed for an APB to pick up Hillenbrand."

After the ambulance had removed Patty's body, Officer Jackson went back to the porch and looked for evidence. He found an empty cartridge clip from a rifle that had hair and blood on it, and two slivers of wood. He then went to the hospital and joined other police officers who examined the body and found wood slivers in Patty's hair.

While at the hospital, Officer Jackson was told there was a second body at 210 West Broadway. When he entered the Evans house he noticed blood on the bedroom wall and in the bathroom, and a male body lying in the northeast bedroom, dressed in a light blue pair of Levis and a shirt.

"And did you notice anything about the body?" the state's attorney asked.

"There appeared to be a bullet wound in the right temple."

"And did you notice anything else in the bedroom?"

"There was a broken rifle stock. And there was blood on the bathroom door jamb and on the side of the sink."

Dr. James Gross was a pathologist at St. Mary's Hospital. He started with the autopsy of George Evans. In his opinion, death was caused by a "laceration of the brain due to a bullet."

"Now, Dr. Gross, directing your attention to the autopsy of Patricia Pence, did you remove any objects from her body?"

"I removed a bullet from the left axilla."

"Did you see any other entry wounds or exit wounds of any other bullets?"

"Yes, she had three. One went from the tip of the shoulder to the left axilla. A second wound of entry was on the left side of the chest with an exit wound on the right side of the chest. And the third entry wound was in the anterior abdomen, exiting from the lateral back area."

"Do you have an opinion as to her cause of death?"

"She bled to death."

"Did you examine the head of Patricia Pence?"

"Yes. I found two lacerations of the right side of the scalp, a posterior one and one above the right ear."

⚬⚬

Anthony Gibbons was awakened by "some commotion in the back yard, a scream" at about seven-fifteen, so he went to his kitchen window to look out.

"Can you tell us what you saw?"

"I seen two people in front of the apartment in our back yard."

"Did you realize who had screamed?"

"It was Patty Pence."

"Who was there with her?"

"Mr. Hillenbrand, and he had a small-caliber rifle."

"And what did you do?"

"I said, 'What the hell's going on?' and I got no response. And I called the police."

"Okay. After you called the police, what do you remember?"

"Well, they was still arguing, and all of a sudden I heard a shot from Henry's rifle."

"And what did you notice after the shot was fired?"

"Patty grabbed herself in her mid-section and said, 'Oh, you shot me,' and then she started to run."

"After the first shot, did you hear any more shots?"

"I did. After Patty took off running, Henry turned and discharged two more shots."

⚬⚬

A sixteen-year-old who lived nearby also had been in bed when he heard screaming. He got up and looked outside.

"I saw a girl running up on the back porch and she tried to open the door and she pounded on the door when she couldn't get in."

"What did she do after that?"

"She was screaming and a man came up on the back porch holding a rifle and started to hit her with it."

"Can you describe for the judge how he started to hit her?"

"Well, he was holding the gun by the barrel, swinging it over her head."

"And what happened to her when she was struck?"

"She fell down to the porch."

♋

On June 29th, 1970, Don Haage was a detective with the rank of lieutenant. He was called at home at 7:40 a.m. and told that Russell Hillenbrand had called requesting Detective Haage to come to his house because his son Henry was there and he believed Henry might have killed someone.

When Detective Haage and Chief Gene Robertson and two more officers went to Russell Hillenbrand's house, Russell told them Henry had already "run out into a wooded area to the east." Russell Hillenbrand and Detective Haage went into the woods in that direction but couldn't locate Henry.

"So after going to this wooded area, where did you go next?"

"We received a radio report telling us a jeep-type vehicle was coming down Miles Hill southbound and the passenger could be Henry Hillenbrand."

"Upon arriving at the vehicle, what did you observe?"

"Henry Hillenbrand was exited out of that jeep-type vehicle, placed in handcuffs, and transported to the Streator Police Department. He was taken into the squad room and his handcuffs were removed."

"After the Miranda warnings were read to him, was there any conversation with the defendant?"

"He said he wished a policeman would've seen him walking with that rifle and things wouldn't have happened that did happen. Also told us Patty Pence was there when he shot Evans. Told us that after he shot Evans, he hit Patty Pence over the head with the rifle. Her head started bleeding pretty bad. He said he took off his shirt, tried to stop the bleeding, got her out into her car, and drove her to his place."

♋

The first witness the next morning was Leroy Patterson, Henry's brother in law, the teenager who had gone with two friends to rob and shoot the old man they called the German.

"Leroy, where do you reside?"

"Missouri State Penitentiary."

"How do you know Henry Carter Hillenbrand?"

"He was my brother-in-law."

"Who is Otto Hanson?"

"He's a guy me and my sister worked with down at the trailer plant."

"Tell the judge the conversation you and Tom had concerning Otto Hanson."

'Well, we talked about the way he felt towards Otto whenever Faith—she went out with Otto, you know, and I guess it made Tom kind of mad or something."

"Did he ever indicate he'd do anything to Otto Hanson?"

"He was going to get to him some way. He didn't say what, you know, but he had it in for him."

⁓

Eighteen-year-old Michael Little had been driving home from Granville about nine thirty when an armed man got into the back seat of his car at a stop sign. The state's attorney established that Henry held a gun to the back of his head while they drove to Chicago.

Michael testified that he was "dumbfounded" after Henry let him go and "instead of pulling over and phoning for a police officer, I looked for one by going down one-way streets, speeding, I ran a couple red lights and stop signs trying to find a police officer."

He testified that he drove home to Ottawa, told his mother what had happened, then called the Sheriff's Department, and they took him downtown for questioning. A few days later "I was arrested for aiding and abetting." Those charges were later dismissed.

⁓

The state rested. Dozens of Missouri people were in town, lined up to testify to Tom's robust Christianity and good citizenship in McDonald County, but it was hard to see how that would counterbalance the brutality of the murders he'd committed fourteen years before in LaSalle County, Illinois.

Thirty One

Robert Wayman was the first defense witness. He testified that Tom Elliott was a good husband and father and a generous neighbor, even more so after he became a Christian.

"He cut wood for two families. In one, the guy was disabled. He cut wood for an old couple and he took them groceries, meat, anything they needed. And he brung us a lot of things. He gave us a hundred dollars after lightning struck our home and said, 'Don't worry about paying me back.' He even helped build the new jail office—volunteered his time.

"Tom would help anybody. He brung an Indian family to our home one night from church, and my wife got up and fed them. Tom gave them all the motor oil he had, and he had sixty dollars and he gave that and then he had to charge his oil and gas the rest of the week."

༄

"Tom was always a good person and he always worried about people," said Betty Wayman, Bob's wife, "but after he became a Christian he just—you could just tell the love of God was with him."

"So this being saved changed him compared to before?"

"It sure did."

༄

Lowell Evans, a Baptist preacher, said Henry had donated five hundred pounds of dressed deer meat for his home for wayward children. Phillip Collier, fellow Christian and logger, said Henry had been a good business partner who handled the books, a hard worker—"I couldn't keep up with him"—and a counselor and preacher in the Bunker Hill Church after he was saved. More witnesses testified to Tom's generosity, kindness, and trustworthiness with money.

༄

William R. Hunt, a preacher, the son of old Bill Hunt, said his father had told him about Tom's bringing wood.

"My father's eighty-six, and if Tom didn't see him out in the yard he'd wake him up and say, 'I just stopped to check to see if you were all right.'"

"Have you preached in the church where Tom attended?"

"I was going to preach the first time I met him, but he took up my time exhorting."

"In other words, he was exhorting and you were listening?"

"I was enjoying."

༄

"Reverend, what was Tom's religious attitude as you knew him in Missouri?"

"I just wish all people claiming Christianity would put that kind of effort behind it," Bob Melton said. "In all my years in the ministry, I never found one quite as ardent in his efforts and quite as sincere in his devotion to learn about the Lord."

༄

"He was really tickled when Thomas was born," Faith said. "He's proud of him. They're real close."

"In your opinion, is he a good father?"

"Yes."

"Did he help you take care of Jeremy, too?"

"He did, but Jeremy was only three or four months old when I left. Then he got religion, and he got me interested in religion with him. He was coming over to the house and he'd bring us wood and stuff and come see Thomas, and we eventually got back together."

"Okay, looking at your marriage relationship, why did you get separated?"

"The second marriage could've worked if I'd of let it, but being married at the young age I was and never going out, then after the first divorce being on my own for a year, I feel like I got more … bull-headed. I become rude to him. I didn't give the marriage a chance. After he came back from Canada I mellowed down some and he got to see the boys."

"During the course of your marriage, did Tom ever strike you a blow with his fists?"

"If he had, I wouldn't be sitting here today. Not on his side, anyway."

"Was there any time in your life, Faith, you'd say Tom wasn't a good father?"

"He was always a good father. Never once did he ever lay a hand on either one of them."

"Do you believe his interest in religion was genuine?"

"I know it is."

Deloris Patterson, Faith's mother, corroborated her daughter's account.

∽

Russell Carter Hillenbrand, Henry's father, gave a lot of rambling testimony about Henry's being a bad student but a good boy. Martha Hillenbrand said Henry was no trouble as a little boy, a good student, a problem-free teenager and young man. She took a deep breath, ready to continue.

"Mrs. Hillenbrand, you may step down," the judge said. She stood, but before stepping down she looked at her son and spoke in a clear voice.

"I just want to tell Henry, as his mother—I still love you, son."

"Thank you," said the surprised judge. Many in the courtroom had tears in their eyes, not the least of whom was the defendant.

∽

On Wednesday, the fifth and final day of testimony, Henry Carter Hillenbrand, age thirty-six, alias Thomas Charles Elliott, took the stand in his orange jumpsuit. His face was freshly scrubbed, his hair and mustache neatly brushed.

Defense Attorney Walter Stodd quickly got Henry to the point in his relationship with Patty where he wanted to marry her.

"She agreed about us getting married but she didn't want to get married right then. She said she wanted to go out with other fellas 'cause she never got a chance to date no one except me."

"Was there any friction between you and Patty?"

"There was friction between me and Patty the time I almost fought with George in Rokey's Tavern. I told him I didn't like the idea of him taking Patty places and getting her drunk and seeing what the heck he can get off her."

"What did he say?"

"He said, 'She's with me and she don't want to be with you.' And I asked him, 'Are you in *love* with her?' And he said, 'I'm not in love with her but she's good-looking and I'll keep going out with her no matter what you say. You said she could see other guys.' I said, 'Yes, I did, but I don't want nobody using Patty and making a tramp out of her. If you love her, that's fine, but you or nobody else is going to be using Patty.'"

"What did he say then?"

"He started toward my face, but Patty come between us and said she didn't want us fighting, and that was the end of it."

"Henry, did you plan to kill Patty?"

"No!"

"Did you plan to kill George?"

"No."

Mr. Stodd got Henry to tell about the escape, kidnapping Michael Little, working at Idle Hour stables, driving with Frankie Brown to Missouri, settling there, the jobs he'd had while living in Missouri, his poaching deer and donating meat.

"Do you consider yourself a religious person?"

"I do."

"When was it you believe you got saved?"

"It's not when I *believe* I got saved, it's when I *know*. It would be in 1980, September."

"Now, this term you used, 'got saved,' what does that mean to you?"

"I never was a person that cared to go to church. I always felt there was a God but I always felt I was unworthy—I knew I killed two people and felt I'd never go to heaven anyway, so what's the sense of getting involved?

"And then Leon read the scripture to me about Paul on the road to Damascus, how he went around persecuting, killing Christians, and he told me how Jesus loved sinners and if I confessed with my mouth and believed in my heart, you know, that I'd be born again.

"So I confessed, just opened my heart, and it was like something awful inside me fell away—I can't put it into words, but I *knew* I was a born again Christian. Like, even though I was running away from the law all these years and I wasn't incarcerated in no penitentiary, I felt like I was in prison within myself. But once I confessed my sins and said yes to Jesus, I felt real freedom and I felt the new man within me."

❦

All Tom Henry could hope for was that the judge would focus on the man he'd become and not on the man he'd been.

Thirty Two

Thursday was reserved for closing arguments. In criminal procedure, the state goes first followed by the defense, followed again by the state.

"Your honor," the state's attorney said, "the murders Henry committed clearly were violent." He asserted that Henry's behavior of "threats, lurking, and looking" amounted to pre-meditation. He said George's actions might have amounted to strong provocation if Henry and Patty had been married, but they weren't. He said Henry's history in Missouri showed a recurring pattern of such behavior, and Henry's incarceration would not cause hardship to his children because Henry didn't care about them anyway.

Henry had a history of prior delinquency, he said, proven by the Germosik burglary, and a long sentence was necessary to deter others whose spouses cheat on them from resorting to murder. He also said that Henry's good deeds in Missouri "weren't really all that significant."

Henry had proven by living as a fugitive that he had no remorse. If he had remorse, the prosecutor claimed, he'd have come back to face justice in Illinois.

"Your honor, as state's attorney I recommend to this court that the defendant be sentenced from one hundred to three hundred years in the Department of Corrections of this state for each of the murders of George Evans and Patricia Pence, and that those sentences be served consecutively."

❦

After a recess, Mr. Stodd began his argument for the defense.

He pointed out that most of the evidence should not have been allowed because it occurred after the crimes.

"The aggravation evidence the law allows is *prior* criminal acts, not future ones," he said.

He told the judge these crimes were not committed for compensation and there was no pre-meditation. He argued that there was, indeed, "severe provocation" because Henry and Patty had lived together and had a child together. He said Henry had no malice, "he was surprised Patty was dead, and he certainly didn't want to kill her."

As to the burglary, Henry "was afterwards very sorry and upset, and that is part of what gnawed on him," he said. "Observation of Henry's conduct over thirteen years shows the circumstances are not likely to reoccur." For years in Missouri, Henry had a useful citizenship and "the witnesses paint a clear picture that Henry is now a man that believes in Jesus Christ," in charity, and in "the love of God expressed as love of neighbor as a way of life."

Therefore, he concluded, the evidence showed that there was no need to incarcerate Henry, and he asked the court to be "as lenient as the law allows."

In rebuttal the state's attorney said, "This is a dangerous man. He hasn't changed during thirteen years, at least as of 1980. Henry Hillenbrand needs to be incarcerated for an extended period of time so society can be protected from him and his vicious and violent acts."

⌒〜⌒

Courts routinely offer defendants the "right of elocution" prior to passing sentence upon them. Henry chose to exercise his right, and his speech to the judge occupies some twenty-four pages of transcript. Here is a brief summary:

"I was really in love with Patty—I loved her more than I ever loved anyone in my whole life, before or since. The night before it all happened I'd been drinking, and whether I was drunk or not at the time, I certainly wasn't in my right mind. It was a crime of passion, and it tormented me, still does. I'm sorry—not just for killing Patty but also for killing George. I'd do it all different if only I could.

"I did poach deer in Missouri, which is illegal, but that's something a lot of hunters do there. I never had much money, but I provided for my family the best I could and I love my boys. After I got saved, I tried to be as good a person as I could. It wasn't always easy but I put a lot into it. I hope to have some years of freedom at the end of my life, but I'll leave that in God's hands."

⌒〜⌒

Judge Bower's sentencing statement, which he read from the bench the next morning, Friday, February 24, 1984, began by acknowledging the positive changes Henry had made during his years as a fugitive. He went on to say that it was too little, too late.

"Too late to save the life of George Evans. Too late to save the life of Patricia Pence. Too late that God entered his life through his consciousness. Too late that he began doing good works for his fellow man."

Bower ticked off the horrible details of the vicious double murder, recapitulating the testimony of the witnesses.

"These killings are not random, thoughtless acts but rather show planning."

He said Henry's good life meant little, since "there was ample reason for the defendant to live a good life in Missouri. He really couldn't afford a traffic ticket.

"Our world is full of violence and people who too easily resort to violence to solve their problems," he said. "This resort to violence must be crushed. Strong sentences are necessary to deter others from committing the same crime. Society needs to be protected.

"It is the order and judgment of this court that the defendant be committed to the Department of Corrections of the State of Illinois and sentenced to imprisonment and confinement in a penitentiary for the murder of George Dwight Evans, as charged in this indictment. The court fixes the minimum duration of imprisonment at fifty years and the maximum at one hundred fifty years.

"For the murder of Patricia Jean Pence, as charged in this indictment, the court fixes the minimum duration of imprisonment at eighty years and the maximum at two hundred forty years. The terms will be consecutive. That for Patricia Jean Pence will not start until the term has been completed as prescribed by this court for George Dwight Evans's murder.

"The defendant is now committed to the custody of the sheriff of LaSalle county for delivery to the Department of Corrections."

Thirty Three

Tom Henry

About seven forty-five in the morning, the second day after I got sentenced, they shackled my wrists and legs and drove me to Joliet.

The first thing I noticed at Joliet was everyone else was getting N numbers while I got an L number—L40686. Then after they processed me at the Annex, two guards took me across the street in a van, walked me through the double gate in the front, then one guard took me to the Tombs. The Tombs is where all the big gangsters go, and the troublemakers.

I asked the guard, "How long I got to spend in here?"

"I don't know. I just have orders to bring you here."

The first day wasn't too bad. I was by myself, pacing, smoking Bugler, reading my Bible. There must be some law about letting a prisoner have his Bible, because that Bible came with me through all my moves.

The second night was a dandy! All the inmates started throwing sheets and mattresses and blankets onto the gallery, then they threw matches on the piles. Pretty soon there was a big blaze going, with thick black sooty smoke billowing up from the heap. I started choking and couldn't breathe.

I grabbed one of my sheets off the bed and got it wet in the sink—I later learned it's faster to dunk it in the toilet—and hung it up in front of the cell as a smoke filter. It wasn't perfect, but it helped.

There wasn't nothing to do. I'd roll the mattress up and tie it tight with my sheet, put it up edgeways by the bars and climb on top of it, then I'd grab the top bars and pull myself up the last few inches and hold there as long as I could to see out the window. Then I'd jump down. I did that a lot.

Most guys went to regular cells and came out for meals and stuff. I was always locked up in my cell. If this is the way prison life is, I'll never make it!

A guy come and asked how I was coping, did I have any problems.

"Are you a counselor?" I asked him.

"I'm a psychologist."

"I don't want to talk to you. There's nothing wrong with me." I was afraid I'd give them a chance to lock me away for good.

"A lot of people with problems say they don't have any," he said. "I'd like to talk to you."

248

"I'm sorry, sir, but I won't talk to you."

After he left, I got to thinking about it. I can't do much worse than this. What can it hurt to talk to the guy? A couple days later he came back around and I called him over. When I got close to the bars, he backed up a little. So I backed up to make him more comfortable.

I asked him, "Why am I here?"

"Well, in your report, the prosecuting attorney says you're an escape risk with suicidal tendencies."

We talked for a long time, and I told him all about my story.

Finally he said, "After talking to you, I believe you're all right and I'm going to talk to someone about getting you out of here."

Well, nothing happened. That was just a line of bull.

A week later the warden came walking through. It was hard to see down the gallery, not like here where we can use our mirrors. There they have the cement walls jutting out about two feet on each side of your front bars, so even if you had a mirror, which I didn't, you couldn't see sideways. I had to guess when he'd come back along and I called out of my cell.

I told him my story and asked why I was here. He said he'd check on it.

A guard come by later with a note that the warden was going to call Springfield to ask them about my case. About two o'clock the next afternoon, they moved me to be with the rest of the guys in population. I was put into a cell with a gang chief from Cook County jail, a big black guy I called Boss Hog. I'd been in the Tombs for about three weeks.

A guy in street clothes showed up at the cell. I already decided if this was another psychologist I wasn't going to talk to him. But he wasn't. He was a counselor and he was there to decide what joint I was going to go to. I knew I didn't want to go to Pontiac, 'cause George's brother worked there. Menard was the obvious choice, me being white and older.

The whole three weeks in the Tombs, I never got a phone call or anything to write with. Right after I got into population, I wrote a letter: "Dear Mom and Dad: You won't believe it. This is just an hour drive from home. You can come for a contact visit."

They came the day after I was shipped to Menard.

I thought my special treatment was over, so I was real surprised when they took us down to Menard on the bus. They loaded the bus with everyone hooked together on the chain, two to a seat. I was in the front seat by myself right behind the driver, handcuffed to the same chain, and my feet was also cuffed to this hook welded to the floor.

Here I am, alone, special chains—you should of seen how the other guys on the bus looked at me. We're all criminals going to a maximum security joint, so you know no one came here for stealing gerbils from the pet store, and this one guy—me—is so bad even the ordinary security of buckling him to the human chain ain't enough. He has to be specially bolted to the floor and watched. Well, I figured that's okay, I'm an escape risk so they have to be careful, but as soon as we get to Menard I'll be in population just like the others.

But when I got here, they put me in South 1-01 on deadlock! My meals were brought to me, plus they brought me clothes from the clothing house. They did get me out to escort me to the Bureau of Identification to get my picture taken.

Spider, who was president of the Bikers, talked to me about joining them.

"I know you don't want me to hook up with the Bikers," I said. "I had training wheels on my tricycle till I was fourteen."

All the gang big shots stopped by the cell. They heard I came from the Tombs and how I was double-chained by myself on the bus and they saw how I was locked up now. When I told them I was on the run for thirteen years, they perked up their ears.

Spider said, "You ain't got to stay like this."

"I didn't think prison was this bad," I said.

"Want a job in the kitchen?"

"Anything to get me out of here."

So Spider talked to someone and I got a job.[43]

∽

The guard that came to release me from deadlock told me I was supposed to move to South 4-45, then report to the kitchen for work.

---

43 The prison allowed gangs to manage assignments (along with virtually everything else), an illegally corrupt and corrupting system. By forcing inmates to deal with gangs, the prison administration gave the gangs power, and the gangs gave the prison a form of discipline, but what a brutal and capricious form of discipline it was!

I got to work right after lunch. I was the water boy—I went around from table to table during supper pouring water. The guard who give me the stainless steel water pitcher warned me not to lose it or I'd go to Seg.

During supper that evening, my very first day on the job, the big riot happened.

I was pouring water on the black side when it all kicked off. I heard shots outside but I didn't know what was going on.

They started hollering names: Northsiders, Latin Kings, Black Stones, Metros, Bikers, Black Disciples, Latin Disciples, Vice Lords.... I didn't know what they was talking about. Then they started throwing trays, food, chairs, even tables. What a mess—we had spaghetti that day. Guys were going around with knives, pipes, all kinds of homemade weapons.

I was scared and didn't know what to do, so I got under one of the tables. With my pitcher in my right hand—I still thought I'd go to Seg if I lost it—I grabbed the table legs with my left hand, pushed the table sideways with my shoulders, and started to drive my way over to the white side.

Somebody hit my table and spun me around. I looked over the table. There's all these blacks coming with metal trays, so I duck back down and start scooting along with all my strength using the table as my shield. Now I can't even tell where I'm going. I don't want to stick my head up again, so I just take them out with the table top.

I'm still trying to get over to the white side and I run over this guy who was crawling and one of my table legs catches him in the head and knocks the table out of my hands. I stumble over it, then fall onto this other guy who's already on the floor.

Meanwhile, the guards started to shoot and the goon squad[44] marched in the front doors. A Northsider chief who saw me with my pitcher still clenched in my right hand shoved three shanks in it. I hadn't never seen a shank before. We got jammed up about five deep standing against the wall, then the guards told us to move out of the chow hall to the street.

As I'm walking out the door, a guard calls out to me to put down my pitcher.

"The man back there told me not to lose it," I said.

"Set it down on that table!"

---

44 Also sometimes called the "orange crush," this was a team of guards outfitted in orange protective padding with nightsticks, mace, and the like, prepared to rush a violent inmate.

Good thing I'd already stuffed the shanks into my pants. We went outside and they made us all lie down in the street. I edged my way over to the flower bed in the middle of the street and scratched a depression in the dirt and buried the shanks.

They singled out a number of inmates they noticed doing the fighting, made them lie in a place by themselves and handcuffed them so when they got them back into the cell house the troublemakers would be marked. But this one guy had a handcuff key and crawled around un-cuffing them. They held their hands together and threw the cuffs out onto the gallery when they got back to the cell house.

I told the gang chief where I buried the shanks but they never found them—the place got searched with metal detectors.

My first day of freedom, and after a couple hours on the job I'm locked up again!

❦

The next morning, they brought Heart Attack from the East House to cell with me. He was into making homemade cards, so I started making cards too. At first I copied his patterns, then I started drawing my own designs. Most of the cards I drew were about deer and animals, and I sent them to my boys.

Pretty soon guys wanted to buy my cards, so I got into selling them. I sent some down home and Faith sold some at work for spending money. Then the owner at Valley View truck stop wanted a steady supply of my cards to sell, but I couldn't make enough. Bob and Betty sold some and sent me the money, which I sent to my boys.

❦

Six sparrows lived in the West Cell House. After we got off deadlock, I started bringing bread from chow and throwing it on the gallery. I liked to watch the sparrows fly from the windows to the bars across the gallery, then down to the gallery floor for that bread.

After a while I put the bread on my cell bars. One sparrow finally got brave enough to come and get it, then they all did, real skittish about it. That first fellow got so brave he came into my cell to get it if I sat in the back. I got to know him and I named him Bobby.

One day I was watching Bobby on the bar across the gallery while I was coloring a greeting card when all of a sudden he fell over dead. I went to the bars with my mirror and saw that these two guys in the next cell had rubber bands and paper clips.

I screamed at them.

"What did that little sparrow ever do to you? He might've been the only thing in this damn place that never hurt anything, and you had to go kill him, you stupid ..."

Then I got to thinking about how many hundreds of sparrows I've shot that weren't hurting no one. I thought of that chicken hawk, too, the one I shot who died in the cage I locked him in.

I shuffled to the back of the cell, sat on the toilet, and put my head in my hands. I asked God to give me some chance to do something good to make up for some of the bad I've done.

Maybe putting me and you together so I can tell my story is God's way of answering my prayer.

Thirty Four

The day finally arrived when I said goodbye to Tom Henry and was transported back to jail to await my fate. There was never any question whether the prosecutor would retry me. The only question was would he prevail.

In the years since my first trial, new studies had been published that contradicted the state's primary expert. And we'd discovered evidence of a real suspect. Shortly after the murders, the man we now suspected had handed his wife surgical scrubs splattered with blood and told her to wash them. Unfortunately she hadn't come forward with this information until years later, following a divorce.

So I wasn't worried about the trial. You might say I was confident.

The prosecution's case was languishing until, at the eleventh hour, they called a prisoner to the stand who told the court I'd confessed to him in prison. The witness said I came to him for legal help and in order to get the best advice I could, admitted my guilt to him. It made no sense, but it was a good performance.

With that the state rested.

To counteract this inmate's "confession" we called three Menard inmates to the stand, among them Tom Henry, who testified that this witness was a known liar and braggart—and no jailhouse lawyer.

All we needed to do now was to put our suspect on the stand and ask him where he got those bloody scrubs just after the murders, why he took my five–year-old son for a walk through the cemetery just before the murders, and most importantly where he was at the time of the murders, something he'd lied to the police about. But the judge refused to subpoena him.

So the jury was allowed to hear a bogus confession but not allowed to hear our genuine suspect answer some highly pertinent questions.

Yet as it turned out, the jury saw right through the lies. After the trial they said they'd been ready to acquit before the defense presented its first witness. Not only had the prosecutor failed to prove his case, they said, he'd proved himself willing to endorse a witness he knew was lying.

I will be eternally grateful to that discerning jury from Decatur.

෬෧

My acquittal gave me the chance to rebuild my life—to do good, to live well. But for a time, I floundered. I immersed myself in work to crowd out thoughts of murder and prison. Early on I tried attending a Brethren meeting, but as the congregation sang the opening hymn, memories of my family sitting next to me in services just like this one overcame me and I fled from the room.

A psychologist told me I still needed to grieve—with the police spotlight on me from the instant I learned my family had been murdered, I'd never had a chance to mourn properly. He advised me to summon memories of my family, to welcome them, even if they caused pain.

So I replayed family stories in my mind and with my friends. Like the time we were all driving to Grandma's and our engine quit and the cold swept through the car as if a window was open, and I said, "Let's all pray," and Becky started her prayer, "Dear Lord, we thank you for this good time we're having." Or the time in church when Gracie bent down to reach something under her seat and fell forward onto her head and her legs kicked up and her heel caught in the opening between two seatbacks of the pew ahead and she was left standing on her head, so shocked she didn't utter a sound.

In time I decided the psychologist was right—the more I thought about Susie and Becky and Gracie and Benjy, the stronger I got. The memories brought happiness along with the pain, and the balance improved as I healed.

∾

Six years after my release, I sold my share of an Ohio prosthetic-orthotic practice and moved to Florida to start work on *Tom Henry*. I conducted interviews and wrote a couple hundred pages of manuscript, but my heart wasn't in it.

I set the book aside and started a business designing and manufacturing orthopedic braces, which grew for a decade until 2009, when a competitor made an offer for it that would give me the time and money to invest in *Tom Henry*.

I searched my soul: was I ready to return to the darkness? Only one way to find out. And as it happened, once I settled into the writing I found the work to be satisfying and healing.

∾

Now, as I approach my sixtieth year and take inventory of my life, I find that I've been blessed. That conclusion might seem difficult to justify, given my story. Perhaps the best way to explain it is to repeat what I recently told a friend who was commenting on my business success as we sat by my pool sipping single-malt and watching a foursome ride by in golf carts.

"I've led a charmed life," I said, "if you don't count that one part in the middle that was pure hell."

Afterword

As of this writing, September, 2012, Tom Henry lives in the Menard Correctional Center. He's been an inmate in the Illinois Department of Corrections since February 27, 1984.

In prison, Tom Henry is known by his birth name, Henry Hillenbrand. A current picture and his criminal information may be viewed on the Illinois Department of Corrections website (http://www.idoc.state.il.us) by doing an inmate search. He can be contacted by writing to:

Henry Hillenbrand, L40686
Menard Correctional Center
P.O. Box 1000
Menard, IL 62259

More information about Tom Henry—and about me—is available on my author website, www.authorhendricks.com, where you can view pictures and hear excerpts of Tom Henry dictating his story in our prison cell, and where you can sign up for news and updates about him.

∽

I currently live in Orlando with my wife, Gazel. I can be spotted around the neighborhood walking two dogs—a black Lab and a white Bichon—playing tennis, or riding my Harley.

By the time you read this I hope to be working on my next book, an account of the murders of my family, my conviction and incarceration, and my struggles, both against my unjust conviction and against prison corruption.

I can be contacted at www.authorhendricks.com.

Photos

Tom Henry in his cell making greeting cards

Pantagraph photos, taken
during a multi-media
interview of David.

Below, David's manuscripts,
books, papers and typewriter
can be seen on his top bunk.
He slept underneath
the bottom bunk
to keep his work space free

David on "Main Street"
inside Menard Correctional Center

David sitting on the edge of Tom Henry's bunk

Tom's house,
"Lodebar, a place so bad cockroaches wouldn't live there"

Thomas and Jeremy pose

on the planter/church sign

Tom Henry

designed and built.

This picture was taken after

their father was in prison

and the church was

no longer in operation.

Patty with '60s hair style

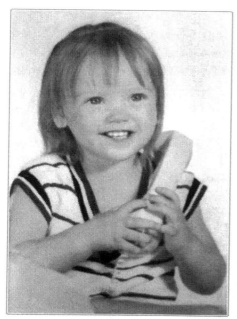

Winkie,
2 years old,
at the time of the murders

Henry Hillenbrand,
mischievous boy all dressed up

261

Prom picture of the happy young couple.

Made in the USA
Middletown, DE
30 April 2018